Will Our Generation Speak? offers Christians an invigorating challenge, and Grace Mally does so with a message that grips the heart. Penetrating yet practical, it beckons young believers to boldly embrace the call to action as a witness for Jesus Christ. This book brings a fresh perspective to the greatest mission of all. The world needs this message, and every young Christian needs this book!

—**CHUCK BLACK,** Author of *The Kingdom Series* & *The Knights of Arrethtrae*

"*Will Our Generation Speak?* is a wonderful, practical, and very timely publication. Never before in history has the Church so needed to speak up and to speak clearly. This book does that and it tells you how to do it, with practical examples and inspiring heart-warming personal experiences. It's fuel for your fire, diligently gathered by the author so that you can let your light shine."

—**RAY COMFORT,** Founder of Living Waters, cohost of *Way of the Master*

"Witnessing often makes people nervous, but it's important that we share our faith. Grace Mally shares practical tools that work!"

—**THE DUGGAR FAMILY,** TLC's *19 Kids and Counting*

"Grace has an open and engaging writing style which makes for an enjoyable read. The personal anecdotes she relates are interesting and encouraging, and her tips are simple and practical. Although specifically targeted toward the younger generation, this book provides an excellent guide for Christians who struggle with witnessing at any age."

—**MICHAEL FARRIS,** Chancellor, Patrick Henry College

"I have had the privilege of meeting the Mally Family several times over the years. Sarah, Stephen and Grace are bright, articulate and "on-fire" for the Lord! … In her new book, *Will Our Generation Speak?*, Grace challenges her peers to get out of the 'pew-sitting' business and into 'people getting' mode. She gives wonderful, practical examples of how the Lord has used her humble obedience to share the love of Christ, as well as the gospel, to more folks than most adults two and three times her age. There is no doubt in my mind that God is going to use this to powerfully challenge a generation mired in complacency. I can only pray that her cry to her generation to be bold will have an impact on the older generation as well. Oh, how we need more young people in the world today who are not ashamed of the gospel, and who are willing to open their mouth even though they may be mocked or ridiculed for their faith."

—**CARL D. KERBY,** President and Founder, Reasons for Hope

"The Christian church has long needed a stimulus for effective witnessing from a Biblical worldview. In this book Grace Mally fills that need. She rightly places creation thinking as the foundation stone of such a worldview, and a primary witnessing tool for the Christian. She identifies creation truth as an 'attention-getter' and 'conversation-starter' without peer. This method will be followed by every fruitful Christian."

—DR. JOHN MORRIS, President, Institute for Creation Research

"Our mission at Summit is to call rising generations from aimlessness to fearlessness and we're seeing it happen! Grace Mally is one of those leading the way, and in *Will Our Generation Speak?* she shows how to break the ice and introduce people to the good news of the Gospel. In the little hippie town where I live, people are evangelistic about all kinds of things – vegetarianism, Wicca, Communism, you name it. They're enthusiastic. They're sold-out. The question for believers is, 'If God made them, Christ died for them, and I care about them, then will I find my voice and introduce them to the truth?' As Grace says in the book, 'Love will find a way. Indifference will find an excuse.' I take this as a personal challenge, and I hope you will too."

—JEFF MYERS, Ph.D., President, Summit Ministries

"If ever young people in America needed to raise their voice and zealously proclaim the truth of God, it's now. In today's post-modern, 'relative' generation, young people have a voice that is heard. We need Christian young people who will rise to leadership. Grace's book doesn't just tell young people to be bold—it shows them how to do it. It is full of real life experience, conversation openers, creative ideas and encouraging stories."

—WOODY ROBERTSON, College Plus

"Grace Mally's timely book, *Will our Generation Speak?* comes as a powerful message for Christ to Christian young people in the adolescent years of this millennium. Not only is Grace a very good writer, but she has built a great file of life experiences, both hers and others, in witnessing for Christ. Just the remarkable number and clarity of real occasions of personal evangelism will convey to the sincere reader that New Testament evangelism ought to be a way of life, a lifestyle for the true Christian. The author gives numerous suggestions and illustrations of planned, group-effort evangelism. Yet the weight of this excellent book emphasizes the great and glorious pattern of an individual life that is driven by love and loyalty to Christ and His gospel, and looks for and makes opportunity for witness for Him in virtually every dimension and experience of life. I highly recommend the thoughtful reading of Grace's book to the present generation of Christian young people in the Western world. May the Spirit of God use this to spark another Great Awakening in our culture for the glory of our Savior, Jesus Christ, and the salvation of multitudes who do not yet know Him."

—DR. DANIEL H. SMITH, Former President, Emmaus Bible College

"What Grace has done in this book is convincingly make the case that all young Christians should be witnesses ... She gives stories of her own experience in witnessing that are truly thrilling. She makes the case that young people can be the most effective soul winners of all. She explains how young people have opportunities to witness that older folks don't have, which I had never thought about. This book will inspire even the skeptic to witness. This book is a must for every Christian young person ... If young people will read it and apply it, we will see revival in America. That's my prayer; thanks, Grace, for helping us all to see the importance of witnessing and the ease in doing it."

—MIKE SMITH, President of HSLDA

"You might be as afraid of a book about evangelism as much as you are of evangelism itself. Take courage, Grace Mally's book is winsome and inspiring! I loved all of her personal stories which tastefully season the book throughout and draw you in from chapter to chapter. You will be glad you read it."

—PHILLIP TELFER, Founder, Media Talk 101

"I'm knocked out by this book. It is so needed and it is very well done. The personal testimonies are invaluable."

—MITCH TRIESTMAN, Author, Speaker, Missionary with The Friends of Israel

"God has entrusted the proclamation of the gospel to each successive generation. *Will Our Generation Speak?* is a clarion call to young people to embrace God's plan for evangelism. This book shows you why you must, and practically how you can, tell others about Jesus. It is Biblical, bold, convicting and inspiring. This is a book whose time has come. I hope every Christian young person in America reads this book!"

—ISRAEL WAYNE, Author, Conference Speaker

"I look forward to getting *Will Our Generation Speak?* into the hands of my grandchildren. Grace Mally clearly, simply, and convincingly provides encouragement to young people that they can be used of God to advance His kingdom. Her illustrations and personal experiences will inspire and motivate her readers to be bold with the gospel of the Lord Jesus Christ."

—NORM WAKEFIELD, Founder, Spirit of Elijah Ministries

"The most compelling feature of *Will Our Generation Speak?* by Grace Mally ... IS Grace Mally. She doesn't just tell us how, why, and where to share our faith—she does it. I was humbled and challenged by reading story after story of how she asked the people God put in her path, 'Do you ever think about what happens after you die?' She serves as a powerful example of the truth that she shares. As a dad, this is a book I'll want each of my teenage children to read. You should too."

—**TODD WILSON,** Founder, Familyman Ministries

"I absolutely loved this book! It had me laughing, crying, convicted and encouraged. I can't wait for my kids to read it!"

—**RACHEL ZWAYNE,** Living Waters

WILL OUR GENERATION SPEAK?

A CALL TO BE BOLD WITH THE GOSPEL

| GRACE MALLY

ILLUSTRATED BY HAROLD MALLY

Tomorrow's Forefathers, Inc.

Library of Congress Control Number: 2012935120
ISBN 13: 978-0-9719405-8-1

DEDICATED TO MY DAD

DAD, I ADMIRE YOU MORE THAN ANY OTHER MAN ON EARTH. IT IS BY WATCHING YOU THAT I LEARNED TO SPEAK OF JESUS. THANK YOU FOR COACHING ME IN SHARING THE GOSPEL. THANK YOU FOR YOUR PRAYERS FOR MY LIFE.

TABLE OF CONTENTS

WITH GRATEFULNESS

DAD—Thank you for reading draft after draft and for contributing so many insightful thoughts. More than that, thank you for teaching me these things and exemplifying them long before this project began. Your zeal and vision for spreading the gospel provide continual fuel for the rest of us. I love how you are an overflowing fountain of witnessing ideas! Thank you for being such a strong leader for our family and for teaching me to love the Word of God. And thank you for the wonderful illustrations you drew for this book.

MOM—You encourage me so much. Thank you for all the praying-for-you and encouragement texts and notes. Thank you for putting my projects and priorities above your own, sacrificing in so many ways to help me to get this book completed. You have strengthened and encouraged me over and over again—always understanding, always taking the time to stop and pray with me. I have learned so much from your example of kindness, sensitivity, and humility. I love spending time with you!

SARAH—Thank you for the literal *months* you've put into helping me edit! It has been so much fun to work with you. I'm never going to forget all the hilarious moments we experienced during the editing process. You have helped me in about every way imaginable in this book process—spiritually, emotionally, practically, editorially. You started helping me with this book years before the writing began ... going out witnessing with me and teaching me, by your example, to seek the Lord wholeheartedly. I love being your sister!

STEPHEN—-Your logical perspective, reassuring words, and comic relief have encouraged me a lot through this book journey! From playmate to coworker to counselor, you're a totally awesome brother and I'm privileged to be your little sister. Your frequent funny remarks bring so much fun to the family and remind me, when I'm troubled about something, that *it's all going to be okay.* Thank you for your help with the book's layout, content feedback, and practical counsel to say no to other activities in order to get this book done!

ACKNOWLEDGMENTS

Grandpa and Grandma—Thank you for your faithful, kind support in everything I do! Thank you for your continual prayers and godly example.

Nickie Biegler—When you read one of my earliest drafts and helped me to systematically think through the chapters, it was a tremendous help. Thank you for the literal weeks you put into formatting this book. Thank you for the huge workload you have taken on in the Bright Lights ministry so I would have more time to write. Thank you for the dozens of times you have come witnessing with me and encouraged me in the Lord. And thank you for being such a good friend.

Judi Miksch—Thank you for your thorough editing, prayers, encouragement, and for all the times you have spoken wisdom into my life.

Tony Ramsek—Your example and teaching in the area of evangelism have been a gift from God in my life. Thank you for all your help with this book!

Augusta Fernando—You continually inspire me. I'm blessed to know you. Thanks for your editing help and, most of all, your prayers.

Rachel and Bekah May—Thank you for taking care of so many things in the Bright Lights ministry so we could focus on this book. Thank you for your help in wording difficult sections, and for your friendship and prayers!

Rachel Zwayne—Your enthusiasm has meant so much to me. Thank you for all you have done to support this book.

James de Leon—Somehow you created a cover that was exactly what I wanted, even though I couldn't even describe what I was looking for. Working with you has been wonderful, and an answer to prayer!

Tracy and Phyllis Winters—We're amazed at how you go above and beyond in so many ways as you help us with the editing and publishing process.

Brian Thomas—Thank you for your insightful comments and additions to chapters 14 and 15 about apologetics and creation science.

Dr. Jobe Martin (and Mirren)—Thank you for your encouraging feedback and ideas about creation science for chapter 14.

Thank you so much to all my friends who helped with proofreading:
Allison Bontrager, Brooke Butler, Nate Bramsen, Tim Chaffey, Bryan and Julie Gates, Lalo Gunther, Caitlyn Hofmaster, Supriya Injeti, Claudia Juhl, Anna and Melodie Kirk, Abby Kramer, Emily Long, Miranda Melto, John Messerly, Bill and Natalie Naas, James and Zion Opperman, Karen Pilling, Laura Sisson, Jeni Sueppel, Mitch Triestman, Baylie Wintle, Ryan Wolfe, Mark Woodhouse, and Kristin Youngblood.

Thank you to everyone who has shared witnessing tips with me, invested in my life, gone witnessing with me and taught me by your example, and prayed for this project. Thank you also to my wonderful church family at Cedar Rapids Bible Chapel for all of your prayer and encouragement!

NOTE FROM THE AUTHOR

Through the process of writing this book, I have learned in a way I've never known before how God's grace is sufficient and His strength is made perfect in weakness! I often came to the Lord feeling inadequate, and my faith has been built as I have seen Him provide for this book ... over and over again.

STORIES AND REFERENCES

The stories and dialogue I recount in the following chapters were written as closely to "word-for-word" as I could remember them. (I've learned that I have to record stories right after they happen before I forget the details!) Occasionally I changed the wording in a minor way for easier readability or clarity. Some names have also been changed for the sake of privacy.

All emphasis in Scripture verses is added. For clarity, I have capitalized pronouns referring to God in the Scripture references. I have also capitalized Heaven and Hell to bring attention to the fact that they are real locations.

SPECIAL NOTE TO BRIGHT LIGHTS GROUPS:

As you know, BRIGHT stands for "being radiant in godliness, holiness and testimony." Much of the Bright Lights material that has been published up to this point has been for the purpose of encouraging you to walk in *godliness* and *holiness*, set apart for Christ and using your youth for Him. We are excited to now zero in on the third aspect—*testimony*. We are called by Jesus to shine our lights, not only by demonstrating the gospel with our lives, but by sharing it with our mouths! For those of you who have already been through the Bright Lights curriculum, I believe that everything you have learned so far will prepare you for the message of this book.

> *May your starlight be bright in the dark of the night,*
> *A treasure to the world be.*
> *May its message touch more than the sand on the shore,*
> *A lighthouse so others can see.* —Harold Mally

My prayer for each of you is "That ye may be blameless and harmless, the [children] of God, without [fault], in the midst of a crooked and perverse nation, among whom ye shine as lights in the world; **Holding forth the word of life** ... " (Philippians 2:15-16).

CHAPTER

ONLY ONE CHANCE TO BE YOUNG!

To be honest, I didn't want to write this book. I casually brought up the idea to my family around the dinner table one day, unsure of what they would think. A couple days later, my dad invited me to join him as he was sitting on a lawn chair reading in the backyard. He told me he thought a book on witnessing was a great idea and that I should move ahead with this project. As we began to discuss it, I actually started to cry. (I think my dad was a little surprised by my reaction!) I just felt that writing a book on witnessing was such an impossible mountain to climb. However, the more I worked on it, the more excited I became, and the more I saw God using this project to change *me*.

If you are a typical person, witnessing scares you. Maybe it terrifies you. I remember how my stomach used to tie itself in knots at the thought of witnessing. Being nervous isn't necessarily a bad thing; it has some benefits. It keeps us humble and dependent on God. But I have found that what I once considered to be very scary has become much easier with practice. I think Satan wants us to believe that witnessing will be a miserable, frightening experience, when actually it is one of the most exciting parts of our lives in Christ! It is my prayer that this book would provide practical ideas and encouragement to my generation as we endeavor—together—to speak the gospel of Jesus Christ with boldness.

LEXI'S BAD DREAM

One of my favorite places to share the gospel is at a little playground a block from our house. One summer day I began talking with a twelve-year-old girl named Lexi who was swinging by herself.

"Do you ever think about what happens when we die?" I asked her.

Lexi told me that she thought about it sometimes, but didn't know the answer about what happens. As I explained what the Bible says about Heaven and Hell, Lexi said something that really surprised me.

"Just last night I had a dream that I died and went to Hell," she told me in a serious tone of voice.

Wow. Seriously? I was thinking.

"Do you think it's interesting that you dreamed that last night and then ran into me today?" I asked her.

Lexi did think it was interesting and, more importantly, she wanted to know how to go to Heaven. As we sat there on the swings, rubbing our feet around in the woodchips, we talked for over 30 minutes about sin, Jesus, and how we can *know* that we will go to Heaven one day.

It is easy to believe the lie that no one will want to listen to us if we start talking about Jesus—that people just won't be interested. Or maybe we imagine that we will offend people if we try to witness to them. We forget that God is working in this world, preparing hearts for the gospel. He simply desires servants who are willing to go into the harvest and reap! The truth is that many *are* seeking, but we won't know that unless we talk with them. Jesus said, "The harvest truly is great, but the laborers are few" (Luke 10:2).

OUR GENERATION

It was a busy Saturday afternoon and the local mall was full of activity—with the typical combination of serious shoppers, mall walkers, and teens just hanging out. Adding yet more variety to the mixture, a group of about eight friends and I had arranged to meet at the mall to try to get into witnessing conversations. We prayed and asked God to lead us to open hearts.

"What do you think happens when you die?" my friend Jenn and I asked three girls.

They looked at each other with surprised expressions. "We were just talking about this the other night!" they exclaimed. "We have these long debates about what happens when we die, but it never goes anywhere because no one has any answers!"

These girls represent the sad state of millions in our generation. They need answers desperately. If you know Jesus Christ, then you have the one answer they need. It's an answer they do not even know exists—and you *have* it!

It goes without saying that the world around us is a mess. You have heard statistics about suicide, abortion, murder, crime, drugs and divorce. There are approximately 6,000 first-run theaters in this country and about 400,000 churches.[1] Yet which do you think is influencing our country more? Are we as Christians truly being the bright lights, the strong voices of truth, that we should be? The solution for this world's confusion is not to fix all the surface problems, however devastating and shocking they may be. Neither is the answer found in political or social improvements. The answer is for individual people to be brought to Jesus Christ and discipled. This means that individual Christians—each of us—need to be faithfully sharing the gospel, teaching others what God has taught us, and encouraging our friends to do the same.

OVERFLOW

Jesus said that we will be His witnesses (Acts 1:8). What is a witness? A witness is simply one who reports what he has seen to those who did not see it—just as in court, witnesses are brought before the jury. Being a witness is all Jesus asked us to do. He never asked us to convert people because that's not our job, nor are we capable of it. We are only witnesses. Since Jesus is infinitely better than any description of Him we could give, it's a challenge—but a thrilling challenge—to report what we've seen. And, of course, there is still so much about Jesus we haven't seen! But if you have come to Him, you can introduce someone else to Him too. Right after Andrew met Jesus, he found his brother, Simon, and brought him to Jesus (John 1:40-42).

Think about this. If you see a breathtaking view, you are anxious to describe it to someone else. If you hear a fascinating story, you want to retell it. It brings fulfillment—and even increases your delight in it—to share it with someone else. Sharing the gospel should be the overflow of our delight in our Savior. Jesus said that when we come to Him to drink, our lives will overflow with living water for others. "In the last day, that great day of the feast, Jesus stood and cried, saying, If any man thirst, let him come unto Me, and drink. He that believeth on Me, as the Scripture hath said, out of his belly shall flow rivers of living water" (John 7:37-38).

The more time we spend with Jesus—learning about Him, worshiping Him, thinking about the cross—the more we will overflow with fresh insights and joy. People watch us and want to know if we are genuine. When witnessing is the overflow of our delight in Jesus, others will be able to see that what we are saying is *real* in our lives.

Let's zoom way out for a minute. Imagine that you are standing by the crystal clear river in Heaven (Revelation 22:1), say, 2,000 years from now. You are thinking about the short life you lived on earth. Maybe you reminisce about the many things you did that really didn't accomplish anything. Then you think about the people you led to Jesus and your heart throbs with joy. Looking back on your life from that heavenly perspective, it won't matter how popular you were, what you looked like, or how comfortable your life was here on earth. The one thing that will matter is what *Jesus* thought of how you lived your life. So let's start living with that as our focus right now.

ADVANTAGES OF BEING YOUNG

"People will listen to you because you are young," someone once stressed to me, encouraging me to share the gospel. I have come to realize how right he was. Adults are curious about young people and enjoy conversing with us. They are not intimidated by us—they are intrigued. The world *caters* to young people. Just look at how the media and the shopping industry revolve around the rising generation. We, as young people, have a voice.

"Do you need to plug that in?" a friendly, older lady at a local coffee shop asked me as I was setting up my laptop. She was sitting at a nearby table.

"I think it will be okay on battery for awhile. Thank you, though," I replied.

"Do you *like* working on that?" she asked.

I nodded and smiled.

"You *do?*" she said. "Let me ask you something," she continued, lowering her voice to almost a whisper. "What is texting? I hear everyone talking about it—saying that young people do it all the time!"

"Oh, you do that on your phone," I told her, pulling out my cell phone.

"Isn't that amazing!" she marveled, shaking her head.

"It can actually be sort of a waste of time," I remarked with a smile.

"I love observing young people and the things they do," she exclaimed. "We didn't even have a phone in our house when I grew up."

She then asked what I was doing in life. This gave me the opportunity to share about some ministry activities and led into a conversation about spiritual things.

I was surprised to run into this same lady again the following week. I was even more surprised when she pulled out the tract I had given her and told me that she had been showing it to her friends! Notice that this all started because she enjoyed talking with a young person.

THE PHILOSOPHY PROFESSOR

He looks like an interesting person, I thought as I saw a tall, middle-aged man with a suit coat and brightly colored tennis shoes sitting on a bench. I was at a local college helping with an outreach event and hoping to get into witnessing conversations.

"Hello," I said as I sat down next to him on the bench.

"Hello," he said, returning a friendly smile.

"Are you from the college here?" I asked.

"Yes, I'm the philosophy professor," he replied.

What did I just get myself into? I wondered.

"Oh, okay!" I said. "Can I ask you a question?"

"Sure!" he said.

"Do you consider yourself to be a good person?" I asked.

Intrigued by the question, he thought for a minute. Then he said, "Yes, I do."

"There is a 'good person test' that you can take to see if you really *are* a good person. Would you like to try it?" I asked.

"Hmmm … " he hesitated.

There was a lady sitting on the other side of him who had introduced herself as the school counselor and a local pastor.

"I'd like to hear you try it," she told him.

"Okay," he agreed.

"All right, the first question is, have you ever told a lie?"

He said he had.

We continued to talk through some of the Ten Commandments. (I like to bring up the Ten Commandments in conversations because it's a way to help people understand sin.)

"So, if you stood before God and He judged you by the Ten Commandments, would you be innocent or guilty?" I asked.

"I suppose I'd be guilty," he said.

"So, since you don't know when you will die, *if* there is a God, shouldn't it be your number one priority to make sure you are right with Him? There is just so much at stake!"

"I like to think of myself as a pretty good person," he said again.

"One reason I like to share the Ten Commandments with people is because they show us how we really appear to God," I explained. "Compared to other people, we may feel that we are pretty good. But compared to God's perfect holiness we look pretty bad. A sheep may look white against the green grass, but when it snows he looks pretty dirty."

The professor seemed to like the simple analogy. He continued, "I'm far from perfect—but I suppose I don't see myself so bad as deserving of Hell."

"Well, no one *has* to go to Hell. People choose to. God provided a way of escape for anyone who wants it … " I explained.

So here was a secular philosophy professor and a liberal woman pastor talking with a conservative Christian homeschooler—and we were all enjoying the controversial conversation. We talked for over 30 minutes about a lot of different issues. They seemed to think of me as just another student and they didn't mind listening to my "interesting ideas." I probably got away with saying a lot more without offending them than an older person could have. Sure, I didn't give the philosophy professor all the intellectual answers that others could have given, but I realized that I didn't need to. The gospel itself is very simple, and because I was young, the professor didn't expect me to give him scores of eloquent and persuasive scientific arguments. That's another advantage of witnessing when you are young. People know that we are *still young*. There is a lot we don't know yet! (That's not to say we shouldn't prepare. We will talk about this in chapter eight.)

Now is the time to get practice and experience in talking with people about the gospel. The more we do, the more we will learn what the world around us is thinking and believing—and the more we will be motivated to study in order to have good answers to their questions. By the time we are older, think how much experience we will have!

Another reason to witness now is that while we are young we usually do not make people uncomfortable. They don't feel threatened.

Since many young people today are immature, irresponsible, and apathetic,

adults notice a distinct contrast when they see a young person who takes a stand for truth and articulates what he or she believes. This alone can make a strong statement. It causes adults to think, *Here is a young person who is different. They have purpose and maturity. What is different about them?*

WASTING YOUR LIFE STARTS NOW

Let's recap: There are many definite advantages to witnessing when we are young. Adults are not intimidated by us. Young people are more willing to talk with someone their own age. We can get practice without being expected to know all the answers. We have the opportunity to stand out with clear contrast to the typical young people of this world. We have energy. We have time. We have enthusiasm. No wonder Satan wants to distract young people from doing God's work! Think of all the young people whom God used in Scripture: Joseph, Samuel, David, Daniel and his friends, King Josiah, Jeremiah, Naaman's servant girl, Esther, and Timothy, to name a few. We should never believe the lie that we cannot be powerful for the Lord when we are young! Scripture says just the opposite. It says young people are to be an *example* to the believers. "Let no man despise thy youth; but be thou an example of the believers, in word, in conversation, in charity, in spirit, in faith, in purity" (1 Timothy 4:12). In other words, we should be so responsible and mature that no one would have any reason to think little of or disregard our youthfulness. More than that, we should be an example of Christlikeness.

Of course, there are also advantages of being older and having the wisdom that comes from years of experience. But we will not get that experience if we do not start witnessing now.

DEVOTION TO OUR COMMANDER

I believe that one of the last things Satan wants is a host of young people who are excited about witnessing! Thankfully, we have a Commander who is much stronger than Satan, and He cannot be defeated. It is out of love for Him that we devote ourselves to His work. We love Him because He first loved us.

God created a perfect world, but man rebelled and turned away from Him. God would have been justified in destroying the whole human race because of our rebellion against Him. But He chose the path of mercy instead because "He delighteth in mercy" (Micah 7:18). None of us can fully understand how horrible our sin is to God, but we get a snapshot of it when we see how much it cost Jesus on the cross.

The Cost

I imagined myself as a spectator watching a scene unfold before my eyes. First, I saw a man who was helping others—yet not simply in the way that any man might help someone else. This was much different. It was as if tenderness and kindness were just flowing out of him. I could tell He was a good man—GOOD in a way that I had never seen before. Every single thing He did was good. His face was so pure. I had never seen honesty like that, never seen love like that. It's like I finally knew what love was—now that I saw Him. All I wanted to do was to keep watching Him because everything He did was so amazing. Even the simple, normal acts of service that He was doing—I was astonished by them ... by Him, I mean. The way He spoke ... I could just tell He was right, that He spoke the truth, that everything He said was right by definition. And the way He looked at people. I wished He would look at me, but He never did. I was just a spectator. But I knew I would never forget this goodness that I had seen. It was almost as if I was in a daze, not quite able to comprehend it, stunned that this kind of righteousness could even exist. I wanted to just keep watching Him. I felt that I would be content if I could simply watch Him for the rest of my life.

But then suddenly the scene changed before my eyes. I didn't want to believe what I was seeing. People were looking at Him with angry stares. It was more than mere anger; it was rage. He was looking back at them with such ... such ... I don't even know the word ... it was as if He was on a totally different playing field. There was such tenderness in His eyes. A touch of sorrow, an ocean of love. Their rage turned into vehement shouting and accusations, and then I began to watch the most horrible scene of my life. The whips they were holding were cruel and the scourging unbearable to watch. But how could this be? He was so good, so pure, so tender. He was the best person I had ever known. This must stop. I tried to yell out for someone to help, for someone to stop this. But I realized, again, I was only a spectator. Lash after lash. Blow after blow. I couldn't look—especially because it was *Him*. It was the worst possible injustice I could imagine. This could not be happening. It had to stop. It had to! But it didn't. On and on it went. Blood and bruises and jeers. And then I caught a glimpse of His face again. The same goodness and tenderness I had seen before were still there. But I almost hated to see it this time. It just made the whole scene seem worse. The forgiveness, the love. It was all so unfair. He was so … so good.

It only got worse. A cross. Nails through His hands. Nails through His feet. Agony. People laughing. Laughing? I stared in disbelief. This must stop. Please, someone stop this. I cried out to God to bring deliverance, to bring justice. But then—horror of horrors—I could not, could *not* believe what happened next. God, the Father, held a rod as well. It was much bigger than the others, and much worse. It was a rod that symbolized the stroke of justice—the wrath of God for the sins of the world. No! Please, no! This is Your beloved One. This is Your Son! The One in whom is all Your delight. Please, don't! … But then—there was darkness.

Horrified, I imagined the "rod of justice" coming down on the only One who did not deserve it. I imagined the Son being broken and crushed—yet with love and forgiveness and tenderness still flowing from Him. How could it be that God would forsake Him? How could He be pleased to crush Him?

The darkness covered all the land, and I could no longer see His face. But I heard His anguished cry: "My God, My God, why have You forsaken Me?" And in those dark moments I realized that the suffering I could *not* see was far worse than what I *could*.

Stunned and traumatized, I stepped back. I forced myself to breathe. I tried not to comprehend what I had just seen: One so deserving of glory and praise, yet receiving such punishment. I'm not sure how long it was before I realized that I was holding something: I also had a whip in my hand. It was then I understood that my hand also was on the rod that fell on Him. Was I responsible? For this? I realized that I had not been merely a spectator.

At last it was over. It was finished. It—is—finished, for all eternity! It is done! God the Father has seen the anguish of His soul and has been satisfied. Never would I have dreamed that justice would have been this costly. How vast is the extent of my sin—that this was the price. And how immeasurable the extent of His love—that this much He would pay.

—Sarah Mally

"But He was wounded for our transgressions, He was bruised for our iniquities: the chastisement of our peace was upon Him; and with His stripes we are healed. All we like sheep have gone astray; we have turned every one to His own way; and the LORD hath laid on Him the iniquity of us all ... it pleased the LORD to bruise Him; He hath put Him to grief: when Thou shalt make His soul an offering for sin ... He shall see of the travail of His soul, and shall be satisfied" (Isaiah 53:5-6, 10-11).

WHY WE SERVE HIM

"For the love of Christ constraineth us ... that they which live should not henceforth live unto themselves, but unto Him which died for them, and rose again" (2 Corinthians 5:14-15).

We are not dedicated to a system or to a list of rules—we are dedicated to a Man, Jesus Christ. He wants us to serve Him out of love—because we want to! The only reasonable response to His inconceivable love is to yield our lives, service, and affections unreservedly to Him. Not only did He save our lives, He did it by sacrificing His own.

THE QUESTION

Now think about this: out of all the ages of history, God chose for YOU to be living in the twenty-first century because He has special assignments for you—right here, right now. If you obey, He will enable you to do what He has called you to do. The work may be hard, but it is exciting and fulfilling. The Lord is offering us the privilege of working alongside Him! The question is, will we join Him? Remember, the cost is extremely high. This is what Jesus requires: Give all.

"So likewise, whosoever he be of you that forsaketh not all that he hath, he cannot be My disciple" (Luke 14:33).

RUNNING WITH THE BATON

Let's do a quick review of where we are in history right now. Two thousand years ago, Jesus Christ rose from the dead. He ascended to Heaven, and He left His disciples with the commission to take the gospel around the world. The early church began with a small group. There were only about 120 believers gathered in the upper room after Christ's ascension (Acts 1:15). Odds were against them. They weren't professionals. Scripture calls them "unschooled" and "ordinary." But they knew Jesus. And within 50 years, Christianity had spread throughout the whole Mediterranean world. It was said that "they turned the world upside down" (Acts 17:6).

In the generations that followed, persecution was extremely intense. Countless followers of Jesus laid down their lives for the sake of the gospel. Their blood was "seed," an early church father stated.[2] The more they were persecuted, the more the church grew.

This was only the beginning. In more recent centuries, men sacrificed their lives so that the Bible could be translated into our language. Men refused to compromise the truth and led a reformation, bringing people back to the basic truths of the Scriptures. The founding fathers of our nation risked their lives so future generations in America could have the opportunity to obey God freely.

In the last several hundred years, God has continued to work in this world through faithful men and women, and His work has not slowed down. Revivals. Awakenings. Missionaries sent all around the world. The explosion of missions that started in the 1800s has had such a great impact that there are now more Christians in non-Western nations than in Western ones.

Twenty-five hundred languages now have translations of the Bible, or portions of it.[3] God's work has neither declined nor decreased. Countless faithful people have gone before us, laying down their lives to spread the message of the gospel. We are the beneficiaries of their sacrifices. And now the baton has been handed to us. The responsibility rests upon our generation.

As God used the original disciples who were imperfect, ordinary, and lacking worldly credentials, He has continued for 2,000 years to do the same. He uses common people—who love Him—to accomplish His work. (See 1 Corinthians 1).

Today Jesus is at the right hand of God, building His church. In a short while, He is coming back as Judge and King. Very soon, we will see Him face to face. That will be a *very* exciting day! It could be that we are the last generation before Jesus' return. It could be that this is the home stretch for the church—the last lap. The baton—the gospel—has now been handed to us, and there is still much work to be done! In every nation, people are dying without Christ. An estimated 150,000 people die every day (that's approximately two people per second), and those who do not know Christ will be separated from God eternally, paying the penalty for their sins in Hell.

This brings us back to the question each one of us must ask ourselves: What has God given *me* to do?

We have been entrusted with the most valuable news in the world—the saving message of the cross. Let us follow in the steps of those who have gone before. Heaven is watching. The world is waiting.

CHAPTER 2

THE LITTLE ENGINE THAT COULDN'T

As I looked around at the décor in the cozy office, I noticed that nearly everything had something to do with fishing. I had scheduled an appointment with a godly older man, Mr. Garvin, because I knew he loved to witness. He calls it "fishing." He is continually sharing exciting stories of people whom he has led to the Lord. I wanted to glean from his advice and ideas.

While I was in his office, his phone kept ringing, so I listened with interest.

"Can you remember the last time you led someone to the Lord?" he asked the caller.

Pause

"No? Well, have you ever prayed and asked God to make you a fisherman?"

Pause

"Do you want to pray and ask God to make you into a fisherman right now?" he asked.

Good point! I thought. Jesus said, "Ask and it will be given unto you" (Matthew 7:7). If witnessing is a weak or absent area of your life, it may be because you haven't asked the Lord to make you a fisherman. If you truly desire to be fruitful in your witnessing, remember that this is something *Jesus* does in you. Jesus said, "Follow Me, and *I* will make you fishers of men" (Matthew 4:19).

When we see weaknesses or failings in our lives, we have a tendency to respond in one of the following two ways:

- We think, *It is impossible for me to change, so why even try? I would never be able to do that.*
- We have the opposite response and ardently resolve, *I can do this! From this day on, I'm going to be different!*

Both of these are actually incorrect responses. We should not give up, nor should we rely on our own strength. The correct response is to **pray**, asking *God* to change us. That which is impossible for us is *very* possible with God. None of us have the ability to witness as we should, but God is able to make us into powerful witnesses for His glory. If we do not believe this is possible, then we are underestimating God's power and insulting Him through unbelief. None of us have sufficient love, boldness, zeal, or strength—and we are not supposed to pretend we do. We are supposed to walk humbly with our God (Micah 6:8), drawing our strength from Him. "I am the vine, ye are the branches: He that abideth in Me, and I in him, the same bringeth forth much fruit: for without Me ye can do nothing" (John 15:5).

To take this point further, let's consider a far-fetched scenario. Imagine you are taking an architecture class and your professor hands you your assignment: "Build a two-story facility for your church with 12-foot ceilings and plenty of natural light."

You stare at the assignment in disbelief. "You actually want me to *build* something? Not just draw the blueprints, but construct an actual building? That's impossible!"

Then the professor says, "By the way, I've already designed the plans and bought the piece of property. I hired the construction crew and put $10,000,000 in the bank for this project. Oh, and I'm going to be working with you."

Now you are thinking, *Seriously? I can't wait to get started!*

In the same way, witnessing can feel like an impossible assignment. We know we are inadequate and we often don't even know how to start! Witnessing doesn't come naturally for any of us, and there is an enemy trying to stop the work. We conclude it's too difficult. We would prefer to sit back, relax, and return to those forms of ministry with which we feel more comfortable.

Jesus has definitely not given us an easy task. He tells us to go into all the world and make disciples of all nations. No shortcuts. No leave of absence. *How can we possibly carry this out?*

The answer lies in the next few pieces of relevant information: "By the way, if you need anything—just ask. Provisions, strength, wisdom—just ask. There is no need to fear; the enemy has already been defeated. Resist him and he'll flee from you." His directives continue, "You don't need to worry about seeing visible results or numbers—that's not how things are measured around here. Oh, and one more thing—I'll be coming with you."

Jesus is coming with us? Well, that certainly changes things! (To see Scripture's exact words, see Philippians 4:19; John 14:13-14; James 1:5; James 4:7; 2 Corinthians 4:18; Luke 16:10; and Ephesians 1:19.)

Right at the beginning of this book, let's be clear about two things. 1) Witnessing is not easy. 2) We are working alongside our King who created the universe and upholds it by His power.

We state, "It's impossible," but God reminds us, "That's the point!" He tells us to do what is humanly impossible so that we depend on Him for every inch of the journey.

Although Jesus has given us a staggeringly high calling, when we start looking at the details of the work-assignment, we see that there are some things to be majorly encouraged about!

This is God's work, not ours. Success is measured by His standards, not ours. God goes before us and prepares the way. He has His troops all over the earth, and we are just one of the millions whom He can deploy at any minute. He even works for good in spite of our mistakes. God is not limited by anything! Jesus told us to "be of good cheer," because even though we will have trouble in this world, He has already overcome it (John 16:33). We are already on the winning team.

Knowing all of this gives us peace as we work. We realize it's not all on our shoulders. He does the heavy-lifting, the orchestrating, and the brunt of the work. He is the One who draws people to Himself (John 6:44). It is merely a privilege that He allows us to help—and it is actually sort of baffling when you think about it. Here's the best news in the world—and *we* get the thrill of sharing it!

WHO GETS THE CREDIT?

"They're out of gas," my dad said after going inside the small, rundown gas station in "nowhere," Missouri.

"There's just one guy in there, sitting at a table—reading," Dad reported to the rest of us back in the van.

"Why is he even open if he is out of gas?" we asked.

Sounds like a good witnessing opportunity, I thought. *Maybe we could give him something else to read.*

I joined my dad as he walked back in, and the man stood up to greet us. I glanced over at the little table where he had been sitting and was shocked to see a familiar book—one we often give to unbelievers. In fact, we had it in our give-away box in the van at the time.

God must want us to talk with this man! we concluded.

"How do you like the book?" my dad asked him.

In a thick Italian accent, he explained that he believed in Jesus, but he thought that one must also earn his own salvation.

"But if you earn it, then who gets the credit?" my dad asked.

"That's how you earn it—by getting credits! Go to church. Believe. Pray," he said.

Obviously, he didn't understand Dad's point!

"If we earned it, then it would not be by God's *mercy*," Dad explained.

Stumped, the man thought for a second, but then returned to his salvation-by-works mentality.

Now what? How do we convince someone in one conversation that we can't earn our salvation, when he has been thinking that way for his entire life? Often, we can't. But we have a special tool—prayer. The God who put the book in his hands and brought us across his path (on the very day he was reading it!) is the God who is powerful enough to change his thinking too! This is another reassuring aspect of knowing we are working by God's side— on His team. We don't have to bear the responsibility of convincing people or converting them. We simply get the joy of being the message bringer—leaving the results in God's hands. We are only one piece of the puzzle.

Before that trip I had prayed that the Lord would prepare the hearts of the people to whom we would witness along the way. He answered that prayer a little more vividly than I was expecting!

SURPRISES IN STARBUCKS

"Lord, please lead me to someone to witness to," I prayed while running errands.

I walked into Starbucks, just to check if there would be an opportunity there to witness. I was quite surprised by what I overheard!

"It's very interesting," an older man was explaining to another customer. "It's a whole museum in Kentucky based on the book of Genesis. It proves by science that evolution couldn't have happened. Very convincing!"

Okay. I was in Iowa. I was at Starbucks. The Creation Museum was 500 miles away. *Sure, it is an item of growing interest, but people don't just talk about it everywhere!*

It is not a coincidence that I am here, I thought.

I walked over to his table and introduced myself. "I'm sorry to interrupt, but I just had to say something," I told him, "because I have actually spent quite a bit of time at that museum. In fact, I volunteered there for several weeks. I agree—it's a great place and something our country definitely needs!"

If God wants me here for a reason, I'd better see what it is, I decided. I ordered an iced latte and sat down at a table in the café that was not too far from his. Right away he began asking me questions—and soon I found myself fully engaged in a friendly conversation with a laid-back, elderly man who reminded me of a fun-loving grandpa.

After a few minutes of discussion, I laid a tract down on the table in front of him, hoping it would take the conversation to another level. It did.

"Can I ask you a question?" I said.

"Sure," Mr. Grandpa replied.

"Do you think eternal life is a free gift or something we have to earn?"

"What's that?" he asked, surprised.

I restated my question.

He hesitated. "I guess I haven't really thought about it much. What's *your* opinion?"

I love it when people ask that!

"Well," I said, "Romans 6:23 says that 'the wages of sin is death but the **gift** of God is eternal life through Jesus Christ our Lord.' So the Bible says that eternal life is a gift—which is great news for us! I know that I could never make it to Heaven on my own (God's standard is perfection!) but Jesus died the death I deserved."

He seemed to be interested, so I continued, "If you think you have to earn your way, you'll never know when you've been good enough. But the Bible says that we can be sure before we die that we are going to Heaven. First John 5:13 says, 'These things I have written to you who believe in the name of the Son of God, that you may **know** that you have eternal life.'"

"I'll have to say, I really can't argue with you," he said. "Honestly, I don't know why I believe some of the things I believe."

"Well, people teach many different things these days," I replied, "so it's important that we know the Bible well and compare everything with it."

"You sound a lot like my grandson and his wife," he told me.

My ears perked up when I heard this. *Maybe he has a believing grandson who is praying for him!*

"They've been trying to get me to go to church with them," he continued, "and, you know, I should probably go one of these days ... "

After asking him a few questions, I was very surprised to discover that I knew his grandson's wife! Just a few months earlier, a friend had introduced me to a young mom who loves to witness, and I had met up with her to talk about witnessing! Now here I was, witnessing to her grandfather-in-law. Could this be an answer to her prayers?

I knew this was no coincidence.

About 30 minutes had passed now. Here we were, total strangers—still sitting a few tables apart from each other—but having a lively conversation about spiritual things. *And maybe adding some interest to everyone sitting in Starbucks.*

Eventually, Mr. Grandpa came and joined me at my table.

I suppose if we are going to keep talking, it does make sense to sit at the same table!

"What do you think about life after death?" he asked.

I explained that I am 100% sure I'm going to Heaven, not because I'm a good person but because I believe the Bible when it says, "Believe on the Lord Jesus Christ and you will be saved."

There were others in Starbucks pretending to read the newspaper, but I had a feeling most of them were listening to us. My feelings were confirmed when a lady came up to our table and said, "I'm sorry to interrupt, but your conversation was so interesting! I just wanted to know what you were talking about."

"Have a seat!" I offered.

Now there were three of us sitting around the table.

I asked her the same question: "Do you think eternal life is a free gift or something you have to earn?"

"Oh my, honey, you gotta earn it," she said. "You gotta work for it every day, doing what's right, being a good person ... "

"So how do you know when you've been good enough?" I asked.

"Well, if you've been a good person all your life, then you can pretty much know that you're going to Heaven," she said.

About this time, I looked up and was surprised to see a friend of mine, Ally, walk in!

"Ally!" I waved her over. "I'm talking with two friends here that I just met. Do you want to join us?"

Now we had four people around the little table. This was getting really fun!

"You know," I explained, "we may *think* that we are a 'good person' compared to someone else, but we can't just compare ourselves with those around us because God's standards are higher than ours."

"Well, you tell me what you think then," the lady told me.

"Okay," I said. *If you insist! [smile]*

I shared, once again, the good news that we don't have to earn our salvation. This time I used the example of the thief on the cross, explaining that when the thief believed on Jesus, Jesus told him, "Today you will be with Me in paradise." But the thief had not done even one good work to get there. Not one! And even if the thief had done thousands of good works, it wouldn't have earned him a place in Heaven. His sin needed to be paid for, and only Jesus could do that.

"That's right," the lady agreed emphatically, "you can't get there on your own! No, no, we need God's forgiveness!"

Hmmm, I thought, *she just said the opposite a few minutes ago. I wonder if she really understands.*

I replied, "But if God is a *just* Judge, He can't forgive someone merely because they are sorry. A truly good judge wouldn't let a murderer go free, would he? No matter how sorry the murderer was! The reason God can forgive and still be just in doing so is because Jesus took our punishment. *Now* we can go free—and God can still be just [in letting us go free]." "That He might be just, and the justifier of him which believeth in Jesus" (Romans 3:26).

Ally added, "I think it really helps to think of God as a Father. Once we are in His family, we *want* to obey Him and do good works. But we don't do them out of fear, but out of love."

"And we don't do good works to *get into* His family. We are born into His family by believing in Jesus," I explained.

The lady agreed and asked if she could take the tract that was lying on the table.

As Ally shared some of her testimony, I was thinking, *It is no coincidence that Ally walked in just now.*

A guy sat down at the table right next to us and opened his laptop. I wondered, *Is he actually working or is he just listening to our conversation?*

The next item of discussion at the Starbucks Theological Seminar table was the accuracy of the Bible. Before I knew it, two hours had passed in the Starbucks café. I left with the excitement of knowing that *God* had orchestrated our paths to cross, and *God* would still be at work in their hearts. He starts the work. He finishes the work.

When Ally walked into Starbucks, I was so happy to see her—and I was strengthened by her presence and support. There is a special fellowship we experience among believers when we do more than "hang out" together, but rather, actually "pull" together—working side by side in the gospel. But do you know what is even more emboldening than the support of our brothers and sisters in Christ? It is the promise that Jesus made to His disciples right after He gave the Great Commission. He said, " … and, lo, I am with you alway[s], even unto the end of the world" (Matthew 28:20).

Have you ever said to a friend, "I'll do it, if you go with me?" How about having the Creator of the universe as the Friend who is going with you?

ADVENTURE

We all love adventure, right? Inside, we have this innate desire to *be where the action is.* So, what is the most exciting adventure of life? Sky diving? Competing in the Olympics? Getting married? Being a fighter pilot or an astronaut?

The *most* exciting adventure in life is being with God and obeying God. Nothing else even compares. Think of it this way: God designed the universe, orchestrated history, and strategized victory over every spiritual force of wickedness. He is daily deploying His troops to "battle," building toward the most incredible showdown the world has yet to witness (Revelation 19:11), and He has assignments for *you* to do! You are a part of the work the Lord is accomplishing in this world (Ephesians 2:10). He is using your labor for Him to fulfill a portion of the beautiful tapestry He is weaving. Everything God does is important. No matter how small the assignment may seem, each assignment from God is significant, and each one brings adventure!

Witnessing is one of those adventures. There are unknowns. We can't predict how the other person will respond, but we know that God is at work. One might think that unknowns would make it frightening, but it actually makes it exciting. We have to step out in faith, trusting the One who is calling us to action. We realize that we are not actually in true danger, no matter what happens, because the enemy can destroy our body but not our soul (Matthew 10:28). If we allow ourselves to think, "What if this happens," or, "What if that happens," it will only fuel our fear and anxiety. But when believers take their eyes off of their failures and inabilities, and put them on the Lord and His strength—watch out! That kind of faith produces children of God who are overcomers and who greatly impact this world. "For whatsoever is born of God overcometh the world: and this is the victory that overcometh the world, even our faith" (1 John 5:4).

Let's be honest. Do you *feel* capable to strongly impact this world for Jesus? Neither do I. Each one of us is, well, a little engine that simply "can't." But look at who God is!

"Hast thou not known? hast thou not heard, that the everlasting God, the LORD, **the Creator of the ends of the earth, fainteth not, neither is weary? there is no searching of His understanding. He giveth power to the faint; and to them that have no might He increaseth strength** (Isaiah 40:28-29).

"I, even I, am the LORD; and beside Me there is no saviour … Yea, before the day was I am He; and there is none that can deliver out of My hand: **I will work, and who shall [reverse] it?**" (Isaiah 43:11-13).

"Ah Lord GOD! … **there is nothing too hard for Thee** … the Great, the Mighty God, the LORD of hosts, is His name, Great in counsel, and mighty in work … " (Jeremiah 32:17-19).

"My counsel shall stand, and I will do all my pleasure … yea, I have spoken it, I will also bring it to pass; **I have purposed it, I will also do it**" (Isaiah 46:10-11).

"Who is like unto Thee, O LORD, among the gods? … glorious in holiness, fearful in praises, **doing wonders?**" (Exodus 15:11).

DRIVEN TO ACTION

The knowledge of the awesomeness of God should never cause us to lean back and relax—rather it should drive us to action. As we realize the power behind us and the needs in front of us, we are compelled to move forward with boldness. This is exactly what one soldier did about 3,000 years ago, during a time of great distress in the land of Israel. This soldier saw that his people were on the brink of disaster. The angry army attacking them consisted of 30,000 chariots, 6,000 horsemen, and people like the sand on the seashore in abundance. And his own army? Only about 600 men. In addition to the horrendous odds, the 600 did not even have weapons. Impossible situation? Pretty much! The terrified people of the land hid themselves in caves, cliffs, and cellars, and some moved out of the country.

However, this soldier had faith in the power of God. He decided that he would attack the entire army by himself. Yes, just he and his armor bearer. At least that's the way it looked on the surface. It was actually he, *his God*, and his armor bearer. Jonathan saw the need and didn't wait for someone else to do it. He rose up to do it himself. As Jonathan approached the Philistines to attack, he explained his reasoning to his armor bearer. " ... there is no restraint to the LORD to save by many or by few" (1 Samuel 14:6). Jonathan's great faith in God drove him to climb up a cliff, enter the enemy camp, and take on the entire army. The Lord won a great victory for Israel through Jonathan that day. (Read the full story in 1 Samuel 13-14.)

We have the same God. Without faith it is impossible to please Him (Hebrews 11:6), but with faith we can do the impossible—because He does it, not us. He is pleased when our confidence in Him propels us to bold action. The more difficult the odds, the more God gets the glory.

Initiative is taking responsibility and assuming leadership instead of waiting for someone else to do it. It is demonstrating courage and vision because we know the God whom we serve.

Sometimes God opens wide a door for us to share about Jesus. Maybe someone asks us a question or makes a comment about spiritual beliefs, and we get the joy of sharing the gospel. But often it's not that easy. Sometimes God doesn't open the door in an obvious way. Sometimes people do not ask questions. Does that mean we don't get to talk about Jesus? Of course not!

Jesus has commanded us to go and proclaim the gospel. This requires taking initiative, looking for ways to open doors, and using creativity to turn conversations to Jesus.

My dad is continually coming up with ideas of how to start discussions about the gospel.

"I think we should use Thanksgiving as a door-opener for getting into conversations," my dad announced to our witnessing team as we were driving to a shopping mall on a busy mid-November day.

Hmm ... I think that will just make it more awkward, I thought.

We arrived at the mall, prayed, divided in pairs and began looking for people with whom we could talk. Since I was paired up with my dad, we used *his* plan. (Funny how that works out. *[smile]*)

My dad was right; using a question about the holiday made a very nice flow from a normal conversation to a spiritual one. Here's what happened:

"Would you be willing to answer some questions about Thanksgiving?"

my dad and I asked a young couple who were strolling past the food court.

"Sure," they said.

"Great. The first question is, do you have Thanksgiving traditions in your family?"

"Yes."

"Who do you give thanks to?" we asked.

"Well, to God, of course," they answered, with an expression implying *Who else would we thank?*

"What do you thank Him for?" we asked.

"For food and health and family … " they replied.

"Great. Have you ever thanked Him for eternal life?"

They looked at each other a little surprised, and the guy, Daniel, said, "Well, you can't thank God for eternal life until you *have* eternal life—and you can't have that until you're dead."

We took some time to explain from the Bible how we *can* know before we die, and, in fact, how we *must* know before we die. But like most other people, they thought eternal life was something you had to work for.

"If you have to earn it, you can never know *when* you have earned it," my dad explained. "But the Bible tells us that we are not good enough, and never could be."

This was a new concept for them. They were very interested and brought up a number of questions.

My dad asked them, "Why can the death of one Man save us?" This seemed to arouse their curiosity.

Dad explained, "It wasn't really the Roman soldiers who were punishing Jesus—even though it looked that way. It was God. He was punishing Jesus for the sin of the world."

I mentioned that we could never get to Heaven on our own, but that Jesus is the only way. I explained, "He is like the … the … "

"The ticket?" Francisca asked.

"Yes—exactly—He's like the ticket that gets us to Heaven … "

We continued to discuss these things for about 45 minutes. Daniel told us, "I think God is using you as His mouthpiece to speak to us today."

The girl, Francisca, agreed.

"Well, if the Lord is bringing this to your attention, then you should take care of it right away and not put it off," we told them, explaining that we have a responsibility to respond to the Lord.

Sensing that their hearts were open, we continued, "You said you have never asked God for eternal life. Is that something you would like to do now?" We offered to pray with them, and I began looking for a corner where we could escape the busy flow of people walking by.

"We can pray right here!" Daniel said.

If it's okay with them, it's fine with us!

Right there in the busy stream of holiday shoppers, we bowed our heads to pray. First, my dad prayed for them (it's good for non-believers to hear us pray), and then Francisca said she wanted to pray. She confessed her sin and asked the Lord for eternal life. Francisca texted me later that evening expressing thankfulness, and a few weeks later my dad and I drove to her town to take her to a church in her area. We continued to stay in touch.

I was so encouraged by that conversation in the mall! Notice, however, that the witnessing opportunity wasn't thrown into our lap; we had to work for it. Missionaries throughout history have had to labor for these gospel conversations by traveling over mountains, enduring harsh conditions, risking the persecution of unfriendly governments, and laying down their very lives. In light of their hardships, going to the mall with a little holiday questionnaire doesn't feel quite so aggressive or bold!

If we do not make an intentional effort to engage people, it is unlikely that we will have many opportunities to share the gospel. Every time we witness we gain more experience, acquire new ideas, and become a little more comfortable with the process. It takes time to learn—but we will never learn if we never start.

SO HOW DO WE START?

What should we say first? How should we say it? What if no ideas are coming to mind? That's what I wondered one time when Mom was gone for the evening. I was about seven or eight years old, and I had an interesting new task set before me: making dinner for my brother and dad. *What should I make?* This was quite a big decision! I looked in the fridge. I looked in the freezer. I looked in the cabinet. I couldn't think of anything. After pondering my predicament, I suddenly had an idea—frozen corn! I warmed it up in the microwave and set it on the table. "Time for supper, Dad and Stephen!" I'm not sure what my dad and Stephen thought, but they acted like they appreciated the corn!

Without experience, it's unlikely that one would have many ideas of how something should be done. It takes time to learn. We can't expect to know everything about witnessing overnight.

I am not very good at chess. My brother Stephen and I would play occasionally when we were little, and Stephen would have me in checkmate in about eight moves. It was sort of depressing. I hated seeing all my little conquered pieces in a pile by Stephen's side. Soon I would get tired of the game and give up. In future years when people would ask me if I wanted to play chess, I'd simply say no to save myself the embarrassment! Who enjoys losing? However, if I had applied myself and played more often, I would have improved. (Maybe. *[smile]*)

Have you noticed that when you improve in a certain skill or activity, you also begin to enjoy it more? With practice, things that were scary become comfortable. Things that were intimidating become second nature. Things that were petrifying can even become fun.

If you are terrified of witnessing, chances are you have not practiced very much. You haven't learned from your mistakes because you haven't even given yourself the opportunity to make mistakes!

How does someone who has cooking skills that peak at Ramen noodles and toasted cheese sandwiches develop into a gourmet chef? They practice often, they collect good recipes from others and improve them, they learn how ingredients work together, they gain knowledge from those who are more skilled than they are, they read blogs and watch YouTube videos about cooking, and they are not scared to try something new. All of these principles apply to witnessing.

THE BIG CELEBRATION FOR ... WHO IS HE AGAIN?

It's loud, it's busy, and swarms of people are just waiting around for the parade to start. Most people don't even know who St. Patrick was, and with curiosity they receive our little tract called *History of St. Patrick*. Many express gratefulness, and some ask for a second one for a friend. We have found that three people can pass out 1,000 tracts in an hour at the parade. But with 10 or 12 people ... you do the math. It's simply a matter of how many we want to print and fold beforehand! After passing out the tracts, we try to get into conversations. The goal is to cover the gospel with the person you are witnessing to before the marching band goes by!

I approached two guys and a girl who looked like they were in their mid-twenties.

"Hey, I'm taking a survey," (which I now prefer to call questionnaires) I said to a group of three. "Would you mind answering some questions?"

"What's it about?" they replied.

"It's about St. Patrick and the Ten Commandments ... " I answered.

"Oh, we're bad people," they laughed as they took another drink from their beer bottles.

But one of them, who I'll call Joe, said, "Sure, I'll take the survey."

"Okay!" I replied. "The first question is, where was St. Patrick born?"

"Ireland," Joe replied.

"Nope! Nice try, but he was actually English. He was captured as a kid, sold as a slave, and brought to Ireland. Second question: Why do you think St. Patrick was such a great person?"

"Uh … he was Irish and he drank beer?" he guessed.

"Uh, no, sorry," I smiled. "He was a missionary and brought the gospel to Ireland. The third question is, do you consider yourself to be a good person?"

"No, I'm bad!" Joe emphasized.

"Yeah, he is!" his friends told me. "He's going straight to Hell!" they joked.

"The fourth question," I continued, "is if God judged you by the Ten Commandments, would you be innocent or guilty?"

"Guilty. Definitely," Joe said.

"That's for sure!" his friends added.

"Would you like to know what St. Patrick preached about how we can be sure we are going to Heaven?" I asked him.

"Sure," Joe agreed.

"Well, St. Patrick preached that we have all sinned and when God judges us, we'll all be guilty. But when Jesus died on the cross, He was taking the punishment that we deserved from God. It's as if Jesus switched places with us and He took our punishment. That doesn't mean the whole world is going to Heaven now—but it means that those who choose to come to God and believe Him *can*, because He made a way for us to be forgiven."

I was encouraged to see a serious look in Joe's eyes as I said this, and I felt that he was comprehending what I was saying.

His friend interrupted again, "Are you saying that my friend is going to Hell because he is Irish and he drinks?"

"You weren't listening, were you?" I said with a smile.

"He never listens! But *I heard you*," Joe stressed, looking me in the eye.

Those last words stuck with me. His warm response indicated to me that he would at least think about what I had said.

What is successful witnessing? If we feel unsuccessful in our witnessing, it could be that we have the wrong measure of success. Success is not measured by how many we lead to Christ. It is not winning a debate or handing out all the tracts in our bag. It is not keeping everyone happy. It is not even escaping with our life! Successful witnessing is accurately representing Jesus on earth. It is being obedient to the Lord, trusting Him to give the fruit. It is being faithful. It is proclaiming the gospel boldly as Jesus did—no matter what response we receive.

One day we will be able to look back and see all the ways God was putting the puzzle pieces together. In some cases, our witnessing may simply consist of

planting or watering a seed. It could be quoting one Bible verse, handing out one tract, or communicating one concept about salvation. We do not know all that God is doing in people's lives; we only see a small fraction of it. But we know what our job is: to speak of Jesus.

God is calling each of us to do great things for Him. As Jesus said, "He that believeth on Me, the works that I do shall he do also; and greater works than these shall he do; because I go unto My Father" (John 14:12). Most of us set life goals that we think we can reach. But if we can reach them in our own strength it means they are far too small. It means we are not taking into consideration the fact that we serve a God who is able to do exceedingly and abundantly above all that we ever ask or think (Ephesians 3:20).

In reality, the Great Commission we have been given is not completed when someone trusts in Jesus Christ as Savior. That's actually only the beginning. We are also called to *disciple* others, teaching them all the things that Jesus has commanded us. Jesus said, "Go ye therefore, and teach all nations … teaching them to observe all things whatsoever I have commanded you" (Matthew 28:19-20). Yes, this is an enormous assignment. And yes, we have a powerful God!

"And they went forth, and preached everywhere, **the Lord working with them** … " (Mark 16:20).

Justified by Injustice

By His wounds I am healed.

By His blood I am cleansed.

By His bondage I am set free.

By His poverty I am made rich.

He was humiliated to remove my shame.

He became sin that I might become righteousness.

He was rejected that I might be welcomed home.

He became a curse that I might be blessed.

He became an outcast that I might become an heir.

He was numbered with the transgressors
that I might be numbered with the saints.

He stepped down to the lowest place
that He might raise me up to reign with Him.

He died that I might live!

IS YOUR PERSPECTIVE UPSIDE DOWN?

I love scents—and the smell of roasting coffee beans is one of my favorites. That is one of the reasons I love going to Roasters, a coffee shop in our town that roasts their own beans. While sipping my warm drink at Roasters one winter afternoon and catching up with some friends from out-of-town, I noticed a college-age Muslim girl typing on her laptop at a nearby table. I wanted to talk with her, but what would I say? *I could simply ask her where she is from,* I thought, *but wouldn't that be a little awkward?*

Excuses began to bombard my mind (a frequent occurrence when I'm considering witnessing to someone!) *It's sort of awkward to just walk up to someone's table and start talking to them. Maybe she would feel self-conscious or uncomfortable. Sarah (my sister) is ready to leave and I don't want to make her wait for me.*

"What should I do, Lord?" I asked. I couldn't decide. I stood by the door, stalling.

"Lord? Should I speak to her?" I prayed again.

Then I had a thought. *What do I have to **lose** by simply greeting that girl and asking her where she's from? Could it really do any harm?*

In these situations, sometimes the best thing to do is to just try something. In fact, that would probably be a good witnessing motto: *Just try something!*

I quickly prayed again and walked over to her table.

"Hi, so where are you from?" I asked her.

"From here, Cedar Rapids," she replied coolly, a little surprised that I asked.

Great. Now what do I say? I wondered, feeling a little awkward.

"Oh, okay! Well, I have a friend who is Muslim and she's from Egypt, so I just wondered if your parents were originally from Egypt or Saudi Arabia or somewhere in the Middle East," I replied casually, hoping to continue the conversation somehow.

"My parents came from Palestine," she explained graciously. "So right around there."

She seemed happy to talk and the awkwardness disappeared.

"So are you in college?" she asked.

"No, I'm actually working with a ministry for young ladies called Bright Lights,"[1] I told her. When I explained that one of the messages we teach girls is the importance of purity, this struck a chord with her.

"Wow, that is so needed today," she said. "It's amazing what girls do just to get attention. They really cheapen themselves."

"I know, it's really sad," I agreed.

"Here, you can sit down if you'd like," she offered. I sat across the table from her, and we talked for another five minutes or so.

"It's great to meet someone else who thinks the same. It sounds like we have similar backgrounds," she told me.

"Do you come here a lot? Maybe we could meet for coffee sometime," I suggested.

She agreed and we exchanged e-mail addresses.

Six days later, I found myself feeling somewhat apprehensive as I was driving back to the coffee shop to meet with my new Muslim friend, whom I hardly knew. I walked in and found her in the same spot with her laptop. We started chatting right away.

"I'm really glad this worked out," I told her. "I know it was a little random."

"I'm such a random person too!" she said.

We hit it off immediately.

She explained to me about her studies in law, and I explained more about the Bright Lights ministry and our views about purity and relationships.

"In my culture, girls don't start a relationship with a guy until both parents agree," she told me.

"Yes, my family thinks the same way," I said.

"I'm shocked!" she replied. "What denomination are you?"

I shrugged. "Nothing. We just believe the Bible."

(Our family attends a small Bible church, but we are not part of a denomination.)

An hour and a half later, she said, "I'm so hungry. Do you have plans for tonight? Do you want to grab something to eat at the place next door?"

"Sounds great to me!" I replied, and we walked over to the Middle Eastern restaurant next door.

This was the start of a great friendship. Over the past three years, she and I have continued to have lots of good times together—including many in-depth conversations about the Lord. One night after going out for ice cream, I brought her to my house and introduced her to my family. This resulted in a two-hour spiritual discussion with my dad. At midnight, she said she had to leave. She was disappointed because she said it was "just getting interesting." She doesn't know the Lord yet, but we are praying for her.

I think back to how I almost walked out of that coffee shop without meeting this Muslim girl. I am so glad that I didn't listen to those excuses but that I went over and said hi.

THE ALIENS STOLE MY TRACTS!

Sometimes we make dumb excuses for not witnessing: *I'm not in the right mood right now. I might be doing it for the wrong motive. Someone else would be better. My hair is a mess. If God wants them to be saved He will reach them. It's too early in the morning. They look grumpy. I need to pray about it first. They look like they might be a terrorist. I don't have any tracts with me today. They might not speak English.*

The human mind is brilliant when it comes to devising excuses. Seriously, we are amazingly good at this. We can think of an excuse to get out of just about anything! Sometimes we even teach *other* people to make the same excuses we are making. That is why we need to be careful when we spend time with Christians who do not share their faith. We need to make sure that *their* excuses do not rub off on *us!* Since excuses can be a big obstacle, keeping us from being bold with the gospel, let's evaluate a few of them.

EXCUSE: "I DON'T HAVE THE RIGHT PERSONALITY."

It is easy to conclude that witnessing is done best by outgoing people. But interestingly, I've observed that quiet people are often even more bold in sharing their faith. It doesn't matter what your personality is. What matters is that we see people as Christ does—with a deep concern for their souls. This drives us to action. *"Love will find a way. Indifference will find an excuse."* —Anonymous

Naturally, each one of us will handle conversations differently depending on our personalities—and that is a good thing! God made variety. This world is full of unique individuals with distinct, colorful personalities. God is the One who matches up who is going to witness to whom. Maybe *your personality* is the perfect one to witness to the person before you. But remember, human nature is the same, and God can use anybody to reach anybody.

And by the way, shyness *can* be overcome. Once we set our focus on the needs of others, we suddenly realize that sometimes being shy is actually being selfish. When someone is in danger, and we know it but don't tell them—that is selfish. When someone is lonely and hurting and we fail to talk with them, that is selfish. The good news is that we serve a God who turns weaknesses into strengths! If God changed your sinful heart into a clean one, He is also capable of changing your shy personality into one that reaches out.

My mom used to be very quiet. In high school, she usually wouldn't talk to anyone unless they talked to her first. Even after she married my dad and was working in youth ministry, she struggled with interacting with the youth at their gatherings. My dad encouraged her to simply force herself to walk up to someone, introduce herself, and ask them questions about themselves. It was the *loving* thing to do. So, step by step, my mom began to overcome her shyness and get to know others. Now my mom is one of the best people I know at reaching out to others!

SERVING SPRITE

Jennifer was a thirteen-year-old volunteer at a hospital with a special responsibility: to serve Sprite to a paralyzed young man who couldn't feed himself. Jennifer wanted to tell him about Jesus, but she was scared. She was shy. She didn't know how to start. As she rode the elevator to his room week after week, her desire to share Jesus continued to grow. Yet she was so fearful she never managed to tell him. Then … the young man died.

Devastated, Jennifer wondered, *Why didn't I have the boldness to at least say something?* She repented of her selfishness and fear, and she knew she would never forget this young man. Later, Jennifer learned some wonderful news: this young man was from a Christian family and was thought to be a believer. Jennifer was relieved and thankful, but this situation was a turning point in her life. She determined to forsake her fears and obey Jesus—the One who gives us strength when we obey.

As a side note, what if another Christian would have "coached" Jennifer, and given her some ideas of what to say to this young man? Maybe Jennifer could have simply shared a small story from her own life, or shared about a Christian activity she was involved in that week. Maybe she could have read him one verse from the Bible or told him she was praying for him. Small comments often open a door for bigger comments. Witnessing may not have been as difficult as Jennifer imagined.

As we discussed in chapter two, God works through our weaknesses.

Therefore, it may actually be a hidden advantage if you feel "extra weak" in the area of talking to strangers. You are one step closer to being used mightily by God, because you are already learning what it means to be dependent on Him, instead of trusting in your own social abilities.

"That the communication of thy faith may become effectual by the acknowledging of every good thing which is in you in Christ Jesus" (Philemon 1:6).

EXCUSE: "SHARING YOUR FAITH WITH STRANGERS DOESN'T WORK; YOU HAVE TO BECOME FRIENDS FIRST."

Some people think that they should wait until *after* they have developed a friendship with a person before they talk about Jesus. But that's not what we see in Scripture. Think of all the times Jesus or one of His disciples witnessed to a "stranger." A few examples are the woman at the well, the Ethiopian Eunuch, Lydia of Thyatira, and Paul in the market place at Athens. In fact, most of the evangelism stories recorded in the gospels and the book of Acts were with "strangers" in public places. Look for yourself! Building relationships is important, and we know that Jesus *did* build relationships. Yet we can become friends and share about Christ all at the same time. We can build a relationship in minutes, not months. Actually, the longer you wait to mention the Lord, the harder it is because they wonder, "Why didn't you say something sooner if this is so important?"

Jon Speed writes in his book *Evangelism in the New Testament* that the question we should be asking when evaluating methods of evangelism is not, "Is it effective?" but rather, "Is it biblical?" He explains that over 80% of the witnessing encounters recorded in the New Testament are times when Jesus and His disciples shared the gospel with *strangers* in *public places.*[2]

"You know, Dad, maybe I'm doing this wrong," I complained after arriving home from witnessing one afternoon. "Recently someone told me that it's better to make friends with the person first and *then* present the gospel," I said.

"That's called friendship evangelism," Dad replied. "This is what happens," he told me as he got out a piece of paper and a pencil. In really big letters he wrote the word "FRIENDSHIP" and then in teeny-tiny letters he wrote "evangelism."

"Often this is exactly how it turns out," Dad explained. "Lots of friendship but very little evangelism." My dad regrets all the time he used to spend "building relationships" with people who weren't even interested in the Lord.

Don't get me wrong: Making friends with people in order to share the gospel with them is a good plan! It's just not the *only* way. We are not *limited* to that method. If we think that we cannot witness to someone because he or she is not our friend, we are believing a false concept. Think about it practically: We only have so many hours in our lifetime. We have limited human capacity. How many friends could we actually add to our life right now? Then think about the rest of the people in the world. Do they not get to hear about Jesus simply because they don't have a friend who is a Christian?

ARE YOU AN ANGEL?

Let me set the scene: Towering above you stands a 456-foot rollercoaster. Standing beside you are people in line—some terrified, some ecstatic. Most of them have already been waiting for hours.

My friend, Brianna (twelve years old) and her brother Chuck (fourteen) were also standing in line. They heard the teenage girl in line in front of them complaining about how afraid she was to get on the ride. Her boyfriend was trying to comfort her, reminding her that she had been in just as much danger in the car on the way there.

Chuck, who loves witnessing, seized the opportunity and asked, "Do you know where you'll be going when you die?"

"Well, yeah—Heaven," the girl said.

"Are you sure?" Chuck asked.

"Pretty sure," she said.

"Have you ever lied? Or hated somebody? Or stolen?" Chuck asked.

She said yes to all those things.

"Are you an angel or something?" her boyfriend asked Chuck.

"That's what I was thinking," the girl inserted.

"Maybe," Chuck smiled. After he assured them he wasn't an angel, the teenage couple began asking Chuck and Brianna questions.

"Now I'm scared. What if I go to Hell?" the girl asked.

"I'm not condemning you or anything but it is reality—I would go to Hell too if it wasn't for Jesus in my heart. He loves you and wants to save you," Brianna explained clearly. She and Chuck emphasized that we are not guaranteed tomorrow so we should not put off coming to Christ.

The "speed line" they were in took longer than usual, and this gave them time to finish the conversation. Both the girl and her boyfriend prayed to ask Jesus for salvation—and it didn't stop there! Another man standing in line overheard the conversation, and he also wanted to place his faith in Christ!

The thrill of the rollercoaster ride was nothing to Chuck and Brianna in comparison to the thrill of seeing these people come to Jesus.

What if Chuck and Brianna had believed that sharing the gospel wouldn't "work" unless they already had a friendship intact? They never would have started that conversation.

I could tell many similar stories to make this point, but let's move on to tackle the next excuse.

EXCUSE: "I MIGHT MAKE A MISTAKE OR SAY THE WRONG THING."

This is actually a good fear. It should drive us to our knees and to our Bibles. But it should not keep us from sharing our faith!

In college, my dad was zealous for the Lord and actively involved in ministry. But he felt inadequate when it came to witnessing. He concluded that since sharing the gospel is such an important task, it shouldn't be done by "trial and error." Now Dad claims he was wrong. Now he says, "Of course you witness by trial and error! How else will we learn? You may think of things afterward that you wish you had said differently, but that just helps you be more prepared next time."

EXCUSE: "I DON'T KNOW ENOUGH."

What if someone asks me a question that I can't answer? If you have ever been afraid of this, just remember that you aren't the only one! We all feel inadequate. Well, at least we all *should*—because we all are! Even the wisest Bible scholar could make this excuse for not witnessing. But if you are saved, you know enough to lead someone else to the Lord. You know how *you* came to Christ, don't you?

There have been many times when I did a poor job of answering people's questions, but I'm still glad I talked with them. For one thing, I became more aware of the common questions people ask and more motivated to learn the answers, so I'd be ready if I was asked that question again. In addition, I know the Lord can use what I said even if it wasn't much. God used the Samaritan woman's testimony only minutes after she met Jesus. He used the rebellious prophet Jonah. He used the boy with the two fish and five loaves. He used Naaman's little servant girl. He even spoke through a donkey! He can certainly speak through us, in spite of our limited understanding.

Remember, we have the Holy Spirit to teach and guide us (1 John 2:20). The fact that we "don't know enough" should be a strong motivator to study God's Word—but it should never keep us from sharing the little that we *do* know.

EXCUSE: "I DON'T HAVE THE GIFT OF EVANGELISM."

When Jesus ascended to Heaven, He commanded *all* His disciples to preach the gospel and make disciples. The mandate was not just for Peter and John. Many people do not witness simply because they do not feel God has "gifted" them in this area. However, the ability to share the gospel is not a gift given only to some. It's the *responsibility* of everyone who knows Jesus. Actually, the only place in Scripture that evangelism seems to appear as a "gift" is in Ephesians 4:11. When read in context, we see that Christ "gave some to be evangelists" for the *equipping of the church*. In other words, it appears that God gives certain individuals the gift of "equipping the rest of the church to share their faith more effectively." I like the way Jon Speed explains this:

"This concept [God only gives some people the gift of evangelism] comes from a misunderstanding of Ephesians 4:11, which states: 'And he gave some, apostles; and some, prophets; and some, evangelists; and some, pastors and teachers.' Ephesians 4:11 has been lumped together with the spiritual gift passages of Romans 12 and 1 Corinthians 12 ... The only problem is that this is not a spiritual gift passage. The word 'gave' is a verb in Ephesians 4:11. The word 'gift' in the spiritual gift passages is a noun. (1 Cor. 12:4; Romans 12:6) Ephesians 4:11 is not referring to a gift, but to an office or function in the church. ... So, when someone says 'I don't have the gift of evangelism,' a fitting

DON'T BE A BYSTANDER!

response might be 'I'm not asking you to teach the church to evangelize … But you do have a responsibility to share the gospel, as all Christians do.'" [3]

EXCUSE: "I TRIED IT AND IT DOESN'T WORK."

I love Indian food. My good friend Augusta, from India, is a fantastic cook. I am always excited when she brings her amazing Indian dishes to the fellowship meals we have at church. There is one thing, however, that Augusta openly confesses that she does not do: bake. She explained to me that when she was young, she and her mom tried making bread. They had to go to an international store to get the ingredients and attempted to follow the directions carefully. But the bread was a complete disaster (it turned out like a rock!) and she hasn't tried making bread since.

In a similar way, a loving mother and her kids began sharing about Jesus with a girl at a park. This girl was very responsive, but her father became angry when he realized what was happening. He shook his fist at them as he drove away with his daughter. This sweet family felt horrible. They told me they hadn't witnessed to anyone since that situation happened—a year earlier.

It is easy to get discouraged because of perceived failure and conclude, "It just doesn't work," or, "It's not for me."

First, we need to understand that even though a conversation may not have gone well from our viewpoint, this doesn't mean it was not successful. Not everyone will respond well, but that doesn't mean we failed.

Secondly, we need to learn how to "fail well." Each of us has made a lot of mistakes in our lives, and each of us will make some mistakes when witnessing—it's guaranteed. That is a big part of how we learn. We shouldn't quit, we should simply learn to do it right. If we have a bad experience and decide, *I'm never doing that again!* to protect ourselves from future failure, that's a "quitter" attitude. But Proverbs 24:16 says, "For a just man falleth seven times, and riseth up again."

EXCUSE: "THEY LOOK BUSY. I DON'T WANT TO BOTHER THEM."

"It looks like they're having a private conversation," I told my friend Jessica, glancing at a guy and girl sitting together on a picnic bench. Jessica and I were looking for someone to witness to, but we were hesitant to approach them because they *did* look occupied and we didn't want to interrupt.

"Well, we'll just ask. If they don't want to talk, then we'll leave," we decided.

We approached their picnic table and explained that we were doing a little questionnaire and wondered if we could ask them a few questions.

"Sure!" they said.

Right away, we learned that the guy spoke Spanish and very little English.

Okay, this might make it a little difficult, I figured. But God had everything prearranged. Jessica had recently taken three years of Spanish, and she was happy to have someone with whom she could practice! This provided a perfect opportunity for me to have a one-on-one talk with the girl, Miranda. She responded to my questions with a hungry, humble heart, clearly confessing her guilt before God.

"I'm really at the end of my rope right now," she said and began to cry.

A verse from Psalm 34 popped into my mind about how God is near to the broken-hearted. As I shared the verse with her, I explained about Jesus and salvation. I was so glad that the Lord brought me to her at a time in her life when she was aware of her own need and willing to listen.

Meanwhile, Jessica was having a nice talk with Miranda's boyfriend

in Spanish. Just think—we almost didn't talk to them because "they looked busy."

Many people in this world are actually very lonely and really appreciate a friendly person striking up a conversation with them. Of course, if they don't want to talk, that's okay. We certainly don't want to annoy people. We can always move on to someone else. But we won't know if we don't ask!

EXCUSE: "I HAVE SO MUCH ELSE GOING ON, I DON'T HAVE TIME!"

Mrs. Naas, a godly friend and role model for me, once looked me in the eye and emphasized, "People come before the program." This is what she meant: If we let our life be controlled by a multitude of "good activities" which we have scheduled, but ignore the *people* God brings into our path, we are not acting like Jesus. That thought stuck with me!

A Christian man in town who had been a chaplain at our local hospital for 17 years explained to me that many people are open to spiritual things on their death beds. He had led many to Jesus. But what he said next surprised me. All the other chaplains he knew were *not even believers!*

"If it is such an open door, why don't more Christians do what you're doing?" I asked.

"Well, you know," he said, "sometimes we're just so busy 'serving God' that we're not serving God."

He's so right. As they say, "*Good* is often the enemy of *best*."

Can you imagine standing before the Lord one day, reporting that you were so consumed with "wholesome activities" that you weren't able to find time for the Great Commission?

EXCUSE: "I CAN'T COMMUNICATE WELL."

I sometimes have trouble communicating what I want to say, and feel inadequate compared to others who are more eloquent. One thing that encourages me is to think about Moses. He was not very anxious to go and speak to Pharaoh—at all! He complained that he was not eloquent, and never had been. But look at how the Lord responded to Moses. God said, "Who has made man's mouth? Or who maketh the dumb, or deaf, or the seeing, or the blind? Have not I the LORD? Now therefore go, and I will be with thy mouth, and teach thee what thou shalt say" (Exodus 4:11-12).

God knew all about Moses' lack of eloquence! In fact, God made him that way for a reason. When Moses continued to plead for someone else to do the job, "the anger of the Lord was kindled against Moses" (Exodus 4:14). Even so, God still responded graciously by supplying his brother, Aaron, to speak for him.

Simply put, just because you are not good at something doesn't mean you don't do it. It appears that even Paul wasn't the most eloquent speaker. Second Corinthians 10:10 says, "For his letters, say they, are weighty and powerful; but his bodily presence is weak, and his speech contemptible." Paul also wrote, "But though I be … [unskilled] in speech, yet not in knowledge" (2 Corinthians 11:6). And in another place he wrote, "And I, brethren, when I came to you, came not with excellency of speech or of wisdom, declaring unto you the testimony of God. For I determined not to know anything among you, save Jesus Christ, and Him crucified. And I was with you in weakness, and in fear, and in much trembling. And my speech and my preaching was not with enticing words of man's wisdom, but in demonstration of the Spirit and of power: That your faith should not stand in the wisdom of men, but in the power of God" (1 Corinthians 2:1-5).

God isn't looking for eloquent speakers. He's looking for hearts that are right before Him (2 Chronicles 16:9). In fact, God gets the most glory when He empowers some of the least likely candidates to do His work. My dad has often said, "God likes to use the underdog." Since our ultimate goal is for Jesus to be glorified, it's actually an *asset* to be a little nervous, weak and young! That way He gets all the glory in whatever He accomplishes through us.

I heard a story of a timid young lady who was going door to door witnessing. She was so scared, she was actually in tears! When the first person answered the door, she was crying as she read her little script explaining the gospel. Yet just as Jesus told Paul, "My strength is made perfect in weakness" (2 Corinthians 12:9), so the Lord was strong in this girl's weakness. The person who answered the door prayed to ask Jesus for salvation!

"When I am weak, then am I strong" (2 Corinthians 12:10).

EXCUSE: "I'LL JUST LET THEM SEE MY LIFE."

Some of the most dangerous lies are the ones that are 95% true. It makes the lie very believable. The idea that it is enough to simply let people see your lifestyle seems to restrain many from witnessing. There is a lot of truth in this lie because it is vitally important that our lives match our words. In fact, what we *do* usually speaks louder than what we say. Yet we must not use this as an excuse for not opening our mouths and speaking. We have been *commanded* by Jesus to share the gospel message! Could He have made it any clearer than this: "Go ye into all the world, and **preach** the gospel to every creature" (Mark 16:15)?

People were extremely affected by Jesus' actions; but they also needed to hear His words. In John 6:68 Peter said to Jesus, "Thou hast the *words* of eternal life."

Maybe you've heard this quote: "Preach the gospel at all times. When necessary, use words." I think that some people use this quote as an excuse to be silent. Let's think about it. Is it truly possible for someone to hear the gospel without words? The gospel IS words. In fact, the word *gospel* means "good news." How can we share *news* without words? The gospel is a message. It's stated concisely in 1 Corinthians 15:1-4.

Yes, the gospel shows in our lives, but that's not enough. If we are going to be biblical witnesses, then we must take initiative to share the gospel with our mouths, because " … faith cometh by hearing, and hearing by the word of God" (Romans 10:17). How can *hearing* happen if we don't speak the words of the gospel? Luke 12:8 says, "Whosoever shall **confess** Me before men, him shall the Son of Man also confess before the angels of God." The question is not, "Will our generation be nice?" but, "Will our generation *speak?*"

CREAM SODA

The solution to excuses isn't simply to knock them all down. The solution is to step back and ask, "Why are we even making excuses in the first place?" Often it's because we *think* we don't want to witness. We *think* we won't like it. We *think* it will be painful. We *think* it will be too hard. But will it really be?

"Sometime we should buy a can of root beer from the vending machine!" my older sister Sarah suggested to Stephen. She was eleven years old and he was five. (I was only one or two years old, so I guess they didn't think of sharing with me!) We were staying on the 16th floor of an apartment building while our family was doing mission work in Hong Kong for four months. There was a vending machine on the first floor, and Sarah and Stephen had been thinking for awhile about buying something from it. When you are only eleven and five and don't have much money, this is a big decision! They thought about it and talked about it for a long time. Finally one day they decided, "Okay, let's do it. Let's split the cost. We'll buy one can of root beer and share it." Root beer was the only kind they liked, so at least that part of the decision was easy. They inserted the money into the machine and selected root beer, but the next second they both said, "Oh no! The wrong thing came out! We wanted root beer—not cream soda!"

Since we were in Hong Kong and didn't speak Cantonese, they figured it would be too much of a hassle to try to explain the problem to someone who worked at the apartment building. Dejected and frustrated, they came upstairs with the can of cream soda.

"You won't believe what happened," Sarah told Mom. "After waiting so long for our root beer, we didn't even get what we wanted!"

"Yeah," Stephen added, "I've never even *had* cream soda!"

But, of course, since they had spent their money they decided to drink it anyway. So Sarah divided it into two cups and they each took a sip.

"Hey, this is pretty good," Stephen said.

Sarah tasted it cautiously.

"You're right—it is!" she said enthusiastically. They enjoyed the rest of the can, and then Sarah said, "We'll have to get this again sometime!"

When Dad came home, they went running up to him and said, "Guess what, Dad? We have a new kind of pop that we like now! Have you ever had cream soda? It's good." Their disappointment had turned into an unexpected blessing. And it must have been a pretty big deal for them at the time since both Stephen and Sarah still remember this—over 20 years later!

How many times do we miss out on blessings because we're afraid to try something new? We stick with what feels comfortable, instead of being ready for whatever adventure God might bring our way. We have an upside-down perspective! We need to stop listening to the lies of Satan who has a way of making good things look bad. He does not want us to pursue those exciting assignments God has for us.

Let's ask God to change us from the inside out, put our perspective right-side-up again, and give us a strong desire to make the gospel known. "For it is God which worketh in you both to will and to do of His good pleasure" (Philippians 2:13).

SINCE WHEN DID UP BECOME DOWN?

"If a commission by an earthly king is considered an honor, how can a commission by a Heavenly King be considered a sacrifice?" —David Livingstone

Think about this from God's perspective. He hears some people timidly praying, "Lord, I am willing to go on the mission field if that's what You really want me to do," or "Okay, Lord, I guess I'll go and witness to someone if You make it clear what I should say." In contrast, He hears others praying prayers that sound more like Isaiah: "Lord, here am I! Send me! Can I go? Please? I want to go! Please use me for Your glory!" (See Isaiah 6:8.)

Whom do you think the Lord is going to send? Which attitude do you think He delights in more? Are we pleading with God to use us for His kingdom? If not, shouldn't we be? Isn't that where it all starts? If we aren't begging to be used, maybe we don't understand what an honor it is or what joy it will bring—not only to us, but to the courts of Heaven.

CHAPTER 4

TRACTS

While washing my hands in a public restroom I noticed two rolls of toilet paper unrolling along the floor, escaping from the housekeeping lady, who looked rather busy. I picked them up and handed them to her.

"Thank you. God bless you, honey!" she said with surprise.

"Oh, you're welcome. Thank you for keeping the restrooms so clean!" I said.

"Oh, bless you, honey … aw, can I give you a hug?" she asked.

She also gave me her business card so I could e-mail her boss to report that the restrooms were clean. I said I would. Then I pulled out a Ten Commandments coin and gave it to her.

"And what is this?" she asked.

"This is a coin with the Ten Commandments on it," I told her. "The Ten Commandments show us our sin. We need God's forgiveness. He will cleanse us from our sin if we ask Him, because Jesus died on the cross for us. Eternal life is a free gift that God gives to those who ask."

Tears began to stream down her cheeks. I was so surprised; I hardly knew how to react! I had only said a few words—why was she so touched? I figured that the *Lord* must have been touching her through me somehow.

I was grateful I had that Ten Commandments coin[1] with me. Otherwise I'm not sure if I would have been able to think of something to say that quickly. But the coin made it easy. Since I was prepared with a "conversation starter," I was ready when the opportunity arose.

Many people say that one of the hardest parts of witnessing is getting the conversation *started*. I agree. I'm planning to share a collection of conversation-opener ideas in chapter 13, but for now, I want to discuss one of my personal favorites—gospel tracts.

TRACTS BREAK THE ICE

Three junior high kids were standing in a little circle in the middle of a convenience store, talking and not doing much. Normally it might feel a little strange to barge into their circle and begin to witness to them. I mean, wouldn't they think it was weird if I, a complete stranger, joined their circle and start talking? Wouldn't that be awkward? Well, no! Not when you have a tool!

Reaching into my purse, I pulled a green card out of my stash of secret weapons and asked the kids, "Hey guys, would you like to try an IQ quiz?"

"Try it!" one girl said to another with a teasing look in her eye.

"Okay," the other said hesitantly.

As is normally the case, she was fooled by the optical illusion, and I pointed out her mistake. The other two kids thought this whole thing was very entertaining. It added some adventure to their day. I gave each of them one of the cards, and they seemed excited to now have something cool to show their friends.

Turning the card over, I told them there were some questions on the back. In a five-minute encounter we were able to discuss God, sin, salvation, and eternity. It wasn't awkward—it was fun! Why? I had a tool with me.

(The small green card I gave the kids was produced by Living Waters.[2] The optical illusion on the front breaks the ice, and I've found that people are almost always willing to discuss the questions on the back as well.)

POWERFUL PIECES OF PAPER

We rarely get to see the fruit that comes from passing out a tract. Usually we hand it to someone, say something nice, leave, and never see the person again. Yet just because we do not see the results right away doesn't mean it won't have a great impact! If we could look into eternity and see the outcome of each tract we gave out, I think we would be handing out a whole lot more of them.

"Hey, Marine—you need Jesus as your Savior," a fellow Marine told Frank as he handed him a tract. Frank took it and, looking around, he noticed that many others had also received tracts. Two Marines were rapidly passing them out to everyone outside the bar in Okinawa, Japan. It was a very ungodly atmosphere, but that didn't stop these bold Marines. Frank wondered what they were so passionate about! He read the tract they gave him, and a seed was planted in his heart.

Three years later, Frank was back in the States working for the Long Island Rail Road. Occasionally, he would find tracts lying on a seat in one of the cabins. He would read them. One time he read a tract together with his girlfriend. The back of the tract said to find a good church that teaches the Bible. So he and his girlfriend attended a Wednesday night Bible study at a local Baptist church, and he gave his life to the Lord.

About 30 years later, as Frank was preaching on a Sunday morning, he told his story. I was in the audience. I had to go up afterwards to ask a few questions!

"What did you think when those Marines gave you that tract?" I asked. "Did you think they were crazy religious fanatics?"

"No, I was interested," he said.

Sometimes we have the idea that if we pass out tracts, everyone will think we are weird—when actually people often appreciate them a lot. I'm sure it's no surprise to hear that Frank now feels strongly about the effectiveness of tracts. He is just one of many Christians I've met, who, when sharing their testimony, point back to how God used a gospel tract to speak to their heart.

TRACTS OPEN DOORS

Oh no! We're stopping? I thought.

I was wrapped up in my coat, sitting comfortably in the back of our van, and I didn't feel like moving. But I knew I should go in and give the employee a tract while my dad bought gas. After a little internal battle, I finally got up and went in. I bought a piece of candy, gave the cashier a tract, and went back to the van. Then my dad went in to pay and didn't come out for about 20 minutes! When he finally came back to the van, he told us what had happened. As he was paying for the gas, the cashier asked, "Was that your daughter who gave me this booklet?"

"Yes," my dad answered.

"This is a good little booklet!" he exclaimed.

The cashier was a Muslim and Dad had the opportunity to share the gospel with him, beginning with Abraham. We were late for church but that was okay! Dad was able to share the story with the whole church, and it was an encouragement for them, just as it was for us.

Passing out tracts is like planting seeds in the ground. Paul wrote, "I have planted, Apollos watered; but God gave the increase. So then neither is he that planteth any thing, neither he that watereth; but God that giveth the increase" (1 Corinthians 3:6-7). It's hard to persevere. Sometimes the excitement of passing out tracts wears off when we get a few cold responses. But Galatians 6:9 says, "And let us not be weary in well doing: for in due season we shall reap, if we faint not." The Lord sees each tract we give, and He is able to cause those seeds to grow.

CHRISTMAS IN THE SQUARE

"Okay, Ashtin, I don't know who to talk to, so I'm just going to pray," I told my eleven-year-old witnessing partner. We were standing in the middle of a Christmas celebration in our town square, sipping hot chocolate, and looking around for people with whom we could share the gospel.

" ... in Jesus' name, amen," I said, finishing my prayer. We took about six steps, turned a corner, and found a group of kids eating popcorn around a picnic table.

Christmas makes conversations easy. In no time at all, we had a talk going and I asked, "What Christmas traditions do your families have?"

After a minute or so, one of the girls said to her brother, "Don't you remember her from Thomas Park last summer?"

They know me? Have I met them before? My mind searched for a few seconds, and then it all began to come back. About six months previously, I had used some optical illusion tracts to get into conversations with several kids on the merry-go-round. These were the same kids!

"I still have the paper you gave me," Victoria told me. "And I've watched the DVD from you, like, two or three times now. I usually watch it when no one else is home so I can concentrate on it." (I had given her a DVD that teaches about the Creator and gives the gospel message.[3])

As we sat with them drinking our hot chocolate, we found that Victoria was very open to learning more about the Lord. We talked for about 30 minutes. When we exchanged contact information, I learned that Victoria worked at a restaurant just two stores down from our Bright Lights office.

A short time later I walked into the restaurant where she worked and met her dad. He greeted me warmly, telling me that his daughter had shown him the pamphlets I gave her. He then added, "I told my daughter, 'That is exactly the kind of person I want you to be hanging out with.'"

Although some people say that the best way to witness is to make a friend, and then sometime down the road, bring them to church or try to witness to them, I believe a better approach is to make friends *through* witnessing. If people receive what we say and want to know more, we can continue to share with them, deepening the friendship which has just begun. If they aren't interested, we can befriend someone else who is. This helps to guide us in where we should invest our time.

CREATING CURIOSITY

It was about 8:30 p.m. and everything was quiet in the little home-decorating shop in the mall. There were no other customers and the cashier looked pretty bored.

Here's a good opportunity! I realized. *She has nothing to do! She would talk to me!*

The only problem was that I *could not* think of how to start.

"When do you close tonight?" I finally asked.

"9:00," she replied.

"Thanks," I said.

Okay, that really went far.

I wandered around the shop, trying to think of something else to say, but nothing was coming to mind. I prayed. I decided to buy a few $.25 dark chocolates, since buying something always provides another natural opportunity to speak with the cashier. As she handed me my change, I decided this was my last chance to say something significant.

"So … I have a question for you that isn't really related to this store," I began.

She listened.

"If someone asked you how they could be 100% sure they were going to Heaven, what would you say?" I asked.

Her eyes widened as she looked at me with an expression of complete surprise.

"I have no idea!" she said.

"Okay," I said and nodded.

There was a little pause.

"Well," I continued, "*IF* anyone ever asks you that question, you can give them this."

I handed her a tract called *"How Can We Know We Are Going to Heaven?"* by Randy Alcorn. She thanked me.

Although I didn't have a conversation with her, at least I had aroused her curiosity to read that tract! Tracts keep speaking after we leave.

"I'LL ADD IT TO MY COLLECTION"

I admit, sometimes it seems that the young people who hang out at the mall these days are getting weirder and weirder. New shades of colors in hair, more piercings, new crazy styles, strange beliefs … you know what I mean. But look at it this way: If these kids are not embarrassed by the crazy things they are doing and saying, then guess what? I don't think we need to be worried about doing something a little unusual too—like having a random, straightforward, candid conversation about eternal truth with them in a shopping mall.

Kids who appear a little "wild" on the outside are usually longing for friendship and acceptance. They often soak up what we tell them, ask questions, and seem to genuinely appreciate the conversation and love.

I like mall food courts because they provide a hang-out spot for kids who are bored—especially on cold, winter days.

"Thank you for being willing to talk with us today. This has been a great conversation," Sarah said, concluding a discussion with a boy named Christian and his friends. They responded warmly. Sarah smiled and added, "I know it's kind of unusual when people you don't even know just sit down at your table in the food court and start talking with you."

They agreed and smiled. However, they obviously didn't mind that Sarah had talked with them, because about half an hour later they called her to come back to their table—their new table, that is, on the other side of the food court. They had another question they wanted to ask and the conversation continued.

A week or two later, when we were at the mall witnessing again, I saw three teens sitting in the food court licking large, colorful suckers and looking bored. I also noticed that they were looking at me with a funny expression, and I recognized that look. It meant: *I think we know her but she looks a little different.* That's what happens when you have a sister who looks similar to you. Anyway, I figured that Sarah had talked to them in the past, so I went up, said hi, and asked if they had talked with my sister.

They nodded.

When I learned that one of them was named Christian, I remembered hearing Sarah tell about her good conversation with a boy named Christian.

I gave him a tract and he told me he'd add it to his collection.

"Collection?" I asked, smiling.

He explained that he still had the two tracts Sarah had given him last time, and he told me that he was keeping them on his shelf!

A few weeks later, as we were passing out tracts at the St. Patrick's parade in downtown Cedar Rapids, guess who Sarah ran into again? Christian!

"I don't think it's a coincidence that we keep running into you!" Sarah said enthusiastically as she gave him our tract about St. Patrick. "And I don't think it's a coincidence that your name is Christian, either! I'm going to pray that you keep thinking about these things ... "

That same day I, independently, also ran into Christian (out of the 10,000+ people at the parade downtown!) I gave him the same tract and talked with him for a minute. Christian seemed surprised (I don't blame him!), but he also had a serious attitude about him.

What was God doing in Christian's life? Why did we keep bumping into him? Why did he end up with five tracts? I don't know, but I do know that God can orchestrate anything to get people's attention. And if God keeps up the pattern with him, he should have *quite a number* of tracts in his collection by now! *[smile]*

People often take tracts more seriously than we would expect. One time my brother, Stephen, handed a tract to a man at the St. Patrick's parade. He told Stephen that he had received one of our tracts every year for the past six years, but still wanted another one to add to his collection.

Actually, most people have a collection—not necessarily of tracts, but of memories of encounters with Christians they've met. Unfortunately, some people already have negative memories. Others may get their only impression of Jesus by what they see in us. It is no small calling to be His ambassadors. May we represent Him in an accurate way to everyone we meet! "Now then we are ambassadors for Christ, as though God did beseech you by us: we pray you in Christ's stead, be ye reconciled to God" (2 Corinthians 5:20).

"¡Hola! ¿Conoces a Jesús?" *(Hello! Do you know Jesus?)*

While a Hispanic friend of mine was in Mexico, he had the opportunity to share the gospel with a man on the street. To my friend's surprise, this man opened his wallet, pulled out a small, folded-up piece of paper, and beamed as he said, "Look! An American gave this to me!"

It was only a simple tract. But apparently, in this Mexican man's mind, the tract was connected with the fond memory of someone who lovingly shared it with him. He had regarded it as a special treasure all this time! And then God brought someone else to water that seed.

TRACTS GO WHERE WE CANNOT!

"Lord, please prepare the heart of the person with whom I am going to talk in here," I prayed as I pulled into the Kinko's parking lot. I walked in and a nice lady helped me laminate my poster. However, I was having a hard time knowing how to turn the conversation to the Lord.

Finally, as we were finishing the poster, I handed her a tract about evidence for the resurrection of Christ.

"Here's something that my sister and I wrote for Easter," I said.

"Oh, I've seen this before," she replied.

"Really?" I asked. I wondered, *How could she have seen it before?*

"Yeah, my son brought it home from somewhere," she said.

Apparently, she had found the tract lying around their house, picked it up, read it, and liked it!

Okay, back up two months. Our family had planned a witnessing event for Easter weekend. We wanted to focus on the message of the resurrection,

so Sarah and I took a few days to read apologetics books and boil down the information into a small tract. It was a great exercise for us. I never realized how much evidence there is from history alone to support the resurrection of Jesus! We put the gospel on the back of the tract and printed about 2,000 of them. Sixty-five people showed up to go witnessing with us on Easter weekend. We divided into teams and took off for parks and malls all around town, passing out the tracts and engaging people in conversation. Then we all came back for pizza and heard story after story of what God had done. It was such an exciting day.

Now fast-forward two months to the lady at Kinko's. I got back in the car after my conversation with her and started thinking about the prayer I had prayed before I went in—that God would prepare the heart of the person with whom I would speak. It was so interesting to see how He did that—two months earlier! I was also reminded that when we pass out tracts, we may be reaching entire families. Who knows where those tracts will go, whom they will reach, or how long they will be lying around people's homes, being read by other family members!

LATE NIGHT CRAVINGS

I really feel like ice cream right now, I was thinking as our family was traveling late one night. It wasn't too difficult to convince my family, so my dad pulled into a McDonald's. While Sarah was ordering, I saw a teenage girl sitting by herself looking bored. Now, how would I begin a conversation with a girl in this situation? I decided to simply hand her something.

"Hi! Here's something for you," I said, giving her a million dollar bill tract.

She took it with a look of surprise as I explained, "It's a million dollar bill."

She smiled, and I continued, "There's a million dollar question on the back. It's 'will you go to Heaven when you die?'"

She was intrigued.

"I like to pass these out," I explained, "because I think the most important thing for people to think about is what happens after they die, so they can be prepared for it."

She nodded and thanked me.

There! See? Thanks to the tract, the conversation was now started. We had a nice talk about life, school, her church background, and other things.

Then she said, "This may sound like a silly question, but would you mind giving me your e-mail address so I could ask you more questions about this?"

We should not assume that people will reject us—or think we are totally weird—if we give them a tract. Often the opposite is true. These underrated, underestimated little pieces of paper are powerful! Don't ever believe the lie that tracts are an outdated, obsolete, or invalid method of evangelism.

TRACT TIPS

I've learned that there are some "do's" and "don'ts" in passing out tracts.

- ### BE CONFIDENT
  If you are bold and unashamed, people will be more receptive. When you pass out tracts, smile. Be confident. Look them in the eyes. Be friendly, and have fun doing it! Be upfront that it's a gospel tract; don't pretend it's something it's not. Assume that they are going to be really happy to receive it. If you act comfortable, they will feel more comfortable too. Treat it like a gift you are giving them, because that's essentially what it is.

- ### KNOW WHAT YOU ARE GOING TO SAY
  "Here's something for you—it's a great message!"
  "We're passing these out today—here's one for you!"
  "Happy St. Patrick's Day!" "Happy Fourth of July!"
  "Here's something for you to read when you get off work."
  "This is a message that changed my life, and I want to share it with you."
  "This is something our family wrote for Christmas this year."
  "Here's something for you. We're trying to reeducate America."
  "Here's something to share with your friends. Make sure you read it first though."
  "This is for you. It talks about the most important questions in life: where we came from, why we're here, and where we're going."
  "Did you get one of these?" (This is a great line to use at fairs or parades. It makes people feel that they are missing out if they don't get one—which they are! If you say, "Do you want one of these?" it is more likely that they will say no.)
  "Have you ever been given a gospel tract before? No? Really? Well, here you are!" or, "You have? What did you think of it?"

  It also helps to be thinking ahead. For example, *I am the next person in line. What tract should I give the cashier? What should I say when I give it to her?*

- ### FIND TRACTS YOU LIKE!
  If you have tracts that you are excited about, you will be more confident with them, and more eager to get them into other people's hands.

Thankfully, there are lots of great tracts available. Make sure the tracts you choose include Scripture and make the gospel clear. For ideas of sources of good tracts, see *www.willourgenerationspeak.com*.

- ## STOCK YOUR PURSE OR WALLET

A friend once showed me the big flap on the outside of her purse and explained how well it worked for tracts—both for storing them and for pulling them out quickly. Ever since then, I have been especially conscious to buy purses with pockets or flaps for storing tracts. Sometimes you only have a few seconds of opportunity to pass out a tract, and the right purse enables you to whip out a tract on the fly just when you need it. For guys—sorry, you're on your own to figure something out! *[smile]*

- ## DON'T LEAVE WITHOUT THEM

If I leave my house without tracts, I often regret that I don't have them. When I have tracts with me, I find that it affects me in two major ways: 1) I am more bold, and 2) I am in more of a witnessing mindset and less likely to miss opportunities when they come.

- ## RECRUIT YOUNGER BROTHERS AND SISTERS

Picture a cute little girl dressed up in a coat and scarf on a snowy Christmas evening. She walks up to an adult, holds up something red and says, "Merry Christmas!" with a cheery smile. Would they turn her down? Very unlikely! It would probably make their night!

Younger kids can do an incredible job of passing out tracts. We have some friends who taught their three-year-old brother, Lance, to hand out tracts. Often when they are at a park, they tell him, "Lance, go give a tract to that person," and Lance runs and does it. People rarely turn him down. I guess it doesn't hurt that he is super cute. Sometimes the smallest people can do the best job carrying out God's work. This is important, not only because they can help with the work, but also because it gives *them* a taste of ministry. They realize, *God used me today.*

▪ KEEP A GIVE AWAY BOX IN YOUR VEHICLE

It is disappointing when you know exactly what you would like to give someone, but you don't have it with you! If you keep a "give away" box in your car that is filled with tracts, DVDs, books, and CDs, this won't happen. The box will also help to remind you that you're a missionary wherever you go!

- ## WRITE YOUR OWN TRACT

  I find it more natural to give people a tract I have written because they receive it as something from *me*, from my life—not just as a piece of literature I am distributing. One idea for a tract is to write out your own personal testimony.

INITIAL FRIENDLINESS OPENS DOORS

I have found that when I am friendly with cashiers or waitresses right from the start, it is more natural to give them a tract when I leave. For example, while ordering at Subway recently, I began talking with the lady who was making my sandwich. Our conversation progressed from discussing the busy day, to our family's travels, to Florida, to the fact that she is engaged and getting married at Clearwater Beach. By the time I paid for my sandwiches, we had become "friends." When I gave her a tract, she took it as a friendly gift and seemed eager to receive it.

It was late at night and the gas station was deserted except for one worker sweeping the floor.

"Hello," my dad and I said, greeting him as we walked in.

"Hey there," he said and smiled.

"How are you?" I asked casually.

"Oh, I'm doing fine. Thanks," he replied.

"Is it okay if we use your restroom?" my dad asked.

"Sure, we're open 'til eleven!" he replied.

"Okay, thanks!" we said.

A few minutes later, as we were leaving, we greeted him again. I pulled out a small booklet that explains about dinosaurs, creation science, and the gospel.

"Here's something for you to read," I said. "We don't think we came from monkeys … "

He smiled and nodded.

"We believe we were created, by God, for a reason. But often people only hear one side of the debate and public schools only teach evolution," I said.

He indicated that he agreed.

"So we are trying to teach the other side," I continued. "And, you know, there is a lot of evidence for design and a Creator. Dinosaurs—for example," I mentioned, glancing down at the pamphlet I had laid on his counter. "The Bible actually talks about dinosaurs and there is evidence that they didn't live that long ago—but during the same time as man."

"Really?" he exclaimed, raising his eyebrows.

"Yeah, archeologists have actually found dinosaur bones with blood vessels still preserved in them—which shows us that they couldn't have been millions of years old, as some people say,"[4] I explained.

My dad joined the conversation and added, "You know, all over the world there are legends of dragons. When these accounts were recorded, most of them were not written as legend, but as true accounts of history. It is also interesting that from all over the world we read of similar kinds of creatures. That's because they were real, and the creatures being described were dinosaurs."

That made sense to the cashier and he nodded in agreement.

"I'm going to read this little booklet!" he told us enthusiastically, picking up the dinosaur gospel tract as we walked out.

Back on the road, Dad and I discussed our encounter with him. We agreed that it had been easy to begin the conversation since we had been friendly when we first walked in. Initial friendliness opens doors.

Let's recap: Tracts break ice, open conversations, create curiosity, keep "speaking" after we leave, continue traveling, arrive at places we can't go, and sometimes explain the gospel even more clearly than we do! They have passed the test of time and are acclaimed by all of the best evangelists I know.

Charles Spurgeon said, *"When preaching and private tale are not available, you need to have a tract ready ... get good striking tracts, or none at all ... therefore, do not go out without your tracts."*

TRACTS KEEP SPEAKING WHEN WE LEAVE

"Let's talk to *them*," I suggested, seeing a group of young people hanging out at a table in the food court. It was a Saturday in December—and you know what's so great about that, don't you? People are out and about, shopping! It's easy to find "fish!" Six friends and I had gathered at one of our favorite fishing locations—the food court. We divided up and began looking for people to talk with.

A few of us found some young people seated around a table who were willing to talk, so we sat down and joined the "party." One of them, Wayne, was especially intrigued by the questions we asked, and he had several questions of his own. Wayne had some rather mixed-up views, and my friends Elijah and James ended up talking to him for about an hour. In the meantime, I was talking with some of the girls at the table.

After awhile, I pulled out some small gospel booklets and asked if anyone wanted one.

"Oh, someone gave us one of those before," one of the girls said.

Who else in town could have possibly given them one of these? I wondered.

I knew that the booklets had only been published recently and I had just ordered them.

"Yeah, we were sitting outside K-mart and a girl just handed it to us, remember?" one of the girls said to the other.

"Wait. Was one of you crying at the time?" I asked.

"Yeah, that was me," one girl said.

"I was the one who gave you that booklet!" I told them, remembering the scenario they described.

They were very surprised. I was quite surprised myself! The memory of our first encounter, about two months earlier, clearly came back to my mind. Our family had stopped at K-mart on our way to clean our church building late one Saturday night (yeah, procrastination). I noticed a few girls sitting outside the K-mart door. One of them was crying and the other was sitting next to her, with her arm around her. I wondered if I should talk to them. I didn't exactly feel like it, and I didn't know what to say either. But when I came out of the store they were still there, so I decided that I would at least do *something*. I grabbed a gospel booklet and walked over to them.

"Is everything okay? Is there anything I can do to help?" I asked.

"No, we're fine," they said. But they seemed to appreciate that I asked. I gave them the booklet and they thanked me. I didn't know what else to say, so I left.

Fast-forward about two months, and here I am talking to them again at the mall. Once we put these pieces together, I asked, "So did you read it?"

"We gave it to *him*," they said, pointing to Wayne.

"Have you read it?" I asked Wayne.

"Yes, more than once," he replied.

Maybe that explains why Wayne had so many questions! Wayne said he lived two hours away—and he seemed quite amazed by these connections. I "happened" to see his friends two months earlier outside K-mart. They "happened" to give the tract to him, and he "happened" to travel to Cedar Rapids and visit the mall at the very time my friends and I "happened" to be witnessing. Of all the people in the mall, we "happened" to talk to him.

"You know, there are no such things as coincidences," I told Wayne.

He agreed.

Now Wayne became even *more* interested in talking with us, so Elijah and James spoke with him for *another* hour or so. They exchanged contact information so that they could meet up again to study the Bible, if he wanted to do that.

God is working in this world. I know that there is a temptation to doubt if tracts really "work" or to feel self-conscious or fearful about passing them out. We all battle fear. But think of it this way: Consider all the Christians in history who were stoned to death or burned at the stake for preaching the gospel. There is a "great cloud of witnesses" (Hebrews 11 and beyond) who have gone before us and brought us the gospel. Now they have passed the baton to our generation. What are we going to do? Are we going to let fear paralyze us so that we won't even give out a tract? What are we afraid of anyway?

Since fear is one of the biggest hurdles we face in witnessing, we are going to discuss several ways to deal with fear in the next chapter.

CHAPTER 5

BUT I'M SCARED!

Of course you are! Join the rest of us. Maybe you even flipped to this chapter first because fear is such a battle for you. I'm guessing that's what I would do if I picked up this book. Fear is perhaps the most common struggle we face in evangelism. Even *Paul* asked for prayer for boldness! He said, "And for me, [pray] that utterance may be given unto me, that I may open my mouth boldly, to make known the mystery of the gospel ... that therein I may speak boldly, as I ought to speak" (Ephesians 6:18-20).

I was standing in a large convention center in Oklahoma City. Trailers were being unloaded, and people were setting up booths all around me. A homeschool convention was beginning the next day. I noticed some young people setting up concession stands. They worked for the convention center but seemed to have finished their work, and now they were just standing around talking.

I should go witness to them, I decided. But as I began walking towards them I chickened out and decided to walk past them into the restroom first ... you know, just to think some more about what I would say. *[smile]* I took a moment to decide which tracts to give them. I prayed. I felt so nervous! I shouldn't have, though. I mean, they were just some other young people my age, and I had nothing to fear. But I still felt intimidated. I prayed again. I thought some more about what I would say. I fixed my hair. I stalled. *Why is this so hard? What am I actually fearing? Will I have to go through these "fear battles" my whole life?* I wondered, half complaining to the Lord. Finally I realized, *It is not helping anything to keep stalling like this. The longer I wait, the harder it will get. I'm just going.*

"Hey guys! Here's something for you," I said, handing them million dollar bill tracts.

They smiled, thought the bills were cool, and my fears vanished.

This isn't so hard! I concluded.

"There's a million dollar question on the back," I told them.

"If we answer the million dollar question, do we get a real million dollars?" the girl asked.

"Well, you can try!" I laughed.

"Will you go to Heaven when you die?" she read. Her expression immediately indicated that she didn't want to talk about this.

"So, what do you think?" I asked. I figured if I could get her to express her thoughts it might get a conversation going.

"Well, according to 'theology,' if you accept Jesus into your heart and believe in Him you will [go to Heaven]," she replied, with some disdain in her voice.

"According to 'theology,'" I repeated, smiling at the way she phrased it. Obviously, it was not *her* theology.

The guy didn't seem to want to talk much.

"Let me ask you another question. Is going to Heaven a free gift or something you have to earn?" I said.

"Earn," the guy, Chris, said without hesitation.

"So what *are* your religious beliefs?" I asked the girl, Destiny. She sort of smirked and glanced at Chris. I wanted to know what her smirk meant, so I decided to just ask. "What's your issue with Christians?" I inquired.

"I don't have an issue with Christians, exactly," she said. "It's just that my aunt is a youth pastor and is always trying to push me into church stuff … "

These young people were pretty typical to ones we often talk with—they had a degree of Christian knowledge but not a true understanding of the gospel. They brought up one of the most common arguments that non-Christians love to use: hypocrisy in the church.

"I'm not trying to trash anyone," Chris said, "but there are a lot of Christians who don't even read the Bible. In fact, there are a lot of people who are Wiccan or other religions who actually know the Bible better than Christians do, because they read it so they can argue with Christians."

I acknowledged that what he said could be true in some cases.

"Let me be honest with you, I'm actually not a Christian," he told me.

I smiled and nodded. *(Like I hadn't already figured that out!)*

"Actually, I have been looking into becoming a Wiccan," he said.

I told him it was good to be honest about where he stood.

"Could you give me a brief summary of what Wiccans believe or what your goals are?" I asked.

"Well, there aren't really any goals," he said. "Basically, you just be good so that you can be reincarnated as something better."

He didn't seem to know too much about it. He said he thought all the religions were very similar. I disagreed, mentioning some of the differences between the various world religions.

"They can't all be true, because they teach very different things!" I told them. "But there *is* one common denominator between most of them. Almost all religions are based on self-effort. They teach that you have to be 'good enough' to go to Heaven (or to get reincarnated as something better). But the Bible says it's about a relationship—a *relationship*—with God," I emphasized, "not a list of rules. Once the 'sin problem' is taken care of, we can have that true connection with God. And *that* is what really changes a person—transforming them so they are not a 'hypocrite-Christian' anymore, like the people you were referring to."

They were listening attentively, especially Chris. After we had talked for awhile, Destiny said, "You know, I am surprised you were willing to stay and talk to us even after you learned that he was Wiccan."

"Yeah," Chris added, "a lot of Christians are pretty condemning. In fact, there's a verse in the Bible that says not to condemn or you will be judged in the same way."

"I agree that *sometimes* Christians handle things in a wrong way, but there's a balance there," I said, searching for words. "What I mean is ... if I saw a friend walking off a cliff and didn't do anything about it because I didn't want to come across as judgmental—"

Chris smiled a little, seeing the point I was trying to make.

They needed to go, but Chris asked, "Hey, what's your name?"

"Grace," I replied.

He shook my hand warmly.

"Nice to meet you. I'm Chris."

As I walked away, I thought, *That was such a fun conversation.* Their response went from being cynical to warm and friendly. I knew that they now had the experience of an enjoyable conversation with a Christian, new thoughts to think on, and tracts in their hands.

I remember almost floating back to our family's booth thinking, *If all I did for the rest of my life was get into witnessing conversations, it would be a great life!*

Before the conversation, I had been so scared. After the conversation, I was so happy! Hmmm ... this seems to be a common pattern.

"THIS WITNESSING THING IS WAY TOO SCARY."

DEALING WITH FEAR 101

Witnessing is about a mile outside most people's comfort zone. It's typical that one might feel afraid before handing out a tract or initiating a witnessing conversation—especially if it's the first time he or she does it. The first time we do anything can be a little scary. How about the first time you got on a horse, prayed out loud in a group, drove a car, had a job interview, or gave a speech? We are scared because we aren't sure of ourselves. We don't know if we will do a good job. But things usually get easier as we do them. Experience gives us an understanding of what will likely happen, so that we aren't living in the world of the unknown. Experience is acquired through lots of practice. As we practice, our skills increase and we become more confident and less afraid.

What skills are we developing in our lives right now? Why is it that many parents encourage their children to overcome their fears when it comes to playing in a recital or giving a speech, yet when it comes to witnessing, few parents take the same initiative to help their kids be stretched and grow? Isn't sharing the gospel one of the most important "skills" we should develop? What higher goal could there be for a parent than to raise a child who is a mighty soul-winner for Jesus? Of course, parents shouldn't force their kids to witness, but they can definitely give training and encouragement. We must not be conformed to the pattern and thinking of this world (Romans 12:2), but choose to make God's priorities *our priorities.*

Imagine standing up to give a speech, but having no idea what you are going to say.

Scary? Absolutely! However, if the message is clear in your mind and you have already given this speech two dozen times, would you be so afraid? Probably not!

I used to be scared at the mere *thought* of witnessing because I didn't know what I would say. I remember praying, "Lord, if You show me what to say, I'll go witness to that person." However, my perspective changed when I realized that I should become equipped beforehand so that I was *ready*. Once I had some good conversation-starter ideas and a simple plan of how I was going to present the gospel, my fear began to turn into excitement.

Preparation and experience reduce our nervousness, but that's just a start—just an introduction to this chapter. They pale in comparison to the three biblical, fear-crushing weapons we are going to talk about next.

1. FAITH

A boatload of promises, sure and certain, have already been given to us by God. Let's claim them, stand upon them, and never let go of them! We're talking about *promises* here: promises made by the everlasting, never-changing, all powerful God! Jesus has promised to provide for all of our needs (Philippians 4:19); to keep us from falling (Jude 24); to do the work for us (1 Thessalonians 5:24); to give us victory (Romans 8:37); to give us peace throughout the journey (John 14:27); and to be with us until the end (Matthew 28:20). These are just a sampling.

Take a look at these promises: Psalm 34:17; Psalm 145:18-19; Proverbs 1:23; Isaiah 26:3; Matthew 6:33; John 14:12-17; Romans 8:26-28; Philippians 4:7, 9; 2 Timothy 2:13; 1 John 2:25-27; and Revelation 22:4-5, 12. These are still only a fraction of what is promised us in God's Word.

Do we actually believe these promises? If we could see Jesus right by our side, do you think we would be afraid of witnessing? Faith is being sure of what God's Word tells us to be true (Hebrews 11:1).

God's comforting promises and words of assurance flood the pages of Scripture. David writes in Psalm 34:4, "I sought the LORD, and He heard me, and delivered me from all my fears."

When Paul was witnessing in Corinth, God strengthened him by reminding him of His presence. "Then spake the Lord to Paul in the night by a vision, 'Be not afraid, but speak, and hold not thy peace: For I am with thee ... '"(Acts 18:9-10).

Paul experienced some tough times while witnessing, but he specifically wrote about the strength he received from Jesus' presence. "At my first answer no man stood with me, but all men forsook me: I pray God that it may not be laid to their charge. Notwithstanding the Lord stood with me, and strengthened me; that by me the preaching might be fully known, and that all the Gentiles might hear … " (2 Timothy 4:16-17).

Although preparation and experience help to build our confidence, true confidence comes from the knowledge that we have the King of all creation with us, supporting us as we go. *That* brings comfort. We may never feel adequate or capable, and that's okay—it's good, in fact. *He* is adequate and *He* is capable. The practice and experience we accumulate as we go shouldn't build our trust in ourselves, but in God. We simply remember all the times that God was faithful to bring to mind the right words—just when we needed them—and we know He will do it again. It's not that we think, *Well, I did it before so I can do it again.* We could not have even one fruitful conversation if it wasn't for the Lord working through us! As we step out in obedience, we remember, *He helped me last time and He will help me this time too.* We are confident only because He is faithful. But if we look inside ourselves for the confidence and strength we need, we will either become anxious or we will become arrogant.

THE MYSTERIOUS DARK FIGURE

How do you react when you get scared? Well, at our house, we always know when something startles my mom because she screams—and I mean, *screams!* Sometimes I'm peacefully reading in my room and, all of a sudden, I hear one of those piercing shrieks. I race into the kitchen to see what's going on and Mom will say something like, "Sorry about that! I just opened the fridge and the yogurt splattered all over the floor."

[Sigh!] One would have thought that the house was about to blow up.

One chilly evening, my mom was home alone. Dad was at an event and none of us kids were born yet. As Mom was cleaning the house, she opened the front door to shake out her dust mop … and there, right in front of her, was the dark figure of a man. She let out one of her blood-curdling screams. Now, the man was actually my dad coming home, but my mom couldn't see him very well in the dark. Guess how my dad reacts when he gets scared? He freezes! Dad was so scared by my mom's screaming, he wasn't able to move. Mom was so scared to see this man just standing there, she couldn't stop screaming! *Some people are just made for each other, aren't they?* I'm surprised one of the neighbors didn't call the police!

THE PRISON OF STRAW

Just as my dad was frozen and unable to move, so our fear often immobilizes us, keeping us from opening our mouths and attempting great things for God. The sad thing is that the fears we entertain are usually not even true. They are make-believe and empty. They trap us in a prison of straw.

It is easy for us to believe lies about witnessing because we are entering the world of the unknown. The unknown scares us. I guess that is why we used to be scared of the dark when we were little. (Well, some of us used to be.) I remember how I used to run up our basement stairs really fast, hoping nothing was chasing me. We as humans have the tendency to imagine the worst, but our fears are often irrational. We imagine that things will turn out worse than they actually do.

Satan is the father of lies. It is his native tongue—the language he speaks (John 8:44). It is how he has operated in this world from the beginning. Often he mixes truth with lies to make the deception more subtle. He says things like this: *"They'll reject you. They will be offended and your attempt will backfire. You are going to look stupid. You aren't capable of doing this. Look—you are stumbling in your own walk with Christ, how could you even think of witnessing? Let more mature believers do it. Just wait awhile until you are ready and then start witnessing. Remember last time you tried witnessing and really messed up? It's just going to happen again. This is not your thing."*

Satan doesn't have anything with which he can truly threaten us, so he makes up lies to scare us away from witnessing. The question is, *Why do we listen to him so much?*

REPLACE LIES WITH THE TRUTH

How do you get the darkness out of your bedroom? You turn on the light. It's as simple as that. How do you get lies out of your mind? By filling your thoughts with the light of God's Word.

We all face fears every day. We can't necessarily keep fearful thoughts from coming, but we *do* have the choice of how we are going to respond to them. Will we let the thought bind and immobilize us, or will we take the offensive position and replace the lie with the truth? (See Romans 8:6 and 12:2; 2 Corinthians 10:5; and Colossians 3:2.)

When I was little, I used to talk with my mom about various fears I had. She always had the same response: she prayed with me and took me to Scripture. She wrote out Bible verses for me on cards and had me memorize them and quote them to myself whenever I was afraid.

The most effective way I have found to deal with fear in witnessing is simply to quote 2 Timothy 1:7 to myself: "For God hath not given us the spirit of fear; but of power, and of love, and of a sound mind." We have an amazing Father in Heaven who knows exactly what we need for this task! Power, love and a sound mind. Think of how those things strengthen us to witness. As children of God, fear is not something we have to be imprisoned by—ever! That's not the kind of God we have. The fruit of the Spirit is love, joy, peace, and so on (Galatians 5:22) *not* dread, doubt, fear, and confusion. Our God is a God of victory and strength.

Here are some fear-conquering verses to study or memorize: Isaiah 31:6; Isaiah 43:1-5; Psalm 31:24; Psalm 34:4; John 16:33; Philippians 4:13; 2 Timothy 1:7; Hebrews 13:6; and 1 Peter 3:6, 13-14.

"FIERCE MAY BE THE CONFLICT; STRONG MAY BE THE FOE"[1]

The storm was so violent that the boat was literally covered with waves. Jesus and His disciples were sailing across the Sea of Galilee. The disciples had been through plenty of storms, but this one was so bad, they concluded they were going to die! They woke Jesus, saying, "Lord, we perish!" But Jesus replied, "Why are ye fearful, O ye of little faith?"

Let's stop right here. From this statement we see that Jesus clearly connected their *fear* with their lack of *faith*. Fear is the opposite of faith. When we have faith, we're not afraid. When we're afraid, it's because we lack faith.

It really comes down to this: Do we believe God's promises to us, or not? Do we truly believe He is with us, helping us? Do we believe He is in control? Do we believe He is all powerful and all loving? Do we believe that *He is the One who has led us in this path*? If so, why are we afraid?

In reality, the disciples had nothing to fear. Why? They had simply been following Jesus. Jesus was the One who had led them into the boat! As the previous verse states, "And when He was entered into a ship, His disciples followed him … " (Matthew 8:23).

When God commands, He supplies strength to carry out the command. God told Joshua, "Wasn't *I* the One who commanded you? Then be strong and courageous!" (My paraphrase of Joshua 1:8.) When the Lord commands, there is safety. It's safer to be in the middle of a storm in God's will, than in your own bedroom in disobedience. But why does God allow us to experience situations that make us feel afraid? It is because He wants us to cry out to Him for help! "Call upon Me in the day of trouble: I will deliver thee, and thou shalt glorify Me" (Psalm 50:15). Then, when He delivers us, it strengthens our faith—again and again. God grows even greater in our eyes, and we worship Him more. Our relationship with Him is strengthened. We are then ready to take on bigger challenges! And God will never allow the trial to be more than we can bear (1 Corinthians 10:13).

"Then He arose, and rebuked the winds and the sea; and there was a great calm. But the men marveled, saying, What manner of man is this, that even the winds and the sea obey Him!" (Matthew 8:26-27). After seeing that awesome miracle, the disciples were now more afraid of *Jesus* than they had been of the storm a few minutes earlier! That's how we should be too (Proverbs 19:23).

The moments when fear and doubt penetrate are the moments in which we fail to hold up the shield that God has provided for us. "Above all, taking the shield of faith, wherewith ye shall be able to quench **all** the fiery darts of the wicked" (Ephesians 6:16).

I think it is helpful to mentally visualize holding up our shield of faith. The enemy says, "This is going to be too hard for you." We say, *"Faithful is He who called me, who also will do it."* And we hold up our shield! The enemy says, "If you witness to them, they might not be your friend anymore." We say, *"I am not ashamed of the gospel of Christ because it is the power of God."* And we hold up our shield.

It is by faith in the Lord and His Word that we overcome. Faith squashes fear. "And this is the victory that overcometh the world, even our faith" (1 John 5:4).

WHAT DID I GET MYSELF INTO?

It was a sunny summer morning in our neighborhood and everything was quiet. I had been reading a book on witnessing and was feeling eager to share the gospel with someone. I strolled down to the park near our house, promising the Lord that I would witness to whomever I found there. (I am not suggesting you do this, by the way. *[smile]*)

I was in for a little surprise. Instead of a young mother with a stroller, I found a pick-up truck and four big construction men.

Something must be wrong here, I thought. *Surely God doesn't want me to witness to them! What would I say?* I quickly turned around and started walking home, no longer feeling quite so cheerful.

But wait! I stopped abruptly. *I can't go home. I made a promise to the Lord.*

I turned around and slowly, very slowly, continued to walk toward the park, taking small steps. *Really* small steps.

I can't believe I'm doing this, I thought. However, I knew that I must not allow fear to take over. In situations like this, my favorite fear-conquering verse (2 Timothy 1:7) really helps!

I reached the merry-go-round where two of the workmen were preparing their paint. Handing them each a gospel tract, I said, "Hi! This is something for you to read when you are on break."

"Oh, what is it?" they replied. They were cordial and warm, and my fears melted away.

"It's a little card that talks about eternal life," I explained.

"Oh!" they replied, "well, what do you believe?"

I love it when people ask that question.

"Actually, I was just going to ask *you* that," I said. "Would you like to answer first?"

"Well," one of them replied, "I believe in God—and that there definitely is an after-life."

"Like Heaven and Hell?" I asked.

He hesitated a little (not really wanting to answer) and then said, "Tell us what *you* believe."

Okay!

"Well, I'm a follower of Jesus Christ and I believe the Bible," I replied.

"Are you a certain denomination?" they asked.

I shook my head. "I just believe the Bible. What about you?"

"Catholic. But my friend here is Methodist, right? He's not a very good Methodist, though … he's going straight down there," he joked.

It was obvious that they didn't understand the gospel, but they were very friendly and eager to talk. I figured God had me there for a reason. I quickly prayed for the right words, and suddenly I remembered a new witnessing idea that my dad had just explained to me the day before.

"Do you mind if I ask you another question?" I asked.

"No, go right ahead!" they replied.

"Okay. There are three situations in which God will not forgive sin. Do you know what they are?" I asked.

"Well, um," one of them replied, "I think God will forgive any sin, I mean as long as you confess it and everything. I don't believe there's anything that God won't forgive."

"Well, this is kind of a trick question," I continued, "but I think you'll agree with me when I tell you the answer."

"Okay, what's the answer?" they asked.

"The first situation in which God will not forgive sin is if we don't ask! God wants us to repent."

They agreed.

"The second situation in which God will not forgive sin is if we don't ask sincerely—like a little child who says 'sorry' with a bad attitude just because he has to."

They understood.

"And the third situation in which God won't forgive sin is ... " and my mind went blank. "It's um ... " I couldn't think of it.

Uh-oh.

I prayed.

"Oh yes," I remembered, "the third situation in which God will not forgive sin is if we don't 'give credit to whom credit is due.' In other words, God won't simply 'let us off the hook' because we say we are sorry." (No judge on earth would do that, and God is far more righteous than any earthly judge!) "We need to give the credit to the One who paid the penalty for our sin. Jesus took our punishment and became our substitute, and God wants us to give His Son the credit He deserves!"

They didn't quite know how to respond, but I figured I had given them some food for thought. I told them to go to the website on the back of the tract, and I moved on to the two guys who were scraping the slide.

(Note: Normally I do not witness to men when I'm alone. But I felt this was a safe situation. However, see more about "safety and discretion when witnessing" in chapter 12.)

"Wow—do you have to scrape that whole thing?" I asked them.

"Yup ... we're repainting it," they replied.

"Well, here's something for you to read when you are on break," I said as I handed them an IQ quiz/tract.

"So where are you guys spiritually in your life right now?" I asked them.

They gave me a kind of funny look. Maybe I could have started with a more neutral question, but I just said what came to mind.

"What do you mean, 'spiritually'?" they questioned.

"Let me ask a different question. If you died tonight, got hit by a car or something, and God asked you why He should let you into Heaven, what would you say?

"Uh ... I have no idea," they said.

"So you've never thought about it before?" I asked.

"I guess not," they replied.

"You know," I commented, "we are going to be dead a lot longer than we'll be alive."

"That's for sure," they replied.

"So," I continued, "I just want people to think about eternity and be certain they are right with God. It's easy to get distracted by work, school and other activities, and not focus on what really matters."

The expression on their faces told me that this wasn't an encounter that happened to them every day *[smile]*, but they didn't seem offended—just intrigued.

Sometimes we assume the wrong things. We assume that people have already heard the gospel and rejected it, and that they will reject us if we share it with them. Or we assume they have no interest. But often that is not true. Many people appreciate the fact that we are willing to speak with them.

"Hey, it's really hot today," I told the construction guys. "I live right up the street. Would you like me to bring down some lemonade?"

They looked at each other with a little smile and replied, "That'd be awesome!"

I returned with some iced lemonade, which they seemed to really appreciate.

Well, that didn't turn out so bad! I concluded as I walked home again.

Witnessing is entering the world of the unknown. But that makes it exciting! Each time we get to see how God is going to work *this one* out. We can stand on the promises of the One who knows the unknown. However, if we remain in that prison of straw we will miss out.

2. FEAR OF GOD

Allison's face was beaming. She was twelve—a great age for witnessing. She had been a valuable part of our witnessing team and an example to all of us. We were glad she was joining us for another afternoon of witnessing at the mall.

"Excited?" I asked as she arrived, noticing her countenance.

She nodded energetically with a big grin.

I enjoy witnessing, too, but I wasn't feeling *that* excited about it at the moment.

Good thing enthusiasm is contagious.

After an hour or so of talking with people, our team regrouped to discuss how things were going. Just then, a conspicuous group of wild-looking teenagers walked past our table.

"Should we go talk to them?" Sarah asked.

"I tried a few weeks ago and they didn't want to talk," I replied.

"Oh, okay … " Sarah said.

"Maybe *I* could go talk with them then," Allison piped up, "since they don't know me yet!"

Sarah and I looked at each other with a little smile. *That sounded like something Allison might say!*

"Sure! If you want to … do you want someone to come with you?" we asked her.

"No, it's okay," Allison said as she grabbed some tracts and headed their direction.

She went straight over, greeted them, and handed them tracts.

"What do you think happens when someone dies?" she asked them.

The kids became very uncomfortable and gave a silly answer, but they took the tracts. Do you think it made an impact on them? Was Allison "successful"? Of course! Encounters with friendly strangers always have some kind of impact. We can pray that those kids become very conscious of their need for God.

Later I asked her, "So Allison, what is one of the main tips that helps you be so bold?" Allison told me that she purposes to "never let herself be embarrassed." That wasn't exactly what I was expecting her to say, but after thinking about it, I realized what she meant: *She doesn't let concern for her self-image keep her from doing bold (and maybe unusual) things to reach others for Jesus.* This is actually a very freeing concept. It is when we fear what people are thinking of us that we are ensnared.

Allison could go boldly because she knew she had nothing to lose. If they responded well—great! If they laughed and mocked—who cares? Yes, we ought to feel compassion for people who mock or reject, but there is no reason to let their reaction discourage us. Allison's job was merely to be a messenger.

THE FEAR THAT GIVES COURAGE

Each of us has an approval drive. We desire to please. We want to be accepted. The question is, to whom are we going to look for that approval? Some of the Pharisees believed in Jesus, but they wouldn't talk about Him openly because they were afraid of being put out of the synagogue. "For they loved the praise of men more than the praise of God" (John 12:43).

The simple remedy to cure our "fear of man" (fear of what people think of us) is to care much, much more about what Jesus thinks of us. The fear of God frees us from the fear of man. We simply have to ask ourselves, *"Whom am I really serving?"* Consider the words of Paul, " … do I seek to please men? for if I yet pleased men, I should not be the servant of Christ" (Galatians 1:10).

When our greatest concern is what the Lord thinks of us, we won't care so much about what other people think. After all, they won't be the One judging us when we stand before the Judgment Seat of Christ and give an account of our lives (2 Corinthians 5:10). This truth brings incredible freedom. There is no way we can please everyone, and trying to do so only complicates life and brings a snare. "The fear of man bringeth a snare: but whoso putteth his trust in the LORD shall be safe" (Proverbs 29:25).

And you know what? If you demonstrate courageous love and speak out, not worrying about what people think of you, people will most likely respect you even more. People admire courage. But whether they respect you or despise you, it's not going to matter in eternity.

"I live before the audience of One—before others I have nothing to gain, nothing to lose, nothing to prove." —Os Guinness

HEALTHY FEAR

I'm scared of treadmills. But I didn't used to be. One time at a hotel when I was about ten years old, I decided to turn the treadmill up really, really fast and *then* jump on. (I know. *Smart.*)

I fell down right away. I panicked, and instead of letting go, I kept hanging on to the front (again, *smart*). The rubber belt kept running—burning the top layer of skin off my knees and ankles. **Ouch!** Finally, I let go and slid off. I used a lot of Vaseline for the next few days! Now I definitely have a healthy fear of what a treadmill can do to me!

Is all fear bad? No. The fear of the Lord keeps us from sinning. Healthy fears keep us from doing foolish things. There *is* a time to listen to fear—to be cautious. My dad emphasizes this to me frequently *[smile]*. For example, we do not witness in back alleys at night because we fear harm—and that is a good fear! We simply need to know what to fear and what *not* to fear.

I don't have a very strong fear of heights, and this has caused some emotional trauma for my family, especially my sister. Sarah *still* tells me the story of how I tried to jump into a swimming pool from the second story when I was one. *[smile]* Healthy fears are good and have their place.

THINGS USUALLY TURN OUT BETTER THAN YOU
IMAGINE. BUT THERE ARE EXCEPTIONS.

Most of us have a healthy fear of doing something socially unacceptable in public. In a way, that's a positive thing—it keeps us acting appropriately. But we need to realize that *witnessing* is not socially unacceptable! Not by God's standard—and He's the King. He sets the rules for what is socially acceptable. Since Jesus told us to go, we have the highest authority behind us. "Where the word of a king is, there is power: and who may say unto him, What doest thou? Whoso keepeth the commandment shall feel no evil thing: and a wise man's heart discerneth both time and judgment" (Ecclesiastes 8:4-5).

Given what we know about eternity, witnessing is the truly *socially acceptable* thing to do! In the face of danger, people must be warned. It would be cruel to remain silent. God is able to give us the wisdom to know what is appropriate to say in each situation and to share in love, showing respect to others. Witnessing is not pushing your beliefs on someone else—it's educating them graciously in what we have learned and proven true.

In the end, people are often grateful when they realize we are genuinely concerned for their welfare. For example, while I was talking with some girls in a food court one busy December day, I explained that God takes sin seriously and will judge us one day. The girls seemed concerned and wanted to know more, so we talked for over an hour. Near the end of the conversation, one of them emphasized to me, "I really like the way you are doing this—how you just sat down and talked with us for awhile—because people need to know this!"

3. ZEAL

A zeal for the message and a zeal for people will overcome the fear that stands in our way. Let's think about public speaking again. If you are passionate about what you are saying because you know your audience desperately needs to hear it, public speaking is not nearly as frightening. You just get up and say it! You aren't thinking so much about *yourself*—you are thinking about your *message* and *them*. You aren't worried about your speaking style, appearance, or the fact that someone else could do a better job.

Have you ever been praying for unsaved friends and thought with longing, *If they could just understand the gospel—if they would only accept it—it would fill their emptiness, lift their gloom, soothe their wounds, unshackle their chains ... and save them from eternal death!* We know they need to be introduced to Jesus, the One who described His mission in these words: "He hath anointed Me to preach the gospel to the poor; He hath sent Me to heal the brokenhearted, to preach deliverance to the captives, and recovering of sight to the blind, to set at liberty them that are bruised ..." (Luke 4:18).

When we deeply desire for them to know the same Deliverer who has rescued us, it is not difficult to open our mouths. It is hard to keep them closed! A strong internal drive to get a vital message across overrides the fear that would keep us silent. "There is no fear in love; but perfect love casteth out fear" (1 John 4:18).

Imagine a father who sees his toddler being attacked by a mountain lion. Would he not put his own life on the line to rescue his helpless little son? Of course he would, because love overcomes fear. Love is strong, and it drives people to do very bold things in frightening situations.

If fear paralyzes us and keeps us from sharing our faith, we must ask ourselves, "Do I truly care about people? Do I love the Lord? If so, how can I be silent?" "To him that knoweth to do good, and doeth it not, to him it is sin" (James 4:17).

Love is not merely a warm feeling toward someone. Love is taking action to help others. It is having compassion for their desperate situation and doing everything in our power to rescue them (which is introducing them to the Rescuer). Love does not think of self; therefore, it does not fear. It always thinks of others. Jesus demonstrated this kind of love to the highest degree when He died on the cross.

Amazingly, *His love* is the kind of love we are supposed to imitate. "Herein is our love made perfect … as He is, so are we in this world" (1 John 4:17).

But emulating Christ-like love is way beyond us, right? Actually, no, it's not—since we have God's Spirit in us. God does not call us to do things that are beyond us. Though it is not possible for us alone, it is possible since He is living in us. Children of God all over the world are killed daily for the sake of the gospel. We, too, can choose to lay our lives down daily, taking action to love people by proclaiming the gospel.

Our love for others springs out of our love for God, and we love God because He first loved us (1 John 4:19). *His* love is what ignites our zeal. "And we have known and believed the love that God hath to us" (1 John 4:16).

If we ever doubt God's love for us, it only takes one look at the cross to remember it. But we shouldn't just *look* at the cross, we should stop and gaze at it—meditating on the tremendous price paid for us, the suffering Jesus endured in our place. The more we comprehend Jesus' incredible love for us, the more we love Him in return. And the more we love Him, the more we will love others for whom He died! (1 John 4:20-21). We have awesome news to tell them. It is our zeal for the message of the cross and our zeal for people that supersedes our fear and selfish concern for ourselves. Love prevails. Fear is cast out.

LET'S REVIEW OUR THREE FEAR-CRUSHING TRUTHS:

- Faith. When Jesus calls, He enables. The problem arises on our side when we refuse to believe.

- Fear of God. The fear of what God thinks trumps the fear of what others think.

- Zeal. A passion for the message and a passion for people will override the fear that stands in the way. Love takes action.

STILL AFRAID? SO WHAT! I'M GOING!

It's not all about what we feel—it's about what we do. John Bunyan, author of *The Pilgrim's Progress*, was imprisoned because he would not stop preaching the gospel. He told the judge, *"If I was out of prison today, I would preach the gospel again tomorrow by the help of God."* [2] A footnote from *The Pilgrim's Progress* gives us an inner look at John Bunyan's perspective on fear: *"Pilgrims! mind this. It is as much your duty to strive, in the strength of the Lord, against unreasonable doubts and slavish fears, as against sin. Nay, are they not, in their own nature, the worst of sins? They spring from infidelity, and dishonour God's precious truth, glorious grace, and everlasting salvation. —Never, never, then cherish or give way to them, but resist, and shut the door of your hearts against them."* [3]

Fear does not merely trouble us and keep us from witnessing. Fear dishonors God, because it implies that we don't trust Him to carry us through. Fear damages our lives and it keeps us from doing a lot of good. When God said, "Fear not, for I am with you," do you think that was simply a suggestion—or was it a command? God does not merely give good advice—He gives commands.

So, for the glory of God, let's trample that prison of straw, hold up our shield of faith, live only for our Commander's approval, keep our eyes on the cross, and **speak**!

In the next chapter, we are going to discuss one of the first things we should communicate—a piece of information that drives people to the cross.

CHAPTER 6

FULL OF GRACE AND TRUTH

About six junior high girls joined Sarah and me as we headed to our town's art festival—a family-friendly event with lots of kids' activities, numerous food stands, and dozens of art vendors. It's a great atmosphere for witnessing. My friend Morgan and I spotted another girl sitting on the grass with her friend.

Perfect.

"What do you think happens when someone dies?" I asked as we began talking with her.

"Interesting you ask, because my grandparents both died recently," Avery said.

"Wow, that must have been difficult. You've probably been thinking about this a lot recently," I said.

"Yeah."

"So what do you think happens when someone dies?" I asked again.

"I think they go to Heaven," Avery said confidently.

"Okay … so do you think God will punish sin?" I asked.

"I think that God is very forgiving," she replied.

"Do you think Hitler is in Heaven?" I asked.

"No, oh, no," she said emphatically. "He killed, like, a *lot* of people."

"So where does God 'draw the line' between who goes to Heaven and who goes to Hell?"[1] I asked, trying to communicate the point that God *does* judge sin.

"Well, I think God will forgive unless you have committed too much sin," Avery said.

"What did Adam and Eve do to get kicked out of the Garden of Eden? Are you familiar with the story?" I asked her.

"Yeah, they ate the fruit, right?" she replied.

"Right. All they did was eat a piece of fruit! That's all! But the reason it was so serious was that God had specifically told them not to—and they disobeyed."

Avery nodded.

"So this shows us that the only thing we need to do to be separated from God is to break just *one* of His commands. Even if the only thing we've ever done wrong is told one lie, we've still fallen short!"

I continued, "When I was younger, I honestly didn't think about Heaven or Hell that much—until one day it occurred to me that I wasn't completely sure I was going to Heaven. I was scared that I would go to Hell. It was at that time I asked God to save me," I told her and explained the gospel.

"Yeah, to be honest," Avery said, "I haven't thought about Heaven or Hell that much, and I thought I was a pretty good person. But now that I have been thinking about it, I've been reminded of a ton of bad things that I've done."

We talked for a long time there on the grass, and Avery expressed that she wanted to ask God to save her. What brought her to that conclusion? It wasn't because I told her, "Jesus wants to come into your heart," or, "Jesus will make your life easier." No, it was because I showed her she was a sinner and *needed* a Savior. People must understand they are lost before they can be saved.

WHO CALLS FOR A LIFESAVER?

Think about when *you* were saved. What led you to Christ? Often when people share their testimony, they explain that it was the knowledge of sin and fear of its consequence that drove them to Jesus. If we are going to be honest with people, we need to explain the truth about sin and God's justice. How can people repent of their sin if they don't understand what it is? Who calls out for a lifesaver if they don't think they are drowning?

Like a schoolteacher, God's Law teaches us what sin is. Galatians 3:24 says, "Wherefore the law was our schoolmaster to bring us unto Christ, that we might be justified by faith."

When used with gentleness, the Ten Commandments can be a great tool to help someone see their sin.

"Have you heard of the Ten Commandments?" Sarah asked some teen girls at the mall.

"Yeah! Isn't the first one like 'freedom of religion' or something like that?" one of the girls replied.

Um, not exactly.

Sarah began explaining the Ten Commandments to them.

"Have you ever taken God's name in vain?" Sarah asked.

"*Oh* yeah!" the girl said, implying *I do it all the time.*

"God's name is holy," Sarah explained. "Using His name in vain is called blasphemy. In Bible times, the Jews wouldn't even *mention* God's name because it was so holy."

"Really? Oh my G—" the girl exclaimed.

Immediately she clasped her hand over her mouth and looked very embarrassed.

"I just said it," she said sheepishly, looking around at her friends.

This really got the girl's attention! After that, she listened pretty attentively as Sarah went on to explain about Jesus and the cross.

After a little while, I came over and joined the conversation. To my surprise, the girl recognized me.

"Remember? We met at Gordmans last week!" she said.

Then I remembered. I had met a friendly girl at Gordmans and given her a tract in the shoe aisle. I found it interesting that God led me to her again the very next week!

"Maybe it's a sign!" she said.

"Could be!" I agreed.

At least now she knows the gospel more clearly.

THE LAW OF GOD: OUR MIRROR

Instead of simply telling people that they are sinners, we can direct their attention to the Law of God and let them see for themselves. That way *we* aren't judging them; we are encouraging them to *judge themselves* by God's Law. We are simply Christ's witnesses, acknowledging that we too have broken God's Law, but have found forgiveness in Christ! Let me illustrate.

"Here's something for you," I said, handing million dollar bill tracts to a mom and her daughter who were standing in a gas station aisle. They happily took them and read the entire back of the tract out loud. I stood there and waited to see how they would respond.

"That is really cool!" they both exclaimed.

"So, what do you think?" I asked. "Let me ask you this: If you died today, do you think you would go to Heaven?"

"Oh, I know I would," the mom said confidently.

"Really? How do you know?" I asked.

"Because I've been a really good person."

[Okay, let's stop the story right here and think about the significance of such a statement.]

Deadly Lie: "I think I'll go to Heaven because I'm a good person."
This is something you will hear people say over and over and over again. But if it was possible for us to be good enough to get to Heaven, then Jesus would not have had to die! (See Galatians 2:21.) If we earned our way to Heaven, then *we* would get the credit. That means *we* would get the glory. Heaven would be full of proud sinners who reached Heaven on their own merits. Justice would be a joke, and God's standards would be lowered to ours. But the Bible says, "For by grace are ye saved through faith; and that not of yourselves: it is the gift of God: Not of works, lest any man should boast" (Ephesians 2:8-9).

[Back to the story.]

"You know, it's easy for us to think we are 'good' because we feel we've never done anything really bad and we're better than others we know," I said to my new friends. "But what we really need is to see ourselves as *God* sees us, because He's the Judge, right?"

They agreed.

"One thing that helped me to do this was a little 'good person test,'" I told them. "Would you like to try it?"

They both smiled, especially the daughter, and agreed.

"Okay. By the way, what are your names?" I asked.

"Brianne," said the daughter.

"Mary," said the Mom.

"Okay, I'm Grace. The first question is, have you ever told a lie?"

They said they had.

"Have you ever stolen anything? Even something small like a dollar bill or piece of gum?"

"No," the mom said, "in fact, one time I found $10 on the floor at a store, and I turned it in to the store."

"What about you, Brianne?" I asked.

"Yeah, I've stolen money from my mom," she said, glancing her mom's direction with a smirk.

"Ah, confession time," I said, smiling. They were smiling too.

"Next question—have you ever dishonored your parents?"

Brianne said she had.

"I ran away from home," her mom said. "Does that count?"

"Yeah, I'd say so … " I replied.

"So those are a few of the Ten Commandments—which is the Law God gave us. When we judge *ourselves* we think we are pretty good, but when we look at God's Law we see how bad we are."

They seemed to be following my point, so I continued, "So if you died today and God asked you why He should let you into Heaven (after all, you've broken His commandments), what would you say?"

"Well … we've changed our way of life and now we are doing better things," the mom said.

[Let's pause again.]

Counterfeit Answer: "But we've changed now."
This is another common response, so we need to know how to answer this when we are witnessing. It reveals that people have completely missed the point! They agree they have sinned, but they think that since they are improving in character, it will all be okay. In other words, they are still trusting in themselves! But even if they *could* change and be perfect from now on, that still wouldn't take care of the sin they've committed in the past. And besides, they *can't* change—not according to God's standard, that is. They may learn to make better decisions in life, but true righteousness means that every single word, action and thought is completely perfect. One hundred percent perfection with no mistakes! Only one Person has that kind of righteousness.

[Back to the story.]

"Sure, and that's good," I told them. "There is profit in doing what is right. But if you stole a large amount of money and then told the judge, 'But I've changed and I'm living a better life now,' that wouldn't be enough. You would still have to pay your fine or your time in jail."

"What about repenting and forgiveness?" Brianne interrupted.

[Pause.]

Misunderstood Concept: "God will always forgive."
It was good that Brianne thought of the concept of forgiveness, but there were some critical things she did not yet understand about God's character.

Maybe you've heard similar comments: "My God is a God of forgiveness." "Doesn't God simply forgive all?" Or, "I was always told that God forgives unconditionally."

Yes, the Lord desires to forgive, but people must understand how God is able to *justly* forgive. God cannot simply overlook sin. He wouldn't be a good judge if He did that. Moreover, God does not forgive sin merely because people confess it. That would be like a police officer letting a thief go free solely because he admitted to the fact that he was shoplifting.

We have only two options: 1) We personally pay our own penalty, which would mean eternal separation from God, or 2) Someone else pays it for us.

But is it possible for someone else to pay? How would that work? Let's think it through. Every human being is on spiritual death row because of our crimes against the King of the universe. Therefore, for someone to pay our penalty, that substitute would need to *die*. He would have to be someone who was not already on death row himself. He could not have any sin of his own for which he would need to pay. He would also have to be of Adam's race. Whoever it would be would become not only our Savior—but also our Master and Lord. We would owe Him our very lives because He saved us, and we would be deeply grateful to Him for all of eternity!

Only God Himself could pay such a price. And He did! He sent His Son to become a Man and die as a substitute in place of those on "death row." Then Jesus conquered death by rising from the dead. God can now forgive the sin of those who repent and ask for mercy—while remaining completely just—because the penalty has been paid. Therefore we give all the credit to the One who paid the enormous price. "Ye know that ye were not redeemed with corruptible things, as silver and gold ... But with the precious blood of Christ" (1 Peter 1:18-19). We are more than forgiven, we are redeemed.

[Back to the story.]

"Yes—good point," I told Brianne (responding to her question about forgiveness). "But if you broke the law, you could not expect the judge to just let you go free. A good judge doesn't simply pardon everyone. God is holy and just, and we've broken His law. That's bad news!"

She agreed that this would mean they'd be in trouble.

"So, let's say you had a million dollar fine to pay—and no money. You were standing there before the judge and then someone came along and said, 'I love you and I am going to pay your fine for you.' How would you feel toward that person?"

"Really grateful," Brianne said.

"And I'd feel like I owed him something ... like my life," her mom said.

"Yes. And that's exactly what Jesus did for us when He died on the cross," I explained.

Once we have explained about sin and the cross, people need to know what they must do to be saved: **believe**. (Pretty simple, huh?) Acts 16:31 says, "Believe on the Lord Jesus Christ, and thou shalt be saved."

When I am explaining to people what it means to *believe* in Jesus for salvation, I like to use the words "repent and trust." Believing in Jesus is not merely acknowledging the facts. It is repenting of our sin and depending entirely on Him.

While Brianne and her mom and I were talking, a friendly gas station employee called to us, "Hey, there's stools over there if you guys would like to sit down!"

Hopefully he was listening to our conversation. Sometimes we are reaching more people than we know.

About this point I realized, *We've been talking for a long time. My family is probably in the van waiting for me.*

I don't know how Brianne and her mom were responding in their hearts to the gospel, but they seemed to appreciate the talk and we left on warm and friendly terms.

When we use the commandments of God to show people their sin, it's like holding up a mirror for them so that they can see how dirty they actually are (James 1:23-25). The Law of God exposes our sin. When our sin is exposed, we realize our need for help. When we realize our need for help, the gospel makes sense! In fact, it suddenly becomes the most wonderful news in the world.

AN URGENT NEED TO KNOW

To put it simply, we want unbelievers to understand two truths. We want them to see the truth about themselves—that they desperately need to be rescued. And we want them to see the truth about the Rescuer—that He is perfect in justice and rich in mercy. Most people don't understand either one of these truths.

"Here—something for you," I told a girl at the park as I handed her a tract. She thought it was cool and began looking at it right away.

She and her group of friends thought that you get to Heaven by "being good," so I used the same approach with them as I did with Brianne and her mom, walking them through the commandments of God to give them a glimpse of how "good" they actually were. I could see the look of conviction in their eyes. They acknowledged that death could occur at any time, and the worst thing that could possibly happen to anyone would be to go to Hell.

"But God forgives!" one girl said. (Sound familiar?)

"But if you were standing in court," I explained, "you couldn't say to the judge, 'Won't you just forgive me?' and expect the judge to say, 'Okay, sure.' No, if he is a good judge, then he *has* to punish the crime. In the same way, God *has* to punish sin—and the punishment for sin is Hell."

"Then everyone is going to Hell," they said.

"Except," I clarified, "there is one way—a narrow path—that God provides for those who are willing to take it. Do you guys know what it is?"

They threw out a few ideas. I decided to wait for a few more minutes before sharing the good news, as I tried to establish a correct understanding of sin. But one of them, Josh, interrupted, "So what's this 'path thing,' like, to Heaven, that you were talking about?" he asked with urgency in his voice.

I guess he can't wait any longer! I concluded, glad to see his eagerness.

"Well," I answered, "first we need to understand that we cannot get to Heaven on our own or by being 'good enough.'"

"Yeah, I know that!" he agreed.

I guess I already made that point strong enough!

"Okay, well then, because God loved you, Josh," I explained, "He decided to take the punishment for your sin. That's why Jesus died on the cross. God became a man, Jesus, and died a horrible, bloody death on the cross. And God put on Jesus our sin, and also the sin of the whole world" (Isaiah 53:6).

"That must have been pretty heavy," Josh remarked.

"Yeah," I agreed with a smile, "but Jesus rose from the dead and He's coming—"

"Okay," Josh interrupted me again with concern, "I just need to know the way to get to Heaven. Do you have, like, a pamphlet or anything that explains it?"

(Hmm ... do I have a pamphlet that explains it ... ?) [smile]

"Well, to find the answer," I told him, "you need to go to the Bible. Don't trust what people tell you. You need to see what God says. The Bible says, 'For God so loved the world that He gave His only Son, that whosoever *believes in Him ...* '" I quoted.

"Believes in Him," Josh repeated to himself, trying to understand what he needed to do.

"But it's not simply 'believing in God,'" I clarified. "Even demons believe that God exists—and tremble. It's like putting on a parachute. You can believe the parachute will save you, but it won't actually help you until you *put it on.* It's the same way with Jesus. You have to trust what He did for you on the cross and ask Him to save you."[2]

I encouraged each of them to get alone with God and talk to Him about this. They seemed to indicate that they would—especially Josh.

"Thank you so much for talking with us!" they said warmly after asking many more questions.

A few weeks later I met them at the park again. They were very friendly and Josh said he had been reading the Bible. "Thank you again for talking with me that one night," Josh told me.

You see, once Josh understood his sin, he became very anxious for grace.

PAINFUL WORDS OF HOPE

My cousin Stephanie began thinking about a former classmate one morning. She had explained the gospel to him many times, but he never seemed to get it or even care. They hadn't been in touch for awhile, but Stephanie felt burdened for him. She decided to call him and simply lay out the facts: Hell is real, and we will go there if we do not trust in Christ to save us from our sin. To Stephanie's surprise, he replied, "You know, it really means a lot that you would call and tell me this." He wasn't especially enthusiastic about the message, but you know what he did appreciate? He appreciated the fact that she cared enough about his eternity to be honest with him about the truth.

A well-known atheist magician, Penn Jillette, was approached by a caring Christian man who spoke some gracious words to him and gave him a New Testament. Mr. Jillette was very touched by this man's kind gesture. He shared the story in a short video clip online. I was so moved when I watched it. Mr. Jillette said that he appreciated the eye contact, honesty, and kind words of the Christian man who gave him the Bible, and went on to explain, *"I don't respect people who don't proselytize ... If you believe that there's a Heaven and Hell,*

and people could be going to Hell … and you think, 'Well, it's not really worth telling them this because it would make it socially awkward'… How much do you have to hate somebody not to proselytize?" [3]

Atheist Penn figured out a truth that we as believers should already know and be acting upon. It's easy to tell someone God loves them. It's a lot harder to tell them the truth about sin and God's judgment. But when we do this with graciousness and concern, it shows people that we care enough about them to give them the tough news, even when it is not easy for us to say. If we only tell them what they want to hear, it shows we don't really care for their soul—we just care about what they think of *us*.

"BUT I DON'T WANT TO OFFEND THEM!"

If you are like me and don't especially enjoy confrontation, you may be wondering how to communicate the truth about sin, but still do it in love.

When witnessing, it is possible to offend someone right off the bat by not being kind and respectful. This does not get us anywhere! On the other hand, it's easy to err on the side of being too soft and not warning people because we're afraid of hurting their feelings. Ephesians 4:15 tells us that we should be "speaking the truth in love." Jesus was both tough and gentle at the same time, and that is how we need to be too—sharing the hard truth, but doing it with so much love that people do not doubt that we genuinely care about them. John 1:14 says, "And the Word was made flesh, and dwelt among us … and we beheld His glory … **full of grace and truth**." Randy Alcorn says it well: *"Jesus wasn't 50 percent grace, 50 percent truth, but 100 percent grace, 100 percent truth."* [4]

GENTLENESS AND HUMILITY

"I'm not judging you—I've done these things too," my friend Brad explained. A group of friends and I were at a college campus witnessing, and Brad had just reviewed the Ten Commandments with some students outside a dorm. He continued to explain, "When I was a college student here, I … " and he shared a bit of what his old life used to be like before he trusted Christ. After this, the students seemed to loosen up and be more willing to hear what he had to say next. Brad's simple, humble statements restrained them from putting up a wall of pride and resistance, and opened the door for a great conversation about the gospel.

"Our job is not to convict or convert. That is the Holy Spirit's job. Our job is to converse." —Carl Kerby

People need to understand that we are *on their side* and that this is the whole reason we are talking to them. Colossians 4:6 says, "Let your speech be alway[s] with grace." Remember, always means always! There is never a time to be ungracious. "The words of a wise man's mouth are gracious" (Ecclesiastes 10:12). Yet being gracious does not mean we hold back from proclaiming truth.

IF TRUTH BE TOLD

I met Shannon while she was sitting on her bike at the street corner. She certainly had a unique style, and seemed somewhat rough and hardened.

"Hey, how are you?" I greeted her as my friend and I walked up.

"Doing great, how about yourself?" she responded in a loud, but friendly way.

"Good! Would you like to try an IQ test?" I asked.

She didn't want to do the quiz, but said she'd answer a few questions.

"Is there a God?" I asked her.

"If you believe there is, then there is to you," she replied.

(It always baffles me how people can give this answer!)

I didn't want to debate with her—I just wanted to share about Jesus. But first, it was necessary that she understood why she *needed* Jesus.

"Have you ever told a lie?" I asked her.

"Every day," she said.

"Have you ever stolen anything?"

"Yep."

"I've done those things too," I acknowledged. "So if you stood before God and He asked you why He should let you into Heaven, what would you say?"

"I have been to churches all my life," she said. "I've been to 16 different churches and not once have I been impressed." She proceeded to bring up many "issues" she has with the church and stated that she believed in reincarnation. Shannon had a stubborn attitude and was unwilling to discuss things in a reasonable way. This was evidence to me that she was simply trying to make excuses for the sinful lifestyle she loved. (The saying is true: "A person's morality dictates his theology.")

By observing the way Shannon acted and talked, I guessed that she had had a difficult upbringing and a rough life—and it seemed obvious that she was not currently hanging out with a very good crowd. She was very friendly and very blunt. I decided the best way to get through to her was to respond in a similar, straightforward manner.

"Can I tell you something really blunt?" I asked.

"Sure, go ahead! I've been really blunt with you," she said.

"Okay. When you think about Hell and how horrible it will be, is it worth it to live the way you want to now, knowing that the punishment is Hell?" I said (as gently as possible). "It sounds as if you love the life you are living now so much that you aren't willing to come to God" (Matthew 16:26).

"I didn't say I wasn't willing," she responded. "I am a very good person. If I see someone who needs a scarf, I give them one. If I see someone who needs help, I help them."

(This is a typical response, revealing the heart of man. People don't want to submit to the Savior; they want to justify themselves.)

I explained that God sees all of our righteousness as filthy rags, but that He provided a way of forgiveness for those who will come to Him.

"I didn't say I didn't love Him," she said.

"But you are saying it by your actions," I replied.

"If God wants me, He'll find me," she answered.

"Well, maybe that's why I am talking with you right now! Maybe He sent me to you," I replied.

For the first time, she had no response. So I kept going, "God loves you and wants you to come to Him. But He won't force you to come—He gives a choice ... So, if you stood before God and He asked you why He should let you into Heaven, what would you say?"

(Though the Bible doesn't describe this actual scenario, I still use that question sometimes because it reveals where people are putting their trust.)

Shannon stated that she didn't think God would judge like that anyway. So I told her, "Remember, just because you don't believe it, doesn't mean it's not true. I could tell you I didn't believe in your bike, but that wouldn't make it any less real. It doesn't matter what you or I believe—what matters is what's true."

"I believe in reincarnation," she repeated.

"Well, reincarnation isn't true," I said. "The Bible teaches, 'It is appointed a man once to die and then to face judgment'" (Hebrews 9:27).

"I am a very good person ... " Shannon said again.

"Well, you just told me you were a liar," I replied, half-playfully.

"Well, I lie sometimes if it's helping me," she argued.

"But you just said you lie every day!"

"Well," she said, "I don't think anyone should be forcing their view on someone else. We have a free will, and we can do whatever we want, and I don't think it is right for someone to judge others ... "

"Let me make something clear," I responded. "We are not out here trying to push something on you. We are talking to you right now because we honestly care about you, and we don't want you to go to Hell."

"Oh, I know. I think what you are doing is beautiful—because you believe

in it. Don't stop what you are doing."

You see, at the end of the conversation—even after everything I said to her—she was not offended! She said she thought it was beautiful. I think Shannon appreciated the fact that I was willing to be straightforward.

Our tone of voice, humility, patience and understanding make a big difference. It *is* possible to communicate hard truths in a gracious way—to demonstrate both truth and grace at the same time.

LET'S GET THIS STRAIGHT: HOW CROOKED ARE WE?

It's not merely one's individual sins that separate him from God—it's the fact that he is a sinner. His individual sins are merely symptoms of that fact. But it's deeper than that. His heart is sick with sin and it shows up in his actions.

Think about someone who has the disease of leprosy. What is his *true* problem? His decaying hand? No, it is his internal disease of leprosy.

Imagine that you lived in Galilee during Jesus' time, and you wanted to take your leprous friend to Jesus to be healed. But your friend didn't believe that he had leprosy and was unwilling to come. What would you do? You would show him his leprous hand and say, "Look, it's obvious you have leprosy—look at your hand! It's decaying! You need to come to Jesus to be healed!"

That's what we are doing when we use the Law of God to talk to people about sin. Just as a leprous hand reveals that someone has leprosy, so our sinful actions reveal that we are sinners.

Although I often use the Ten Commandments to teach about sin, it's only one tool. It certainly is not the only way to communicate our sinful condition.

Here are a few other ways to explain the problem of sin:

- **Romans 3:23** "For all have sinned, and come short of the glory of God." (Like crooked arrows, we all miss the bull's-eye.)
- **Isaiah 53:6** "All we like sheep have gone astray; we have turned every one to his own way; and the Lord hath laid on Him the iniquity of us all." (Going our own way, independent from God, and living for ourselves is sin.)
- **Isaiah 64:6** "But we are all as an unclean thing, and all our righteousnesses are as filthy rags; and we all do fade as a leaf; and our iniquities, like the wind, have taken us away." (Even our *good* actions are not impressive to God.)
- **James 2:10** "Whosoever shall keep the whole law, and yet offend in one point, he is guilty of all." (It only takes one act of disobedience to separate us from God.)
- **Romans 2:14-15** "For when the Gentiles, which have not the law, do by nature the things contained in the law, these, having not the law, are a law unto themselves: Which shew the work of the law written in their hearts, their conscience also bearing witness." (Even if people have never heard of the law of God, they still have an internal compass of right and wrong—unlike animals.)

In a nutshell, anything that misses the mark of perfection is sin. Anything less than absolute righteousness disqualifies us from fellowship with God.

"PASS ME YOUR TEA"

Imagine that you are observing the following conversation taking place in a small café in the Middle East, year 2010 A.D.

In the group of men who have gathered, there is one who is a follower of Jesus. He is an American, whom I'll call Sam. (This is a true story and Sam is a friend of our family.)

As the men drink their traditional tea, talking loudly and having a good time, they decide to ask the foreigner, Sam, about his beliefs. Sam is ready for their question and says to one of the men, "Here, let me have your tea."

Sam took the cup of tea, swished around a bunch of saliva in his mouth, and spit into it. Now there was a big wad of saliva floating on top of his friend's tea.

Gross.

"Hey, he spit in my tea," the guy said in disbelief. "He *spit* in my tea!"

If anyone's eyes weren't on Sam before, they were now.

Sam handed the glass back to his Muslim friend with a smile.

"Here, drink it," Sam said.

"I'm not going to drink that!" the guy exclaimed looking at the wad of saliva—with a room full of his buddies amused by his predicament.

"This is what sin is. It's the gross things we do," Sam explained. "It pollutes our lives. It is disgusting to God. We can't get rid of it—no matter how much good we do."

"Hey, waiter," Sam called, "pour some more tea in here."

The waiter poured more tea into his friend's glass.

As more tea filled the glass, the wad of saliva didn't go away, but surfaced at the top again.

"Here, *now* you can drink it," Sam said, giving it back to his friend.

"I am not drinking that," his Muslim friend insisted, as the others listened with humored interest.

"How much tea would we have to add to make it pure again?" Sam asked. Then Sam made his point: "See, you can add more 'good works' to your life, but the sin is still in the middle of your heart. I am guilty of sin, and I know you are too. We can't even live up to our own standards. How much less can we live up to God's standard?"

There is no religion on earth that can remove sin from our hearts. Only Jesus Christ can do that by washing us with His blood.

IT TAKES HUMILITY

Hmmm … should I get coffee or tea this morning? I wondered as I looked at the options at the concession stand.

One of the employees was especially nice. I wanted to witness to him, so I gave him our tract about evidence for the resurrection of Christ, hoping it would start a conversation. He thanked me and kept working. I wanted to say more, but I couldn't think of the right way to get started. I stalled for a long time, putting cream and sugar in my tea to give me more time to think. Finally I prayed, *"Lord, open a door."*

Right then, this employee, Calvin, walked by and asked, "So, was that like a poem you wrote or something?"

There we go! [smile]

"No, it's about the evidence that we have that Jesus rose from the dead," I explained, giving him a short summary of the tract. From there a very interesting conversation emerged. As we were talking, a friend of mine, Curt, who also likes to witness walked up and joined the conversation.

Calvin thought you had to earn eternal life and said, "Nothin's free. I know; I've been behind bars and I know the consequences there are."

"Hey, man, I served a year and a half in prison, I know what you are talking about," Curt said. (Curt gave his life to the Lord in prison and has a neat testimony.)

"I served 24," Calvin said, and Curt and Calvin chatted for a few minutes about their prison experiences. I was thinking, *Curt was just the perfect guy to have walked up right at this moment …*

I told Calvin, "Imagine you were facing life in prison. Then someone came along and paid your fine—"

"Did your time for you," Curt inserted.

"So you could just go free," I said. "That's what God did for us."

"It's like this, man," Curt explained, "if I was giving you $100, what would you have to do to take it from me?"

"I don't take anything free. I need to pay my fine," Calvin replied.

"Well, it takes a lot of humility," I explained, "to come before God and admit we deserve Hell and need His salvation."

Though he didn't fully agree with us, Calvin did promise to read the book I gave him.

Calvin had difficulty with the idea of *humbling* himself to admit he needed salvation. He is not alone in his resistance. Remember Naaman, captain of the Syrian army? He was revered for winning great victories for the king, but now he faced leprosy. His wife's young Israeli maid did a great job "witnessing," and when the king of Syria heard that someone in Israel could cure Naaman, he sent a formal letter and costly gifts to the king of Israel, asking for Naaman's healing. The king of Israel, however, thought the whole thing was a political trick. "Am I God that I can cure a leper?" he asked with alarm.

Elisha, however, said, "Let him come to me." So the great general came to Elisha's house with his horses and his chariot. But Elisha didn't even give Naaman the honor of coming out to meet him. He simply sent a messenger telling him to "go wash in the Jordan."

Naaman was enraged. He was expecting Elisha to greet him properly and call upon his God to do a great miracle worthy of a high-ranking general. He considered Elisha's response to be a great insult. No respect. No honor. Just "wash in the Jordan"? *What's so great about the Jordan, anyway?* he wondered as he angrily turned around to leave.

At this point, Naaman's servant gave him some profound advice. "My father," he said, "if the prophet had bid thee do some great thing, wouldest thou not have done it? How much rather then, when he saith to thee, Wash, and be clean?" (2 Kings 5:13).

In other words: "Think, Naaman! This is your life we are talking about. If Elisha had told you to do something dangerous or difficult, wouldn't you have at least *tried* to do it? All he is telling you to do is dip in the river. How could you possibly refuse?"

Naaman saw the logic in his servant's argument, washed in the Jordan, and was completely cleansed (2 Kings 5:14).

Many people today are just like Naaman. The way to be saved is too simple for them. It's too humbling. They don't want to submit to God's way.

I remember talking to a Muslim friend at our kitchen table about this. She replied, "But I want to earn it myself!" She wasn't getting our point. Or maybe she was, but she didn't want to humble herself to accept it. You see, it's a natural response of our pride to want to earn our salvation.

God simply says, "Wash and be clean." But to wash requires humility. One has to acknowledge he is dirty. This requires repentance—agreeing with God about our sin.

Part of our job, as witnesses, is to speak the truth about sin and coming judgment. However, let's not take our eyes off the fact that this is only the *first* part of the message. The core of the message is not one of doom or misfortune at all—it's the opposite. It is a message of amazingly good news. (Remember, that's what the word *gospel* means: good news!) The worst news in the world prepares the way for the best news in the world: God is offering grace.

"For the grace of God has appeared, bringing salvation to all men" (Titus 2:11). It's our job to spread the word!

HOW MANY WAYS CAN I SAY, "IT'S FREE"?

What is grace? One definition could be "an undeserved gift."

When the prodigal son returned home deserving punishment, but the father gave him a hug, kiss, robe, ring and party instead—*that* was grace (Luke 15:11-32).

When our greatest efforts were like disgusting soiled rags, but God replaced our rags with the beautiful, white robe of the righteousness of Christ—*that* was grace.

When we could do absolutely nothing to get to God, yet He reached down, picked us up, cleaned us, and brought us into fellowship with Jesus Christ—*that* was grace.

God's grace takes us from one extreme to the other: From eternal destruction to eternal joy in God's presence. From criminals to ambassadors. From His enemies to His bride!

Consider these words: "But God, who is rich in mercy, for His great love wherewith He loved us, Even when we were dead in sins, hath quickened us [made us alive] together with Christ, (by **grace** ye are saved;) And hath raised us up together, and made us sit together in heavenly places in Christ Jesus: That in the ages to come He might shew the exceeding riches of His **grace** in His kindness toward us through Christ Jesus. For by **grace** are ye saved through faith; and that not of yourselves: it is the **gift** of God: Not of works, lest any man should boast" (Ephesians 2:4-9).

There is no way to earn this. It's a *gift*. It's grace. It's free to us, but only because it cost Him terribly. How could we even *think* we could pay God for this? We can't even comprehend the value, and we certainly cannot contribute anything towards it. If we could, it would cease to be grace. The work of salvation is done. All we can do is accept it or refuse it. Those who accept it get the joy—and challenge—of communicating it to others as well.

James and Ryan, some friends of ours, have been witnessing on Thursday nights at an apartment complex in our town. They told me of a guy, Derek, to whom they had been witnessing for multiple weeks.

"It became clear to us that he really didn't understand grace," James explained.

That phrase stuck with me ... *he didn't understand grace*. How many people simply don't understand grace! It's so simple that they miss it. Derek, like many others, was full of expressions such as, "Try hard," and, "Do my best," but the word *grace*, or even the concept of it, was not in his vocabulary.

"Look, man, you are missing the point!" James and Ryan told him, emphasizing the beauty of the grace God is offering to us. They explained that we can go from being God's enemies, under His wrath—to being His friends, in a close relationship with Him. As they continued to spend time with Derek, he continued to grow in his interest, and now they are studying the Bible with him.

Many recognize the song *Amazing Grace*, yet they don't know what grace really is. If one thinks he can earn his salvation, he doesn't understand grace. How can one earn a gift? Either it is a gift or it isn't. One of the best ways to help someone understand grace is to help them see their great need for it. When they realize how much trouble they are in with God, how helpless they are to do anything about it, and how undeserving they are of His favor—God's grace suddenly becomes the most beautiful thing there is.

Therefore, our goal in witnessing is to explain the truth about sin honestly, while explaining the good news about grace passionately. We need to explain both. We need to be full of truth and full of grace at the same time—as Jesus was. Remember, He was 100% grace and 100% truth! We should be the same.

CHAPTER 7

LISTEN BUT LEAD

"Attention, travelers on Delta Flight number 4131 to Cedar Rapids. The flight has been overbooked. We are offering a $400 voucher for anyone who will transfer to the next flight, departing at 7:45 a.m. tomorrow morning ... "

Sarah and I were waiting to board that flight. After hearing this announcement several times, it dawned on us, "Maybe we should do it!"

An hour or so later we were on a shuttle bus, headed to a hotel for the night. I glanced over and noticed another girl in her twenties. She appeared to be traveling alone, and I wondered what her situation might be.

As Sarah and I were unlocking the door to our hotel room, we saw her again. She was entering the room right next to ours. It was 9:00 p.m. and we hadn't eaten supper yet, but we had free voucher money to use.

"Should we ask that girl if she wants to eat with us?" I asked Sarah.

It won't hurt to ask, we thought, so I knocked on her door. She seemed eager to join us and we went down to the little restaurant in the lobby. During the first 20 minutes of the conversation, we learned a lot about our new friend, Sierra. She had just come from her grandpa's funeral; she had cried the first 15 minutes of her last flight; she had converted to Mormonism two years earlier.

"What were some of the reasons you were attracted to Mormonism?" I asked her.

"When the [Mormon] missionaries came to my door," she explained, "they told me that I should pray, and if what they were saying was true, I would feel it in my heart—the 'Spirit of God' would confirm it to me. And that's what happened."

Now, a number of immediate responses may come to our mind in situations like this, such as, "Feeling something in your heart is not a good way to make decisions," "Mormonism is not true, and I can tell you many reasons why," and so on. But if we are not sensitive, if we are not gracious, and if we don't care about the person as an individual, it is unlikely we will get very far in witnessing to them. That's why this chapter is entitled, "Listen but Lead."

Instead of immediately telling Sierra what was wrong with Mormonism, we talked about who Jesus is, what it means to have a relationship with our Creator, and the problem of sin. We asked her some questions about Mormonism and gently challenged a few of the points she made. During the course of the conversation, God provided in another interesting way: Two other ladies who had taken the same voucher also joined us at the restaurant. One of them asked, "Aren't all religions basically the same?"

Thank you for asking that! I was thinking.

This gave us a perfect opportunity to answer her question in a way that would also communicate truth to our new Mormon friend.

Sarah and I were encouraged by the way the Lord arranged our circumstances that evening. Can you think of a better witnessing situation than having two hours in a quiet restaurant to chat with a young lady who is lonely, hurting and misguided?

The next morning we saw Sierra again and gave her a booklet called *Heaven* by Randy Alcorn, with my e-mail address if she wanted to keep in touch.

Why was Sierra willing to discuss spiritual things with us even though we were strangers? I believe it was because we had first taken the time to get to know her. Sierra was on her way home from a funeral. She was alone. She was sad. If we hadn't taken the time to learn about her situation, we may not have known the best approach to reach her with the gospel. The question therefore is not simply, "Will our generation speak?" but also, "Will our generation listen?"

People are not projects: they are people! We should not treat them like projects, as if we think we can make another little check-mark on our notepad after we talk with them. There is value in listening to people, in taking the time to hear their story. I often have to remind myself to take the time to listen and not do too much of the talking myself. Listening is one of the best ways to demonstrate genuine concern. It shows respect. It also gives us the chance to respond kindly and enthusiastically to what they say. More importantly, listening often enables us to communicate the gospel more effectively. It enables us to understand *them* better and tailor our presentation to them, using terminology they understand and examples to which they can relate. Leading well requires listening well.

WHAT'S THEIR POINT OF VIEW?

A group of missionary kids were sitting on the floor at the airport, enjoying some time together before departing to their various destinations. One of them noticed a beetle walking across the floor and habitually picked it up and popped it into his mouth.

"Eww, that's gross!" another kid responded. He went on to explain, "We always *cook* ours!"

You never know what someone else's perspective may be! Viewpoints held by other people in this world are sometimes quite unique—much more extreme than preferences in beetle cuisine. It is helpful to learn where people are coming from and why. When we pay attention to what they are saying, we will be better able to discern which roadblocks are keeping them from understanding the gospel. Discerning the mental barriers is the first step to removing them.

I couldn't believe it when an Asian guy told me that he had never sinned. *Is he telling me he is perfect?* I wondered. *How will he understand the gospel if he doesn't see his need for it?*

As my friend and I continued to ask this young Asian man questions, we realized that he simply had a different definition of sin. He thought of sin as "big crimes." Since he hadn't committed any big crimes, he didn't think he was a sinner. If we had not discovered his misconception, we would not have made much progress in our conversation with him. If we had said, "You need to accept Jesus into your heart," he would have had no idea what we were talking about!

Witnessing should be much more than a presentation: it should be a *conversation*. Each person has a different worldview and belief system which influences the way he thinks. The gospel message doesn't change—it's the same for everyone. But people are different. Jesus handled people in very different ways. Look at how He interacted with the woman at the well, Nicodemus, the rich young ruler, the Pharisees, Zacchaeus, and others.

Our goal is not merely to listen; it is to *listen, but lead*. It's not necessary to let the unbeliever lead the conversation. They don't know where to take it. We do. The best way to lead a conversation is not to do all the talking, but to ask the right *questions*.

USE QUESTIONS ...

- **To keep people's attention.**
  I find that when I go into "presentation mode" and start rattling off a little message, I sometimes begin to lose people's attention. People typically do not want to listen to a speech; they want interaction.

- **To make sure they understand.**
  You may have just said something really profound, but how do you know that the person you were talking to understood it? It could be that it went right over his head while he was thinking about something else. If we ask questions, we will be able to make sure he is still "with us."

- **To show genuine concern.**
  True social maturity is thinking of others more than yourself. It is asking questions and listening with genuine concern, not just pretending to listen. It is giving others a chance to talk. No one enjoys being with people who are continually talking, especially when they are always talking about themselves. Being a good listener means being a good question-asker. Good question-askers know how to ask appropriate questions at the right time. They are fun to be with because they take an interest in other people and generate stimulating discussions.

- **To steer the conversation.**
  We can direct people's train of thought by the questions we ask. Like this: "What is God like?" I asked three junior high girls who seemed unfamiliar with the gospel. "What's His character? How would you describe Him?" "Loving, good, forgiving, kind," they answered.

"How do you know that?" I asked.

"Church."

"How does your church know that?" I inquired.

"The Bible," they said.

"Okay, so you believe the Bible is where we learn about God?" I asked.

"Yeah."

"I do too. Well, the Bible also says God is just. Do you know what that means?"

They said they didn't. This opened the door to discuss justice, forgiveness, and the way of salvation.

- **To get back on track.**
  People love rabbit trails, but we should be careful not to get too far away from the main point. A good question often gets the conversation right back on track.

- **To show people something about themselves.**
  Jesus often asked questions. Even though He already knew everything about everyone, He still asked people questions because it helped *them* to see things about themselves that they hadn't realized before. (See Matthew 22:41-46; Mark 9:33-37; and Mark 11:27-33.)

- **To avoid awkward silence.**
  When we are not sure what to say next, we can simply say, "Hey, let me ask you another question," and bring up a different topic.

- **To arouse curiosity.**
  "Do you know why Jesus died on the cross?" I asked a junior high girl on a bench at the library.
  "He was doing it for others?" she guessed, with a questioning tone in her voice.
  I continued, "It was a really horrible death being nailed to the wood and hanging like that."
  She agreed.
  "So why did He do it?" I asked again.
  She didn't know, but now she was curious.
  "If Jesus hadn't died on the cross," I explained, "there would be no way we could go to Heaven." I continued to share the gospel. This girl and I ended up talking for about 45 minutes there on the bench, and I was encouraged by her thirsty response. I left her with a small New Testament which she told me she would read.

THE SALTY CHILI

"I'm so sorry about the salty chili. I accidentally doubled the salt," our hostess told us as we were eating chili over tortilla chips with cheese. My family assured her that they hadn't even noticed and that it tasted great. But after she mentioned the salt, I began to think, *Wow, this IS pretty salty!*

We were visiting friends a few hours from home, helping with a church service the next day. That night as Sarah, Stephen and I were up in our room trying to review notes for a presentation we were giving, Sarah mentioned, "I'm thirsty. *Really* thirsty!" As soon as she said that, I realized how thirsty I was too. We weren't making much progress on our planning anymore. Instead, all three of us began discussing which ice-cold beverages we craved most—which, of course, only made things worse!

Finally, I decided to creep downstairs to see if I could find the kitchen. Everyone else was in bed and the whole house was quiet. I had a few problems. First, I had curlers in my hair so I really didn't want to be seen. Second, the house was big, old and dark, and I hadn't even been in the kitchen before, so I wasn't exactly sure where it was. Third, I noticed midway that I would have to pass their grandpa who was sleeping in a chair in the living room. Eventually, I chickened out, and we all had to settle for water from the bathroom sink. In the morning I overheard Sarah and Stephen comparing notes about how many times they had to get up in the night to drink more water from the faucet.

CREATING THIRST

Jesus said, "Ye are the salt of the earth: but if the salt have lost his savour, wherewith shall it be salted?" (Matthew 5:13). Jesus compares Himself to Light, Water, Bread, a Rock, and many other things, but He compares *us* to salt. Of all the minerals in the world, why did He pick *salt?* And how does it apply to witnessing?

I believe one reason is this: Our job, as salt, is to make people thirsty for Living Water—so they will crave Him, seeking the satisfaction that only God provides. We can create thirst by displaying Christ through our actions and speaking of how great He is. We want to give people a taste of Him! This will help them to see that there is a gaping hole in their lives without the Lord.

We are told in Colossians 4:6 to have "salty" speech. "Walk in wisdom toward them that are without, redeeming the time. Let your speech be alway[s] with grace, seasoned with salt, that ye may know how ye ought to answer every man."

How can our speech be "salty"? We can word things in a way that arouses others' curiosity—so *they ask us* for the gospel. When witnessing to people, why make it boring? Instead, let's learn how to capture their attention!

Jesus was continually telling stories, using illustrations and asking intriguing questions. When Jesus talked with the woman at the well, He sparked her curiosity by mentioning "living water" that would keep her from ever thirsting again. Immediately, she began asking *Him* questions. Similarly, when Jesus was talking with Nicodemus, He stated, "You must be born again." This made no sense to Nicodemus, so *he asked Jesus* to explain. Jesus had sparked his curiosity.

One time my dad was checking out at a hardware store.

"How are you?" the cashier asked him.

"Better," Dad replied.

"Better? What was wrong?" she asked.

"I was dead," he said.

Now my dad had her full attention!

"You were dead?" she asked.

"I was dead and now I'm alive," my dad said, explaining that he was spiritually dead before Christ saved him.

LEAVE A STONE IN THEIR SHOE

"What do you think man's purpose in life is?" I asked a girl on a college campus. By her previous statements, it was evident to me that she had an evolutionary, humanistic mindset.

"I don't know, but I'm going to be thinking about this all day now!" she told me.

Asking a good question is like leaving a stone in someone's shoe. It can stimulate their minds to begin searching for truth, bothering them until they find the answer.

In situations where we know we only have a few minutes with someone, a good question may accomplish more than anything else. While sitting in the oral surgeon's office discussing the upcoming procedure of getting my wisdom teeth extracted, I glanced at my dad, knowing we were both thinking the same thing: *How can we witness to this friendly guy who is doing our paperwork?* It can be difficult to know how to start witnessing in those situations. Finally, Dad simply decided to ask him a straightforward question. He figured, *We only have one chance so we might as well try something.*

"So are you a Christian?" my dad asked.

He claimed that he was. (Though, of course, that didn't mean he truly understood the gospel.) After a little more discussion, Dad asked him, "So what keeps someone *out* of Heaven?"

"That's a really good question!" he said, turning from the computer screen to give Dad full eye contact. "Wow—that's deep. I'm going to have to think about that. Actually, I'm probably going to have to think about that for a couple weeks!"

We laughed.

After a little pause, he asked Dad, "Could you just give me a brief answer to that question?"

Although a person may not repent of their sin and turn to Jesus right there on the spot, we can start directing their thoughts in the right way by asking challenging questions. In some instances, we may only have time to make one point before they need to leave, but that's okay. God can bring along another Christian to build on that foundation. Who knows? You may be just one out of two dozen people whom God is going to use to lead this person to Jesus. Sometimes it is better not to overload people with *too* much information all at once, anyway. People have a limited capacity of how much new information they can retain.

QUENCHING THIRST VS. INFORMATION OVERLOAD!

PUT A QUESTION IN THEIR MOUTH

Many people, even many churchgoers, don't spend very much time thinking about what happened on the cross. In a discussion with three girls at Subway, I asked them, "How is it that just because this Man died 2,000 years ago it has relevance to your life and eternal future today?"

"I have *no idea*," one girl answered emphatically. My question had aroused her curiosity, though, and now I had the opportunity to explain the answer to a captivated audience. A person will not search for an answer if they don't have a question. That's why we want to establish questions in others' minds—so we can answer them!

A college student (biology major) once told me that she was an evolutionist and that all the scientific facts point to evolution. But she said she *did* believe in a "higher power."

Instead of debating science, I decided to veer the conversation in a different direction. "If God is good, why does He allow so much suffering in the world?" I asked her.

She suddenly brightened and became very interested. "I have actually wondered that before," she said. "I'm not sure!"

This gave me the opportunity to explain that it's not God's fault there is evil in the world—it's ours. God created a perfect world, but we rebelled against Him. The Bible says that one day God *will* judge the world in righteousness. He will make all things right!

I love using this question about evil in the world because it springboards right into the gospel. You see, God did not create us to be robots. He gave us freedom. This freedom included the possibility of making wrong choices. Man's rebellion against God brought evil into the world—and this is the cause of all the suffering we see today. But when we look at the cross, we see that God is the One who suffered the most. As we consider what Jesus did for us there, we cannot doubt God's love. "But God commendeth His love toward us, in that, while we were yet sinners, Christ died for us" (Romans 5:8).

This question about suffering in the world is a very common question that people ask—and it provides a wonderful opportunity to explain the gospel. But if others don't ask it, we can ask it *for them*—and then answer it!

People need to be challenged to search for truth. Asking thought-provoking questions implies that we *do* have answers ... that there *are* answers to be found for those who seek.

"Why did Jesus come to be born as a baby?" my friend Annie and I asked two other girls at the mall. They thought and thought. They threw out a few ideas but didn't really know.

Before giving them a complete answer, we switched gears and began to discuss some basic concepts. Sin. God's justice. A courtroom scene. The need for a perfect substitute.

"No one can kill God, so God put Himself into a body that could die. But in order to die He had to first be *born*," I emphasized.

"Ah ... I see!" one of the girls said, smiling as it clicked.

The thrill of watching an unbeliever have an "ah ha" moment as they comprehend a truth about the gospel makes me think about what a privilege it is to witness. Since Annie and I had let these girls wrestle with the question for awhile, they absorbed the answer when we finally told them.

A STASH OF QUESTIONS

I know what is going to happen if I try to witness: My mind will go blank and I won't know what to say next.

Is this something you ever fear? If you have a collection of questions in the back of your mind (or on a notepad in front of you), it will dramatically reduce this concern.

- **What do you think happens when someone dies?**
  Follow up questions could be these: "How do you know that to be true?" or, "Have you always believed that way?" or, "What caused you to change your beliefs?"

- **Is eternal life a free gift or something you have to earn?**
  If they say, "Earn," you can ask, "Then your faith is in *yourself*, right?" and, "Then who gets the credit?"

- **What did the thief on the cross have to do to be saved?**
  This can be an eye-opening thought for people who think they can earn their salvation.

- **When did you become a Christian?**
  If they say, "Oh, I've always been a Christian," that's a pretty good sign they are not one. Follow-up questions could be, "What led you to Christ?" or, "The Bible talks about being 'born again' into God's family—which means a very specific point in time that we become God's child. Is there a time that happened to you?"

- **Who do you believe Jesus Christ is?**
  This gets straight to the gospel. I have found this question useful when I am trying to get the conversation back on track if we get distracted following a rabbit trail.

- Do you know what it means to be "born again"?

- How many of the Ten Commandments can you name?
  I learned this idea from a friend, Matt, who would use this as his primary
  starter question with college students. Often people enjoy the challenge
  of trying to name them, and reviewing the Ten Commandments provides
  a springboard to discuss sin and justice.

- Do you consider yourself to be a good person?
  Follow-up questions could be, "Would you like to take the 'good person
  quiz'?"; "If God judged you by the Ten Commandments, would you be
  innocent or guilty?"; "Would you go to Heaven or Hell?"; "Does that
  concern you?"

- Do you think one can know his sin is forgiven before he dies, or does he
  have to wait until after he dies?

- Do you know the meaning of the word "gospel"?
  Explain that it means "good news" and then ask, "Do you know what the
  good news is?"

- If you died today, do you think you would go to Heaven?
  If they say yes, gently probe, "Why do you think so?"; "Are you 100%
  sure?"; "If not, wouldn't it be the most important priority in your lifetime
  to be 100% sure about where you will be for all of eternity?"

- **Have you considered how much evidence there is for the resurrection of Christ?**

  Not only is the resurrection of Jesus Christ fundamental to the gospel, it's exciting to share with people because of the irrefutable evidence that many have not considered before. People may deny the resurrection, but for 2,000 years no one has been able to refute it.

- **Did you grow up with a certain belief or religion?**

  This is another non-threatening starter question which I especially like using with people older than I am.

- **How do you think one can get rid of his guilt and sin before God?**

- **Do you *hope* that there is a God?**

  This forces a person to consider his own motives.

- **Why does God allow evil and suffering in the world?**

  "What will happen when God finally fixes all the evil in the world? How will He do it? What will it mean for us?"

  Or you can present a scenario, such as this: "Let's say God created a perfect world and man broke it. What is God going to do?"

- **Has anyone ever explained the gospel to you before?**

- **Of all the knowledge in the universe, how much knowledge do you think you have?**

  Once when Sarah asked an atheist college student this question, he replied, "A miniscule of 1%." So Sarah asked him, "In the 99% plus that you do not yet know, do you

think it's possible that there is evidence that God exists and that He has revealed Himself?"

"It's possible," he acknowledged.

Notice that he just changed from an atheist to an agnostic. They went on to have a great conversation. This simple question graciously reminds people (especially the "know-it-all" type) that, in actuality, they do not know *everything* and they should at least look into the truth of the Bible.

RESPONDING QUESTIONS

What if they say something really weird and I don't know how to respond? What if I don't know the answer? Easy. We merely ask another question.

- **Where did you get your information?**
  "I believe that when you die your spirit has a choice of where it wants to go," a guy told some friends of mine who were witnessing to him in the food court at the mall.
  "Where did you get your ideas?" my friends asked.
  "A TV show I saw once," the guy replied. A smile came across his face as he realized that he was getting his information from pretty poor sources. Hopefully, their question helped him to see how dangerous it is to base your theology and stake your eternity on something you learn from TV.

- **Why do you believe that?**
  This forces others to defend their position and think about the claim they have just made. It puts the burden of proof on them.
  I've never heard that one before, I was thinking as I listened to a talkative college student explain his crazy idea of what Christianity was all about. I didn't know what to say, but my friend simply asked, "Why do you believe that?"
  The guy didn't have an answer. He just turned around and left. This was a good thing, because we were then able to continue the discussion with his friends who were more interested in the gospel than he was.

- **What led you to that conclusion?**
  This is similar to the last question, but perhaps a little softer. I love using it because it often causes a person to explain about their past or about an experience which influenced their life—and it helps me to understand them better.

- **What evidence do you have to back up your position?**
  "So what do you think about origins? How did we get here?" I asked a man who was attending the National Education Association Convention for

public school teachers. (Answers in Genesis had a booth at the convention to give away free materials and I was helping them.)

"Oh, aliens," he said.

"Ah … so what evidence do you have to back up your position?" I asked.

"Oh, I saw it on YouTube," he replied confidently. "And they're comin'."

"The aliens?" I asked.

"Yeah, we've been trashing this planet and it's comin' … " he said in a warning tone of voice.

"Well, we believe *'it's comin'* all right," my friend Frank (another volunteer at the booth) replied, "but we believe it's the Lord Jesus Christ who is coming … "

The guy didn't want to talk much longer after that!

Here are a few more questions to use in conversations: "Would you like to know the Bible's answer to that question?"; "Did that make sense?"; "Have you heard this before?"; "What are your thoughts?"; "Have you ever read the Bible?"; "What do you think is the main thing God wants us to know?"; "Do you think what I am telling you is the truth?"

WHAT IS WINNING REALLY?

Sometimes when another person's argument doesn't hold up, we feel a little surge of victory. We think, *I was so clever to have just asked that question!* or, *Hurray, I am winning the debate!* or, *Look! They are digging themselves into a hole and can't get out!*

That may be true, but we must remember that our goal is not to win debates—it's to soften hearts. The last thing we want is to win the argument, but lose the person. Our goal is not to make them feel stupid! Another purpose of salt is that it thaws. God is able to use us, as salt, to thaw cold and hardened hearts. To do this, we must demonstrate humility and give soft answers with meekness and respect. We do not want people to put up a wall of pride and resistance—we want them to respond with thirst and ask for Living Water.

"And let him that is athirst come. And whosoever will, let him take the water of life freely" (Revelation 22:17).

CHAPTER 8

KEYS TO CONFIDENCE

"How do you *know* the Bible is the Word of God?" a college girl asked me several years ago at a parade. She asked in such a strong and cynical way that I was caught off guard. I didn't do a very good job answering her question and she left with sort of a, *"Ha, I gave that Christian something to chew on!"* attitude.

I was discouraged. Of course I knew that the Bible was the Word of God, but forming a concise answer on the spur of the moment just didn't work out very well. When this happens, there is a temptation to become disheartened and conclude, *Maybe I should let others who* ***know more*** *do the witnessing. Maybe I'll actually do more harm than good if I try to witness!*

But the solution is actually quite simple: we need to prepare! Preparation gives confidence and reduces fear. After my disappointing attempt to answer that question, I resolved to spend more time studying so I could answer people's questions. I was more motivated to read books, to listen carefully whenever I heard messages about apologetics, and to ask my dad questions. But there was just so much to learn. I wondered, *How can I ever learn all the answers? There are thousands of books on apologetics, and I'm a slow reader!* Thankfully, I realized that it's not as overwhelming as one might initially assume. We don't need a Ph.D. in theology before we start witnessing. The main thing is to be familiar with the Word of God and to know the Lord.

One thing is certain: we should not wait until after we have "finished" preparing to start witnessing. If we did that, we would never witness because there is always more preparation we could do. In fact, one of the ways we learn to witness is *through witnessing!* It is possible for someone who has only been saved for 15 minutes to lead someone else to Jesus. All they need to do is explain how *they* came to Christ.

Jack's Diner was a favorite "fishing hole" of a friend of mine named Earl. He witnessed there so frequently that he earned the title, "Chaplain of Jack's." He led more people to the Lord at that restaurant than at the church he pastored. One time Earl noticed a man at Jack's Diner who looked very troubled. As he began talking with him, he learned that his wife was in the hospital in serious condition.

"Do you know the Lord?" Earl asked him.

"I know about Him," the man replied, having some Bible knowledge.

"Well, you need to know the Author of the Book," Earl said.

Right there at Jack's Diner, this man gave his life to Christ. Guess what this new believer did next? He went right up to his wife's hospital room and led *her* to Christ! Talk about witnessing when you don't know much!

The first point we need to understand is that each one of us should be witnessing now with the knowledge we currently have—even if it's not very much. The second point, however, is that we should be serious students of the Word of God—studying, growing, and preparing to give wise answers. This is going to be our focus through the rest of this chapter.

Think about it this way: we study *other* things. How much time do we spend on math, science, foreign languages, or musical instruments? Should we not put even more of an emphasis on preparing for this most important calling of speaking God's truth to this generation?

"But sanctify [set apart as of first importance] the Lord God in your hearts: and be ready always to give an **answer** to every man that asketh you a reason of the hope that is in you with meekness and fear" (1 Peter 3:15).

The word "answer" is the Greek *apologia* from which we get the word "apologetics"—which means giving a careful, logical defense of the Christian faith. Paul did not merely preach the gospel; he defended it (Philippians 1:7 and 1:16). He *reasoned* with people and gave answers to their questions (Acts 17:2, 18:4,19). He told Timothy, "Study to shew thyself approved unto God, a workman that needeth not to be ashamed" (2 Timothy 2:15).

EMERGENCY CALL

A Muslim friend pulled out a spiral bound notebook and set it on the table at the coffee shop. She was a high school student and wanted to learn more about Christianity. In the process of answering her questions, I explained how amazing it was that the Son of God, Jesus, who was perfect, chose to die on the cross for us—sinful people. My friend, who I'll call Mysha, asked, "Why couldn't an angel have died on the cross for our sins instead of Jesus?"

"Well, angels aren't per—" I stopped mid-sentence.

"They're not?" she replied.

"Well, I mean, they—"

My mind went blank. I had never been asked that before. I knew there were numerous answers to this question, but my mind froze and I couldn't think of any! I told her I would think about it and tell her when I found the answer. Mysha was fine with that. After a few minutes, I excused myself, ran to the restroom, made sure no one else was in there, and called my dad.

"Dad. Why couldn't an angel have died on the cross for our sins?" (Not the most normal way to start a conversation, I know.)

He gave me some initial answers which I communicated to Mysha later in the conversation. Later Dad gave me more answers. Here are a few of them: The only one who would be able to absorb the full wrath of the infinite, almighty God without being totally destroyed would be God Himself. In addition, angels are not of Adam's race and therefore an angel would not be a qualified substitute to die in man's place. Furthermore, if an angel died for us, that angel would get the glory for being our Savior, and men would worship that angel instead of God. But God says, "My glory will I not give to another" (Isaiah 42:8).

Back to the story: Mysha and I continued to spend time together (shopping, going out to eat, cooking) and we had many spiritual conversations, comparing our beliefs. I would often come home and talk with my dad about our discussions. He would give me ideas of things I could have said—things I wish I would have thought of myself at the time. However, I would not have even thought to ask my dad those questions had I not put myself into those new situations where I needed new answers. Witnessing provides motivation to go home and do more studying.

Being stumped by a hard question is not something that we need to fear. We can always say, "That's a really good question. I'm going to go home and study that one. If you give me your e-mail address, I'll let you know what answers I find." An added benefit to this is that it puts us in continued contact with that person so we can have further opportunities to witness to them. If we act as if we know everything, we could drive someone away simply by our arrogant attitude. No one likes to talk with a "know-it-all."

TERRIFIED, AND RIGHTLY SO

Picture a young, unprepared soldier on the front lines of a battle. In terror, he watches his enemies quickly approaching. They are already beginning to shoot arrows at him. This poor soldier has forgotten his shoes and his bare feet are already bleeding from the rocky ground. (I know this sounds extreme and unrealistic, but that's the point.) He does not have any armor, and, therefore, he is an open target. Someone tosses him a sword, but it is of no use because he has never even held a sword before. He knows nothing about battles. The enemy is drawing nearer. Is he afraid? He's terrified!

Now let's change the situation. Let's say this young man had joined the King's army and, knowing there would be many battles ahead, he started preparing. Early each morning he worked to fine-tune his swordsmanship skills. He maintained excellent physical and mental condition. He studied war strategies and sought instruction from veteran warriors and commanders. He maintained the best equipment—sword, armor, shield, shoes and helmet. In addition, he was best friends with the King's Son, who was not only Commander-in-Chief, but the Champion of the military. From Him he received daily instruction and, when in battle, they went together. The young man was equipped and energized because he knew that a strength greater than his own fought with him and for him. He knew that the battle he fought was not his own, but his Commander's. And even if he died in battle, it would be an unspeakable privilege.

This is a very real picture of two types of Christians today. We are not in a make-believe war. There is spiritual combat raging all around us—and it is real. Jesus Christ is our Commander-in-Chief, and our brothers and sisters in Christ are our fellow soldiers. Unbelievers could be viewed as prisoners of war—captured by the enemy. They need to be rescued. Are we running from the battle or are we accepting our mission with joy and preparing for it?

"For we wrestle not against flesh and blood, but against principalities, against powers, against the rulers of the darkness of this world, against spiritual wickedness in high places" (Ephesians 6:12-13). A few verses later, we are told that our feet must be shod with the "preparation of the gospel of peace." I used to wonder what that meant. Then it occurred to me that one aspect of having our feet shod is being *prepared* to share the gospel.

Like the unprepared soldier, many Christians today are "barefoot" and don't know how to use their sword. No wonder they are scared to witness! But when we are prepared we will be more eager to go.

"*[Feet shod with the preparation of the gospel of peace] suggests a readiness to go out with the good news of peace, and therefore an invasion into enemy territory. When we relax in our tents, we are in deadly peril. Our safety is to be found in following the beautiful feet of the Savior on the mountains, bearing the glad tidings and publishing peace (Isaiah 52:7; Romans 10:15).*[1]"
—William MacDonald, *Believers Bible Commentary*

1. KNOW THE WORD

It was an emergency sandbagging operation. Our city of Cedar Rapids, Iowa, was flooding and many volunteers had joined to help. As we were shoveling sand and tying bags, a very interesting, yet friendly debate developed between me and the guy next to me.

"Christianity is so intolerant!" he stated.

I didn't disagree with his statement, but replied, "Well, Jesus *did* say, 'I am the way, the truth, and the life—no man comes to the Father **but by Me**'" (John 14:6).

He paused, looked at me, dropped his argument and exclaimed, "I wish I could quote Scripture verses like that."

The Word of God has a powerful effect on people! When the Word of God comes out of our mouths, it is much more influential than our own words. Whether it enlightens, convicts, or offends, we can be sure it *does* make an impact!

Another time, while talking with a new friend, Victoria, I could tell there were some concepts about the gospel she didn't understand. I was trying to make it clear, but she didn't seem to be getting it. So I pulled out my New Testament and showed her Romans 10:9. "That if thou shalt confess with thy mouth the Lord Jesus, and shalt believe in thine heart that God hath raised Him from the dead, thou shalt be saved." I emphasized the phrase *thou shalt be saved*.

"Can you write that down so I can look it up later?" she asked me.

When I started showing Victoria Scripture verses, instead of just paraphrasing the gospel in my own words, something seemed to change in her response. All of a sudden she had a greater level of seriousness. It was as if it was no longer *me* talking—but *God* talking. There was a greater authority behind my words. When we use Scripture, people are no longer arguing with *us*, they are arguing with Scripture. Plus, no one says it better than God does.

OUR SWORD

"For the Word of God is quick, and powerful, and sharper than any two-edged sword, piercing even to the dividing asunder of soul and spirit, and of the joints and marrow, and is a discerner of the thoughts and intents of the heart" (Hebrews 4:12).

Knowing the Bible is top priority. It is our sword. In order to use lots of Scripture as we witness, we need to be familiar with it. I strongly suggest that you make memorizing Scripture a priority in your life. Of course, you don't have to wait until you know 300 verses before you start witnessing—one

H.Mally

could know only John 3:16 and still be a bold witness. But the more verses we have memorized, the more we have to draw from when we are in conversations.

Some people complain about how hard it is for them to memorize. I believe that this often comes from a misunderstanding about memorizing. You see, the ability to memorize works like a muscle. It takes time to build up and it gets faster as we go. Sure, it may come easier for some than others, but like any other muscle, it has to be developed.

Many who once thought memorization was very difficult or impossible have found they were able to easily memorize large portions of Scripture by developing a *consistent* memorizing pattern in their life. For example, my mom used to think she was a failure at memorizing, but seven years ago, she decided to simply memorize one verse a week and to keep reviewing each verse she learned. Now she can quote about 400 verses. She says this has been one of the best decisions she has ever made.

In the same way, I know numerous young people who are able to quote multiple *books* of the New Testament—not because they have a special ability in this area, but because they have been faithful and consistent in their study. It takes determination to become not just acquainted, but intimately familiar with the Word of God. We won't do it unless we *want* to.

Let's not be content with the verses we already know, but persistently engraft new verses into our minds and lives. You may already

H.Mally

be familiar with many common New Testament verses, but what about the rich gospel verses in the Old Testament? Here are a few to start with:

- "Come now, and let us reason together, saith the LORD: though your sins be as scarlet, they shall be as white as snow" (Isaiah 1:18).
- "And he believed in the LORD; and He counted it to him for righteousness" (Genesis 15:6).
- "But your iniquities have separated between you and your God, and your sins have hid His face from you, that He will not hear" (Isaiah 59:2).
- "But He was wounded for our transgressions, He was bruised for our iniquities: the chastisement of our peace was upon Him; and with His stripes we are healed. All we like sheep have gone astray; we have turned every one to his own way; and the LORD hath laid on Him the iniquity of us all" (Isaiah 53:5-6).

OUR MANUAL

In addition to being familiar with key gospel verses and carrying a Bible with us, we should go to the Word as our manual to teach us how to witness. Here is a practical idea to start with: Grab a notebook and pen and read through the book of Acts. This time, as you read it, specifically ask the Lord to teach you about witnessing. Notice the different ways the gospel is presented. Notice how it is handled with different people. Notice the attitudes and priorities of the disciples. Notice the ways in which *God* worked and provided.

When Joshua was about to embark on a great military conquest, the Lord didn't have him read a book about military tactics; He commanded him to meditate on Scripture (Joshua 1:8). The world's idea of meditation means "emptying" your mind. Biblical meditation means filling it!

"Blessed is the man … [whose] delight is in the law of the LORD; and in His law doth he meditate day and night. And he shall be like a tree planted by the rivers of water, that bringeth forth his fruit in his season; his leaf also shall not wither; and whatsoever he doeth shall prosper" (Psalm 1:1-3).

2. KEEP YOUR LIGHT PURE

"This guy is very intellectual, and you may not know the answer to some of his questions," my dad warned me. "But he'll see your commitment to Christ—and that's important."

I wasn't sure how to feel about our morning's plans. We were meeting with a college student, Gordon, whom my dad had been corresponding with via e-mail for the past several months. Gordon, a sociology major, had been asking my dad a lot of academic questions about Christianity. Now Dad wanted to meet with him in person, and he asked me to come along.

Dad and Gordon had been e-mailing about a wide assortment of topics: the politics of education, textual criticism, peer review, scientific bias, naturalism, mutation of viruses, denominational divisions, and the theological positions of some modern philosophers.

I was half wondering why I was even going, realizing that my dad was right—I probably wouldn't have very much to contribute to their discussion. But my dad explained that this wasn't my reason for going. He reminded me that there is something that speaks even louder than intellectual arguments— it's our commitment to Christ. People want to see if we are genuine. In fact, this is a primary reason why martyrs spark revival in the church. Onlookers watch them die and acknowledge, "Look—they have something so good they are willing to die for it. I want what they have."

It is our *holiness*, not our presentation, that makes the biggest impact in our witnessing. It doesn't necessarily matter how eloquent we are or how much we know. What does matter is that we are living a godly, set-apart life for Jesus and that we are *committed*. Christlikeness speaks much louder than intelligent arguments. "Having your conversation [conduct] honest among

the Gentiles: that, whereas they speak against you as evildoers, they may by your good works, which they shall behold, glorify God" (1 Peter 2:12).

PURIFIED VESSELS

If we truly desire to be useful to our Master, let's consider the instruction given in 2 Timothy 2:20-21: "But in a great house there are not only vessels of gold and of silver, but also of wood and of earth; and some to honour, and some to dishonour. If a man therefore purge himself from these, he shall be a vessel unto honour, sanctified, and meet for the Master's use, and prepared unto every good work."

What is this verse telling us to do? Purge (eliminate) what is dishonorable from our lives. A drastic change ought to occur when someone comes to Christ. He should leave all the dark and polluting things of this world behind. An example of this is when the people of Ephesus burned their magic books publicly (Acts 19:19).

If we do not cleanse sin, worldliness, and polluting influences from our lives, it will hinder our testimony for Jesus. We will be double-minded and distracted. We see a dramatic example of this in the account of Ananias and Sapphira, whose compromise led to a devastating end (Acts 5). Purity of heart before the Lord is what matters!

The world's attraction to sensuality and sin is very evident by its media, entertainment, clothing, music, literature, activities and priorities. Therefore, the life of someone reflecting Jesus' nature will obviously look extremely different (Romans 8:5). If people don't notice a difference in us—if we appear just like the world—something is drastically wrong.

We are told, "Be not conformed to this world: but be ye transformed ..." (Romans 12:2). If we are concerned about "blending in" in order to gain a hearing with people, our method of evangelism may backfire. We will blend into the world instead of being a testimony to it. How will others be drawn to the light if the light looks just like the darkness? *People are less intimidated when you are more like them, but are they more helped?*—John Piper

It is crucial that unbelievers see a *contrast*—a distinct, unmistakable difference between the lives of believers and unbelievers. Think of the difference between a bright, sunny day and a dull, cloudy day. We want unbelievers to see light against darkness, not merely shades of gray. We want them to see that living for Jesus affects *every single area* of our lives. "But ye are a chosen generation, a royal priesthood, an holy nation, a peculiar people; that ye should shew forth the praises of Him who hath called you out of darkness into His marvelous light" (1 Peter 2:9).

In essence, we are called to be holy. God says, "Be ye holy; for I am holy" (1 Peter 1:16). In trying to understand what a word means, it helps to look at the opposite. The opposite of the word "holy" is not merely the word "sinful," as some may imagine. It's primarily the word "common." To be holy means to *separate* from the common and unclean ways of the world (2 Corinthians 6:17) and be set apart for Christ. We are dedicated to Him only. We are His special treasure. Paul described himself as being "a servant of Jesus Christ ... separated [set apart] unto the gospel of God" (Romans 1:1). May that be the description of each of us as well.

"The church today has replaced the doctrine of separation with the doctrine of relevance. As a result, we have lost our saltiness; we have lost our testimony. In seeking to be culturally relevant, we have become ineffective."—Dan Smith, Chancellor, Emmaus Bible College

Christians should not copy culture—they should *set* culture. If we are copying the world or compromising with it, we will not be demonstrating Paul's attitude or method. We see clearly from 1 Corinthians 1:17-23 that Paul did not try to impress the world or be accepted by it. He simply held up the cross of Christ!

INTRIGUE IS GOOD

"I'm sorry I have so many questions, I've just never met a full-blown Christian before," a girl at the park told me recently. I had given her and her friends some tracts and asked them what they believed. This led into a 45-minute conversation, most of which consisted of a steady flow of questions—coming from them, not me. "Do you live with your parents? Do you have a job? Do you think piercings are bad? What do you think about weed? What if it's for medicinal purposes? Do you think God comes before your family? Are your brothers and sisters as religious as you are? Do most people just sit and listen to you? Are you ever worried about your safety? Do you think that drugs are bad? What about smoking? How old are you?"

I laughed and kept trying to redirect the conversation to Jesus—but I realized that they were simply interested in knowing a Christian! They were not trying to antagonize me; we were merely having a friendly discussion. Sure, they recognized I was a little *different*, but that is what they expected from a genuine Christian. People expect Christians to be Christians! They respect the stands we take. They are curious about us. When they see compromise, they take note of that as well. Standing upon a conviction may be criticized by some, but it is noticed and respected by many silent observers.

Of course, being set apart for Christ does *not* mean having a "holier-than-thou" attitude. Pride will not get us *anywhere* when trying to witness! As Christians, it's not that we think we're better than others. On the contrary, we understand how bad we really are—and that's why we've trusted Jesus to save us.

We cannot control the responses of others. But one thing we know—when a Christian stands out in stark contrast in the midst of the darkness, it does not go unnoticed!

I'M ON YOUR SIDE!

If we really want to gain a hearing with people, we should not try to be more like them; we should demonstrate genuine love so they realize that we are their ally, on their side. Most people honestly don't care if you are different from them or even if you seem a little "weird." What they are most concerned about is whether *you* like *them*. People respond to genuine love.

My brother, Stephen, is a freelance photojournalist. He has become good friends with his coworkers, even though he is definitely quite different from most of them (for example, his activities and language are different, he chooses not to work on Sundays, and he has an entirely different worldview). However, he has a great relationship with them.

Stephen stepped into the kitchen the other day as I was cooking and read me a text he had just received. It was from the wife of one of his coworkers, worried about her husband who was facing surgery. It read, *"We may not be religious, but any positive thoughts are more than welcome as we're awaiting a meeting with the surgeon … "*

Stephen was surprised by this text because this lady was actually somewhat opposed to Christianity. But now she was asking for prayer (though she could barely bring herself to say it)! It is interesting to see those who have never before expressed spiritual interest ask for prayer in a tough time. But think about it this way: when someone is in a time of need, who do they go to for counsel or prayer? To their other friends who are just like them? No. If they truly want answers, they go to someone whose life they respect.

If we want to be bright lights and voices of truth in our culture, may we, by God's grace, no longer be tainted by this world (Daniel 1:8) but exemplify the holiness and love of Jesus to those around us.

3. BE READY TO ANSWER QUESTIONS

Why do we need to defend Christianity? Does God need us to defend Him? No. But we are ambassadors for Christ, and the Lord has given us an overwhelming amount of evidence to confirm that everything He said in the Bible is true. Apologetics is an awe-inspiring study, because the deeper we look, the more we find that our faith is built on unshakable ground.

Most people ask the same things, so it is relatively easy to learn answers to the most common questions. Here are some suggestions:

- Read good books about apologetics, but not necessarily material that is way above your level. Make sure you are reading with understanding so you will be able to repeat what you have learned to others.
- Pick five of the most common questions people ask. Write down some concise answers and verses on 3x5 cards and familiarize yourself with them. See ideas and suggested books on our website.
- Begin sharing what you have learned right away—even if it's simply with your brothers and sisters! We normally forget information that we never use.

What happens when someone suddenly gets interested in a new hobby? They read about it, talk about it, spend their money on it, enjoy being with others who have the same interest, and seek to gain skills in that area. It's not *work* to them; it's fun! Let's treat witnessing with the same excitement. Of course, witnessing is much, much more than a hobby—it is our true career and God-ordained life purpose.

NOW THAT WE'VE DISCUSSED THE EVIDENCE FOR THE RESURRECTION, LET'S TALK ABOUT FULFILLED PROPHECY ...

H.Mally

ALTHOUGH MR. BEAR DIDN'T SAY MUCH, JOEY COULD TELL HE WAS LISTENING.

Remember the fictional young soldier mentioned earlier in the chapter? Just like him, each one of us has a choice. Will we prepare? If we don't, we will be more likely to run from the battle. Fear, however, begins to melt away when we have our armor on and our feet shod with "the preparation of the gospel of peace" (Ephesians 6:10-18).

THE MALAYSIAN TRACT RACK

I was standing in a church basement in Kuala Lumpur, Malaysia, looking at the tract rack. One tract especially caught my eye. It was entitled, "Are all religions the same?"

I should read this, I thought. *Maybe it would give me more ideas about how to answer people's questions about this while I'm over here.* I put it in my purse. During some free moments on a bus ride I pulled it out and read it.

Less than a week later, we were boarding our plane to come home. Initially, we were disappointed because we learned that the seating arrangement for our group was scattered around the plane, so we couldn't all sit together. But then we remembered that 13 hours in a plane provides great opportunities for evangelism, so we figured that God had arranged this for a reason. Nickie and I found ourselves sitting next to a young Asian guy.

I admit, I didn't really feel like witnessing at the moment. *Maybe he doesn't speak English,* I thought hopefully as we sat down.

"Hello," Nickie said cheerfully.

"Hello," he replied.

"Where are you from?" she asked.

"The Philippines," he said. His name was Gelix.

We talked about his work, family and background. I was trying to think of a way to make the jump to spiritual things, so I asked, "In the schools in the Philippines, do they teach evolution, creation, or both?" This led to a conversation about evolution, God, and one's personal beliefs.

"So, how do you know the difference between all the religions?" he asked.

I smiled. *God had me read that tract at just the right time!*

"Well, there are many people today who say that it doesn't matter which religion you follow—we're all worshipping the same God. But there is no way that this could be true," we explained. "Christianity is very different from all the other religions. For one thing, it's the only one with a risen Savior. Muhammad, Buddha, and other leaders died and were buried, but Jesus rose from the dead and is alive."

"And it's the only 'religion' that even *has* a Savior," Nickie added. "Other religions just have leaders."

"Christianity is also the only religion that has a cure for sin," I continued, explaining that Jesus took our punishment on the cross. "It's the only religion that is not a 'do it yourself' religion," I emphasized. "Most people in this world are trying to be *good enough* to go to Heaven."

Gelix agreed.

"But," I said, "Christianity is the only religion that says, 'Hey, we can't do this on our own. We can't be good enough. There's no way we could measure up to God's perfect standard.' The only reason we know we are going to Heaven is because God made a way to *save* us."

(Note: Although we were calling Christianity a "religion" in this conversation, it is actually much better described as a "relationship.")

Gelix seemed both surprised and interested in what we said and continued to ask questions. We discussed many things such as life purpose, spiritual warfare, and the danger of polluting influences in our lives. Then we learned that his parents went to a Baptist church. Maybe our conversation with him was an answer to their prayers!

"I think I should start going to church again," he told us.

JUST IN TIME!

One time a girl in our neighborhood asked me, "If Adam and Eve were white, how did we get all the different races?" I couldn't believe she asked. Just the week before, we had studied this very question in our Bright Lights group.

"Oh, I've just been studying this!" I told Kayla. I explained that there is actually a very simple answer. There is only one race. We are all descendants of Adam and Eve. The only difference between colors in so-called "races" is the amount of melanin in the skin. All the "races" could easily have come from one set of parents. Adam and Eve were probably a middle-brown in color.

It is comforting to remember that God orchestrates both our preparation and our witnessing encounters. Often He provides answers right before we need them.

4. TREASURE JESUS

"In a way, I really like witnessing when I haven't done it for awhile," a friend told me. That didn't sound right, so I wondered what he meant. He explained that sometimes he will hear a new insight about the gospel, or view the cross from a new angle, and get excited about the thought. New insights are fun to share and we tend to express them in a fresh and vibrant way.

He continued to explain, "The answer is not to witness less often [so it comes out 'fresh' when you do], but to spend more time thinking about the cross, so that the cross means more to you."

Ah. It was then that his point clicked with me. When Jesus' suffering on the cross means more to us, we will be better witnesses of it.

The gospel is so deep that we could spend our whole life studying it and always be learning new insights. It remains a mystery even to the wisest scholars (Ephesians 6:19), yet it is so simple that little children can explain it (Matthew 18:3). After one becomes a believer, we do not move on from studying Christ's work on the cross to more "advanced" topics. No, we stay beneath the cross for the rest of our lives—treasuring it more and more!

The first meeting of our church every Sunday is a little different from most. There is no schedule, planned speaker or song leader. The focus is purely to spend time remembering Jesus' death, as He commanded us to do (Luke 22:19). Various men in the church stand up and share insights about the gospel, read Scriptures, suggest a song to sing, or pray—but the topic never changes. That's because the topic is inexhaustible—the gospel. It's amazing how many new insights are continually shared as we meditate on Jesus and all He has done for us! During this time, we also break bread and pass around grape juice as Scripture instructs (1 Corinthians 11:25-26). This one-hour service is a major highlight in our week. The more time we spend examining the beauty of our salvation, the more beautiful it becomes to us.

Scripture is brimming with rich metaphors, comparisons, parallels, types, and word pictures that give us a deeper understanding of the gospel message. We should dig for these gems! Treasuring Jesus is preparation for the work that lies ahead. The more we know Him, the better we represent Him.

Witnessing involves much more than the words we speak. Some of us may not be very eloquent, but if we are genuinely excited about our relationship with the Lord and the gospel message, others will see it—and *that* speaks louder than eloquence does. People want to know if what we are telling them is real in our own lives. Therefore, the ultimate preparation is to know Jesus and spend time with Him. "Thus saith the Lord, Let not the wise man glory in his wisdom, neither let the mighty man glory in his might, let not the

rich man glory in his riches: But let him that glorieth glory in this, that he understandeth and knoweth Me … " (Jeremiah 9:23-24).

The way to become a better witness is not simply to practice and critique your method and delivery (though that's not a bad idea). The best witness in court is one who is most familiar with the person and events. Spending time with Jesus is what gave Peter and John boldness in their witness. "Now when they saw the boldness of Peter and John, and perceived that they were unlearned and ignorant men, they marveled; and they took knowledge of them, that **they had been with Jesus**" (Acts 4:13).

"When you are thinking about God all the time, it spills over into what you say," someone once commented. I love that concept. If we are always thinking about Jesus, He is the One we will *want* to talk about. "For of the abundance of the heart his mouth speaketh" (Luke 6:45).

Now let's look at it from the flip side. Not only does treasuring Jesus help us to be better witnesses, but *witnessing* helps us to treasure Jesus more. We understand His work on the cross in deeper ways when we explain it over and over. The teacher learns more than the student. And when we explain the hope we have in Jesus to those who have no hope, we become more acutely aware of what a treasure we possess.

I was sitting in the warm sand with the sun setting over the ocean behind me … in the middle of a great conversation about the gospel. I felt that there was nothing I would rather be doing at the moment. My friend Danielle and I had begun talking with four teens who were building a sand castle. One of them, Brian, was a skeptical seeker and was asking a lot of good questions— making it a very interesting discussion.

At one point in the conversation I gave a description of how good God is. I explained, "Not only did our Creator make the beauty all around us for our benefit, He loves us personally and died to have a close relationship with us!"

Danielle and I shared how our relationship with such an amazing God was the best part of our lives.

"The God you are describing is surreal," Brian replied.

His reaction surprised me. My description of God seemed too good to be true.

"You're right!" Danielle and I acknowledged. "It is way too good to be true! But it's true!"

Brian was obviously affected by our delight in the Lord, and I pray that one day he will come to truly know and enjoy the God he called "surreal!"

The Courtroom

No one looks forward to being on trial—especially if you know you're guilty. And I knew I was guilty. Everyone knew I was guilty.

I trembled as I thought of standing before the judge. I had heard about Him. He was the one whose eyes were said to be like a flame of fire, whose words were like thunder. His rulings were always just. No crime was left unpunished. Every one of His words came to pass. Nothing could be hidden from Him.

I kept my eyes on the floor as I was led into the courtroom. I didn't want to look at anyone, and I wished no one was looking at me—even though I knew everyone was. I was on trial, after all.

The courtroom was not at all like I expected it to be. It was very bright and pure and good—even though for me it meant swift and certain judgment. Every foolish action that had seemed bad to me before seemed 100 times worse in this bright and holy place. As my crimes were brought into the light, they were much more shameful than I had remembered them.

I knew this was much more than a courtroom, and I thought about how amazing it would be if I could be accepted in such a place. I felt a longing in my heart to know the ones who were here. If only I could start all over again. I never knew such a place existed. Such desire welled up in me to be able to stay here—but instead, I was here only to be condemned and cast away. If only things could have been different …

How can I describe the intensity of the guilt that was so heavy upon me? Worst of all was the fact that the one I had offended was the Judge himself. It was extremely obvious to everyone that I was entirely guilty and that He was entirely innocent. Why was He even taking the time for a trial? The outcome was already obvious. Couldn't we skip the painful trial and go straight to the verdict—since we all knew what it would be? But no, the Judge was too upright for that. Justice called for a proper trial. Never before had I understood how beautiful a thing justice was—and never had I hated it more.

I stood there saying nothing, still looking at the floor. The trial began. There was no squirming, no excuses, no rationalizing, no blaming—I was face to face with the fact that I was guilty. My accuser stepped forward and began to speak. On and on he went, describing each one of my transgressions in painful detail.

Why couldn't I simply be condemned and have this whole thing over with? Why must I listen to my accuser name each offense with such hateful glee?

The things I wanted to be kept hidden, the dark secrets that I didn't even want to know myself—that I had tried so hard to forget, to escape from, to cover up, that I wished had never happened—these were all now being fully disclosed with all their gruesome details. I couldn't decide which was worse—the heaviness of the guilt upon me or the severe condemnation that I knew awaited me.

Finally, to my great surprise, someone interrupted my accuser. As I turned to see who was speaking, I discovered something astonishing. I had an attorney! An attorney? How ever did I get one? Was anyone actually on *my* side?

The next shock came when I was told who my Attorney was—He was the captain of the greatest army in the world, and the rightful Heir to the throne. He was also the One who would be the ultimate Judge—not only of my case, but of the whole world. So the Judge that I had offended was also my Attorney? How could this be?

Even more mind-boggling was the fact that my Attorney was actually serious about rescuing me. As I listened to Him, I was amazed at the compassion and love with which He spoke. I had no idea how He could rescue me from my inevitable fate—my need to face justice—but it was an amazing feeling to know that He cared for my situation, even though I had wronged Him so much.

As I listened, I soberly realized how dreadful my condition actually was. The offense had been extremely grievous. The penalty was severe. My Attorney said something about justice not being easily satisfied. I covered my face with my hands. I shut my eyes tightly. I trembled as I tried to imagine such a penalty. I thought of the powerful, offended Judge, uncompromising and swift in judgment.

But then the Attorney said the unbelievable: He said that reconciliation would be possible if a qualified mediator could be found. One who would be willing to represent the offender, appease the Judge, and satisfy justice.

My accuser laughed. He seemed to think it was hilarious that reconciliation was even mentioned as a possibility. How ridiculous. Who could possibly be such a mediator? Who would ever offer to do that? Who would even be able?

Yes, of course, the accuser was right, I concluded. Why did I entertain hope in my heart?

My Attorney broke the silence. He said that He Himself would be this mediator.

The accuser laughed again. What about justice? What about the penalty? What about the fact that I myself had already pledged my allegiance to him—my accuser? My own words were used to condemn me.

My Attorney did not flinch, nor back down. Rather, He said the most inconceivable thing I had heard so far—that He Himself would take the penalty.

I'm sure I'll never know exactly what He endured in my place. But this much I know: the blow of Justice fell entirely upon Him and not one stroke was left for me. The just took the place of the unjust. The King took the penalty of the traitor. The Highest took the place of the lowest. The earth quaked; the sun refused to shine; and Heaven watched in awe as the Prince of Glory gave His life for sinful men. You see, my Attorney filled all three positions: Attorney, Judge, and ... yes ... criminal. He couldn't simply mediate by pleading my case, for I had no grounds of merit. No, my Attorney was mediating by *taking* my place.

When the darkness lifted and I dared to look around, I saw that a piece of paper had been slipped into my hand. There was only one word that mattered to me—it was the word "pardoned." If you have never been in my position, you might not be able to comprehend how significant that word was to me. The mountain of shame, the piercing guilt, the sting of all my regrets, the dreadful consequences awaiting me—all taken away in one unbelievable instant.

I stared at the word again—pardoned. I looked up at my Attorney whom I had also come to know as my Judge and my Friend. And when I looked at Him, I saw He was looking at me. I will never forget the love that I saw in His eyes. And I understood that this was much more than simply a pardon—this was reconciliation.

That's another word that may not mean much to you. But if you had any idea of how awesome and desirable, how tender and kind this Judge is—then you would see that reconciliation with *Him* was a dream above dreams … coming true. This was far more than just pardon. I was accepted and welcomed by Him. And that is something I suddenly realized had been my greatest longing my entire life.

As I was trying to take all of this in, another thing happened that took me completely by surprise. I was handed something else—another piece of paper. I couldn't understand what it meant until someone told me. It was a will, and my name was written on it. I was given an inheritance? From Him? This was a strange feeling for someone who had been hopelessly in debt just moments before.

It was far too much for me to deal with the extreme change of course that had happened to me in one day. I went from being on death row to having the inheritance of the King. The Attorney said it was okay—I would have all of eternity to try to comprehend it.

I woke up, shaken. It was a dream. I grabbed my Bible and opened it up. As I read, the message was very clear. Mercy was available to me now. Not later—but now. The throne of God was open to me now if I would come, if I would repent, if I would believe in the One who died in my place, the One who is the mediator between God and man.

"For there is one God, and one mediator between God and men, the man Christ Jesus" (I Timothy 2:5).

"He made Him who knew no sin to be sin on our behalf, so that we might become the righteousness of God in Him" (2 Corinthians 5:21).

—Sarah and Grace Mally

CHAPTER 9

MOVING THE HAND OF GOD

"Prayer is not preparation for the work; it is the work. Prayer is not preparation for the battle, it is the battle." —Oswald Chambers

"Let's talk to him," my friend suggested, seeing a middle-aged man walking down the sidewalk of the college campus. He was nice and was very willing to take our questionnaire.

"In the past six months has your interest in God increased, decreased or stayed about the same?" we asked him.

"It has definitely increased," he said without hesitation. Then he told us that he had come to the campus that afternoon specifically to pray for students to come to Christ and be discipled!

Amazed, we explained that we had come with about seven other friends specifically to share the gospel on campus!

"When did you get here?" my friend asked him.

"About half an hour ago," he replied.

"That's when we got here!" we exclaimed.

Encouraged and energized, we saw this as a special confirmation from the Lord. I felt that we were there that day because *he* was there praying. It was only the second time we had been to that campus that year. Prayer moves the hand of God. *"Prayer strikes the winning blow; service is simply picking up the pieces."* —S. D. Gordon

If we want to see our generation be outspoken for Jesus Christ, let's ask God to do it. Let's ask Him to send out a whole generation of zealous soul-winners. Jesus specifically instructed us to pray for this. He said,

"The harvest truly is plenteous, but the laborers are few; Pray ye therefore the Lord of the harvest, that He will send forth laborers into His harvest" (Matthew 9:37-38).

The multitudes of the spiritually lost are like a field of grain ready for the harvest. They are waiting for laborers, but the Lord must send the laborers. He is waiting for those who are concerned to ask Him to do so. Thus, the laborers are few because those who intercede in prayer are few.—Oswald Chambers

So let's pray for laborers, and let's ask the Lord to start the work in us!

WHY WAS I SURPRISED?

"Lord, I don't know who to witness to today," I prayed one morning. "Please just place someone in my path for me to talk to. Have someone come to me, Lord!"

That evening, while Sarah and I were meeting with some friends at Taco Bell, an employee came over to our table, pulled up a chair, and sat down.

Okay, this is a little weird, I was thinking. But then I remembered my prayer from that morning.

The employee said that he had read the tract I had given to the cashier, and he wanted to know more about it.

"I am just like the bad people that paper describes," he said, explaining that his past torments him. (The tract was a cartoon that illustrates the Ten Commandments and teaches the gospel.)

Sarah told him that we, too, are sinners, ashamed of things we've done in the past. "The reason we hand out that tract is so that people will realize they are in need," she explained. "If people don't understand they are sick, they won't take the cure. Jesus did not come to help the healthy, but the sick!"

He nodded in agreement. He was from Iraq and said he had been looking into other religions.

"Have you read the Bible?" Sarah asked.

He said he hadn't very much.

Then another employee, Dan (the cashier to whom I had originally given the tract), came to join the conversation. He was also interested in discussing these things.

"Do you think eternal life is a free gift or something we have to earn?" I asked him.

"It's a free gift," Dan said, confidently. "I read the paper you gave me," he explained with a smile.

"Very good!" we laughed and congratulated him.

After we explained the gospel, Sarah told them, "If someone believes that

Heaven and Hell are real, and that Jesus died on the cross and rose again, and that the Bible is true—and we do believe those things—then it would be selfish if we didn't tell others! That's why, more than anything else, we want to share this message with others. We don't know you guys very well, but we do care about you, and we don't want you to go to Hell. I mean, of course, we want you to go to Heaven—"

They nodded and understood. They seemed to respect what we were doing and appreciate our concern for them. We probably talked for about an hour. I was so glad I had asked the Lord to bring me an opportunity that day. How often do we have someone come and sit down with us at a restaurant and ask for an explanation of a tract? On the other hand, how often are we praying for this? When we pray expectantly for opportunities we are not as likely to miss them when they come!

Did you know that even *Paul* asked his friends to pray for opportunities for him to witness? He wrote, " … praying also for us, that God would open unto us a door of utterance, to speak the mystery of Christ, for which I am also in bonds: That I may make it manifest, as I ought to speak" (Colossians 4:3-4).

Paul obviously believed that prayer was essential, because he frequently asked for prayer. His request was not simply for open doors, but also for boldness. (See Ephesians 6:19.) If even *Paul* needed prayer for boldness, how much more do we? When was the last time you prayed for boldness? (Acts 4:29).

THE FAITH TEST

Many *say* they believe God answers prayer, and they *think* they believe God answers prayer, but they prove that they have little faith in prayer because they do not pray very much. I recently heard a speaker ask something like this, "If all the prayers you prayed this past week were answered, how many babies would be saved from abortion? How many persecuted Christians would find comfort? How many tribes would hear the gospel?" And the list went on. I was so convicted. I need to continually ask myself, *Are my prayers small and self-centered or are they big and moving the hand of God in this world? Am I praying for the impossible? If not, why not?*

So let's take a minute and think about it. If all our prayers from last week were answered, how many opportunities would we have to share the gospel? How would our brothers and sisters be doing spiritually? How would our thought life be? What kind of zeal would there be in our churches? How many of our neighbors would we have a chance to reach?

"The prayer power has never been tried to its full capacity. If we want to see

mighty wonders of divine power and grace wrought in the place of weakness, failure and disappointment, let us answer God's standing challenge, 'Call unto me, and I will answer thee, and show thee great and mighty things which thou knowest not!'"—J. Hudson Taylor

WHERE THE REAL WORK IS DONE

About 25 years ago, my dad realized that he had not been praying very much for missions or for the world, so he decided to pick one major religious empire on which to focus his prayers. He made a list from which to choose: the Hindu empire, Buddhist empire, Muslim empire, and a few others. Dad doesn't remember how he finally arrived at his decision, but one night he simply decided: Muslims would be his prayer target.

The following day something very surprising happened. A friend invited him to attend a Muslim Awareness Seminar. My dad was amazed. This friend had no idea how perfect his timing was. Had he asked my dad the previous day, my dad would have turned him down. But how could Dad say no to him today? He had never heard of such a seminar before, but he was interested now!

Dad agreed to come to the planning meetings to help bring the seminar to our town. Guess what happened at the first meeting? They made my dad the prayer chairman. Could God have confirmed (and emphasized) my dad's prayer decision any more clearly?

Unmistakably, God must want me to pray for Muslims, Dad concluded.

My dad prays that God will loosen the enemy's grip on those people—that God would put "cracks" in their defenses so that the gospel can get through. He prays that there would be gospel penetration to the heart of Muslim strongholds abroad. He prays that there would be special interest taken in those Muslims who have traveled outside their homeland and are now in direct contact with Christians in the West. He also prays that God will raise up many who have a heart and burden for Muslims.

HOW SHOULD WE PRAY FOR UNBELIEVERS?

Rather than simply repeating, "Lord, please cause 'so and so' to get saved," let's look at some ideas from Scripture about praying for unbelievers. We can pray:

- That God would open their eyes, turn them from darkness to light, and release them from the power of Satan (Acts 26:18)
- That God would give them understanding and remove blindness from their heart (Ephesians 4:18)
- That God would bring more laborers into their path (Matthew 9:38)

- That seeds which have been planted would be watered and grow (1 Corinthians 3:6)
- That God would draw them to Himself (John 6:44)
- That the Holy Spirit would convict them of their sin (John 16:8)
- That God would grant them repentance (2 Timothy 2:25; Acts 17:30)
- That they would confess Jesus Christ as Lord (Romans 10:9)
- That they would fear the Lord (Psalm 111:10)
- That they would believe the Scriptures (1 Thessalonians 2:13)
- That they would seek the Lord (Acts 17:27)
- That they would take root and grow in Christ (Colossians 2:6-7)
- That God would give *us* specific opportunities to meet needs in their lives and serve them in a way that will turn their attention to God (Matthew 5:16)

PRAYER TRUMPS

Sarah and I stood in the food court at the mall, trying to inconspicuously get a better view of a Muslim girl we both thought looked familiar. Sarah decided to say hello just in case. She told her, "We thought you were another friend … but I guess not, but anyway—hi—nice to meet you."

Although it was an awkward start to the conversation, the girl graciously replied, "Oh, hello, it's nice to meet you!" She seemed eager to talk, so they briefly got acquainted and exchanged phone numbers.

Sarah sent a text to Aisha saying it was nice to meet her, and Aisha texted back warmly. Then Sarah began to pray for her. About one month later, as Sarah was praying, Aisha came to mind. Sarah decided that before letting too much time go by, she should text her and ask for her e-mail address in order to get a little more acquainted. *It's not going to hurt anything, and maybe God will open a door!* she figured. Sarah determined to text her, but before she actually did, she noticed that *she* had received a text—from Aisha! Aisha said she had some questions about religion and asked Sarah for *her* e-mail address! She sent her the questions (an assignment for a school project) and Sarah was able to respond with clear and thoughtful answers that included the gospel.

One afternoon as Sarah was praying for Aisha, she began to think about how seemingly impossible it would be to reach Aisha with the gospel. She wondered if Aisha was trying to convert her to Islam while she was trying to lead Aisha to Jesus. Both are convinced that they are right, and both know how to argue their case. Isn't this a hopeless situation? Of course not. Sarah remembered that she had a secret weapon—something that Aisha did not have. Prayer! That is, prayer to the God who hears and answers. Without the weapon of prayer, it *would* be a hopeless situation. But nothing is impossible with God. His Spirit can convict Aisha of her need for Jesus Christ. He is able to draw her to Himself. Sarah was reminded to not underestimate this invisible, *powerful* weapon! What could be more powerful than moving the hand of God? "The effectual fervent prayer of a righteous man availeth much" (James 5:16).

I was sitting in a local coffee shop, feeling a little nervous, waiting for my unsaved friend to arrive. Although she was very sweet, she was also definitely opinionated and strong in her views, not to mention articulate and intellectual. I asked my dad for some advice, prayed, and called two friends to ask them to pray. I tried to relax and hoped my nervousness would not be obvious.

After my friend and I caught up on news, I showed her the tract about the evidence for the resurrection of Jesus. Then I decided that it would be an appropriate time to go warm up my latte so that she could read it. *[smile]*

As I was standing by the microwave praying, I was reminded of how much more I had on "my side" than she had on hers! In a way, I felt similar to Elisha's servant whose eyes were opened to see the spiritual army God had sent for their help (2 Kings 6:15-17). From an earthly perspective, it simply looked like two girls chatting at a coffee shop. But in the spiritual realm, there was a battle going on—and I knew that I was on the winning side. I realized that I could have complete confidence because of the unseen spiritual help God gives.

I returned to the table, strengthened, and we had an excellent conversation. Though I wouldn't say she was "persuaded," I knew it wasn't my job to convert her anyway—just to give her information and converse with her. I clearly saw the Lord guiding me and giving me words that afternoon.

Often it is when we feel weakest that we are actually the strongest. In reality, we are always weak; it's just that sometimes we feel it more than others. But when we feel weak we tend to pray and depend on the Lord more. And the more we rely on God's strength, the stronger we become. So it is actually a good thing to feel weak! Paul said, "Most gladly therefore will I rather glory in my infirmities, that the power of Christ may rest upon me ... When I am weak, then am I strong" (2 Corinthians 12:9-10).

Every time we are in the middle of a witnessing conversation and cry out in our hearts, "Lord, I really don't know what to say next! Help!" He hears us. "God is our refuge and strength, a very present help in trouble" (Psalm 46:1). The amazing fact that we have access into the presence of God, knowing He hears and responds to our cries, is a truth that transforms the way we look at every situation in life.

"I GET IT NOW!"

Winters are frustrating. That is, if you live in Iowa, it's −3° F, you want to witness, and you are looking for people to talk to. Everyone stays inside and it's more difficult to find them. That's why we often head to the mall in search of people. About seven of us were witnessing one Saturday when my friend Maisie and I began talking with some junior high kids who were friendly but did not seem to understand what we were telling them.

"Okay, explain to *me* now how Jesus' death on the cross saves us," I said to one of the girls named Bailey. I had already explained it twice. I had tried to make it clear that it is not possible to get to Heaven by living a good life—but only through Jesus. I could tell, however, that she was not processing what I was saying. Finally, I simplified my question to something like this: "How do we get to Heaven?"

"By being good?" Bailey guessed.

She is definitely not getting this! And I've been trying to make it so simple!

I felt as if her eyes were blinded, so I cried out to God in my heart to open her eyes. But then Bailey had to go, so we were not able to talk further.

After awhile, the seven of us met in the food court to share how our witnessing conversations had gone. My ears perked up when Sarah began sharing about her conversation with a girl named … did she say *Bailey?*

Sarah explained, "As I was walking through the mall, a girl whose name was Bailey called out to me and said, 'Are you one of those people talking about God?'"

Sarah told Bailey that she was and began talking with her. Bailey described to Sarah how this "one girl" (referring to me) was trying to explain something to her about God and Heaven. She complained to Sarah that she didn't get it, but she wanted to know more.

Apparently, this is what happened: Bailey hadn't needed to leave after all so she tried to find me again and couldn't, but she found Sarah instead (a benefit of having a sister who looks similar to you *[smile]*).

Sarah gladly explained the way of salvation to Bailey more thoroughly, taking her back to the story of the first sin in the garden and gradually leading up to the cross.

"Oh, I get it now!" Bailey told Sarah.

When I heard Sarah share this story, I remembered my plea for God to open Bailey's eyes. I was reminded that the power is not in our explanation or eloquence—the power is in God who hears our prayers!

PRAYER CHANGES US

We pray, not only because it changes circumstances, but because prayer changes us. We care about what we invest in. When we invest time and energy into praying for people we become more concerned about them. We are suddenly more eager to ask how they are doing. Prayer changes our attitude toward people because it causes us to see them more from God's perspective—with compassion.

It is also by prayer that we ourselves are spiritually revived. If we fail to spend time with Jesus, we soon become like dry, thirsty plants (Psalm 63). In my own life, I've observed that the times I get discouraged are often the times I've failed to pray as I should.

Our primary desire is not merely that our requests would be granted, but that we would draw nearer to Jesus. Prayer is much more than a duty: it's the cultivation of a relationship with the One who took our pain and died in our place. We pray because we want to be close to Him. If we desire to have an intimate walk with the Lord, there is no other way than by spending time with Him. How can you be best friends with someone you never talk with? Since the King of the Universe actually desires to be with us, shouldn't we be looking for ways to spend time in His presence as often as we can? "Draw nigh to God, and He will draw nigh to you" (James 4:8). "The prayer of the upright is His delight" (Proverbs 15:8).

When we spend time with the Lord, the things that are heaviest on His heart begin to transfer to ours. A good wife is concerned about her husband's concerns. As the bride of Christ, we should be the same.

In essence, it is by being with Him that we become more like Him. Second Corinthians 3:18 says, "But we all, with open face beholding as in a glass the glory of the Lord, are changed into the same image from glory to glory, even as by the Spirit of the Lord."

Prayer changes us and prepares us for what lies ahead.

NOW WHAT AM I ASKING FOR AGAIN?

Imagine you are a lawyer standing before the Supreme Court of the United States, and you know that a very important case is at stake. Would you simply stand there and mumble? Of course not. You would make your case eloquently. You would know in advance what you were asking for and why you were asking for it. With boldness and respect, you would persuasively make your request.

When we come before the throne of God—the Highest Judge of the Universe—do we have that same attitude? When I heard Roger Magnusen (a lawyer in Minnesota who has appeared before the Supreme

Court) use this example when teaching about prayer, it really challenged me. Do I clearly and boldly make my requests, believing God has the power to grant them? Am I alert? Am I expectant? (Colossians 4:2; Mark 11:24).

If prayer seems boring, it may be that we have forgotten the One with whom we are communicating. We are not speaking with some far-away, abstract being, but with a Person who is near—who is our mighty King. Losing sight of this will cause us to pray mundane, routine prayers, without the excitement that comes from faith. "O Thou that hearest prayer, unto Thee shall all flesh come" (Psalm 65:2).

It takes faith to pray. Why? Well, first of all, we have to believe that it is worth the time and effort it requires to pray. If we do not believe that it is accomplishing anything, we won't do it. But those with faith take the time to pray seriously because they expect God to act. They pray precisely and specifically—not just for themselves, but for God's kingdom and God's work.

Faith is believing that not one word escapes the ears of our Father (1 Peter 3:12). Faith is demonstrating patience and not wavering through unbelief—even when the solution seems impossible. Faith is continuing to pray even when we don't see answers.

Remember the man who was praying on the college campus? While we talked with him that afternoon, he shared that the Lord had led him and his wife to the full-time ministry of traveling around the country and praying at college campuses.

I wrote my phone number on a Bright Lights brochure and gave it to him, in case he needed anything while he was in town.

"Bright Lights? My nieces are in this!" he said.

"Really? What are their names?" I asked with surprise.

"Melanie Thomsen and her sisters … " he replied.

"I am good friends with them!" I exclaimed.

Melanie leads a Bright Lights group in Ohio. I called her to tell her the story. She told me that her uncle (whose name is Rod) had already prayed at over 1,000 campuses throughout the US! I wonder how much has happened as a result of Rod's prayers.

The same day we met Rod, another guy on our witnessing team, James, also approached him (independently from us) to witness to him. When James learned about Rod's prayer ministry, he asked, "Did you ever pray at Indiana University?"

"Yes," Rod replied.

"I was saved there!" James shared.

Rod is not able to see all the fruit of his prayers now, but one day he will. Last I heard, he had prayed at over 1,225 college campuses. This is definitely a demonstration of faith!

We should want to be well known, not to the world, but before the Throne of God—to be someone whom angels recognize as a "frequent visitor" before God's Throne, so to speak.

But becoming a prayer warrior is demanding work! It's one thing to pray hard and long when you face a crisis. But it is another thing to spend sincere, fervent prayer routinely for others and for the work of the Lord. Serious effective prayer isn't just a switch you turn on—just like no one becomes a marathon runner overnight. It requires time, energy and dedication. Faith is the main driving ingredient, along with righteousness and humble gratefulness. However, the more we persevere in this discipline, the more our desire increases. The more we pray, the more we want to pray.

Now, with all of these reminders in place, let's discuss some ways to increase our prayer lives.

TEN PRAYER IDEAS

- **Location.** Sometimes it takes creativity to find a private place to pray (Matthew 6:6). Here are a few suggestions: early in the morning before others get up, in your garage, in an empty vehicle, or somewhere outside (Mark 1:35).

- **Focus.** To stay focused, consider praying out loud, walking as you pray, writing out prayers, or following a prayer list—putting a check after each request when you pray for it.

- **Humility.** Notice that the Bible talks a lot about praying on our knees (Daniel 6:10; Ephesians 3:14). It also frequently mentions fasting—another way to show humility (Matthew 6:16-17; Acts 13:2).

- **Prayer Targets.** One way to combat a sinful or distracting thought is to choose a "prayer target" to pray for every time the wrong thought comes. Years ago, my sister, Sarah, picked an unsaved neighbor girl as a prayer target, and guess what? The girl came to Christ and is now raising a godly family.

- **An Hour.** Try an "hour of prayer" by using a schedule of five-minute segments. See *www.willourgenerationspeak.com* for a sample schedule.

- **Extra Time.** A couple years ago our family decided to implement a new prayer time at the Bright Lights office—3:00 every afternoon. We actually got this idea from Peter and John (Acts 3:1) *[smile]*. It is a great way to refocus in the middle of each busy day.

- **Together.** Praying with our brothers and sisters in Christ is one of the sweetest things we get to do here on earth (Matthew 18:19-20). Our good friend Augusta from India, who joined our church a few years ago, mentioned to us that she felt the ladies at our church should be praying together more often. We agreed, but wondered when we could fit in another weekly get-together with everyone's busy schedule. Finally, we decided: we'd do it on Sunday morning before church. It has become one of the highlights of our week!

- **All Night.** "Do you have all-night prayer meetings here?" Augusta asked us after she had been a part of our church for about a year.

  All night? I was thinking.

  "In our church in India, we did them monthly. I wondered if you did them here," she explained. Sarah and I agreed it was a good idea, so Augusta scheduled one. I admit, I was somewhat useless the first time because I kept falling asleep! But Augusta has continued to schedule them and they have been a great blessing to everyone involved.

Why pray all night? So you can say you did it? No, the primary reason to pray at night is simply because you have a large chunk of time with *no distractions*. Also, there are a number of significant examples in Scripture of praying in the night (Luke 6:12; Luke 18:7; 1 Thessalonians 3:10; 1 Timothy 5:5; 2 Timothy 1:3).

If you'd like to try this with your friends, our routine is something like this: we make prayer lists, pray, and in between prayer segments we sing with a guitar and read Scripture (and some of us drink coffee *[smile]*). At 6:00 a.m. we go out for breakfast. I don't know if I would have believed this if someone had told me beforehand—but our main problem is running out of time! Usually our prayer lists end up being so long, it's hard to finish by the morning. When 5:00 a.m. rolls around we have to start "speed praying" to get through everything!

- **Missionary reports.** Most of us get them. But how much time do we invest in prayer for the needs they mention? Some young people in our town from various churches have recently been organizing a "missions prayer meeting" on Friday evenings. They print out missionary reports and pray for missions and the world for a couple of hours. I have been encouraged by the times I have joined them!

- **Accountability.** One day my friend (yes, Augusta again *[smile]*) suggested that she call me every day at a certain time so we could pray for a specific unsaved friend to whom I had been witnessing.

  Call each other every day? I thought, a little surprised. But the phone call only lasted about five minutes and it was a special time each day. Augusta is committed to praying for unbelievers because she was saved when a group of believers were praying fervently for her.

Think about all of the different activities in which we choose to invest our hours. Not one of those activities will produce the results that prayer will produce. Prayer is one thing we can do on earth that will continue to bear fruit after we die!

THE FARMER'S MARKET

"What are our prayer points for today?" Sarah asked as she was driving. We were headed to a farmer's market with some friends to find people with whom we could share the gospel. On the way there, we decided to review the suggested prayer requests for the day from the "30 Days of Prayer" booklet. You see, it was the first day of Ramadan (the Muslim month of fasting), and many from our church were making an increased effort to pray for Muslims, following the booklet's suggested prayer-points. We were all feeling enthusiastic about our new prayer focus, and I remember thinking, *I've never seen Muslims at this park before, but it would be so neat if we met one today!*

We arrived at the park, prayed and split into pairs. My friends Emily and Melodie began talking with a lady and her daughter by a picnic bench.

"Hello! Are you having a nice day?" they asked.

The lady smiled back and indicated she was.

"My friend and I are taking a little survey, and we wondered if we could ask you a few questions?" Emily continued.

"Oh, I do not speak English ... " she said, with a thick accent.

Undeterred, Emily turned to her daughter and asked, "Do you?"

The girl's English was perfectly understandable and she agreed to interpret.

"What do you believe?" Emily asked.

"I am a Muslim. I am from Indonesia."

"You are a Muslim!" Emily exclaimed. "Are you participating in Ramadan?"

"Yes!"

"Well, I believe the Lord has brought us together, then, because just this very day—the first day of Ramadan—we have begun a month of prayer for Muslims around the world. I don't know a lot about what Muslims believe. Could you tell me?" Emily asked.

This question led into a 30-minute discussion, in which the lady, whom I will call Sameera, said something they did not expect: "I read the Bible. I sleep with the Bible." But with confusion, Sameera expressed, "I do not know who to pray to. I read the Bible, and I read Koran. Pray to Isa [Jesus] or Allah?"

Translating through the daughter, Emily shared many Scripture verses about Jesus.

"I dream about Isa [Jesus]," Sameera said with certainty, yet perplexity. Motioning with her hands, she explained how Jesus was shining in her dreams. "Always bright, always smiling ... and then—He disappears."

Emily got the impression that she dreamed about Him often, and it was always the same—radiant, and with invitation, but then gone.

Soon a van pulled up and Sameera said she had to go, but she gratefully shook their hands. She told them that she was actually on her way to a Bible study.

Bible study? Okay, let's think about this. *She was having dreams about Jesus. She reads the Bible. She is in contact with other Christians. And God led us to her on the very day we began a prayer focus for Muslims.* I don't know what God was doing in Sameera's life, but I do know one thing: coincidences don't exist with God.

In light of all we have discussed, how could we afford to work for the Lord without placing a strong emphasis on prayer? Not only should we pray before, during, and after witnessing, we should ask others to pray for us too. Notice Paul's specific request: "Finally, brethren, pray for us, that the word of the Lord may have free course, and be glorified" (2 Thessalonians 3:1).

What happens when God's people pray? Revival starts. Laborers are sent. Satan's army is weakened. The gospel goes forth. And *we* draw closer to God through the process. The Lord has already given the invitation: "Call unto Me, and I will answer thee, and shew thee great and mighty things, which thou knowest not" (Jeremiah 33:3). How will we respond?

"The one concern of the devil is to keep Christians from praying. He fears nothing from prayerless studies, prayerless work and prayerless religion. He laughs at our toil, mocks at our wisdom, but he trembles when we pray."
—Samuel Chadwick

CHAPTER 10

WHEN THEY AREN'T SO FRIENDLY!

- **SCENARIO 1:** "If this is about religion," a lady at the park told me in an irritated tone of voice, "I'm *not* interested."

- **SCENARIO 2:** "I just want to punch you in the face," Markel said to my friend Jeff.

- **SCENARIO 3:** "You've just made me feel like the worst, most terrible person ever," the girl in the hotel lobby told me defiantly.

- **SCENARIO 4:** %$*!&# #%$@&#

- **SCENARIO 5:** "Good luck in finding people who want to talk," a lady told me sarcastically, after expressing her disinterest.

How should we respond when people "aren't so friendly"? How do we have the perseverance to keep going? What does Scripture say about these kinds of responses? Although most of the stories in this book are accounts of people responding positively, it does not always happen that way. In this chapter we are going to look at the scenarios described above and consider what our response and attitude should be in such cases.

SCENARIO 1: IF THIS IS ABOUT RELIGION, I'M NOT INTERESTED.

"Hi," I said to an older lady sitting on a bench by herself at the park.

"Hello," she replied.

"Is that your grandson?" I asked, trying to think of something to say. She was watching a little boy on the playground.

"Yes," she said, with a small smile.

Pause.

"Can I ask you a question?" I asked.

"If this is about religion," she replied in an irritated tone of voice, "I'm *not* interested. I don't think it's right for people to come out to a park like this and talk to people about religion. I think it's very disrespectful, and if that's what you're doing, I *don't* want to talk about it."

"Oh, okay," I said, and stood up to leave.

What did I do wrong? I wondered. I felt discouraged.

The reality is that people will sometimes get offended when we witness to them. We can expect it, and we should try to not let it dampen our enthusiasm. If people get offended, it does not necessarily mean that we did anything wrong. Jesus' words and presentation were flawless, yet many rejected Him. Similarly, many mocked and rejected Paul. Does that mean Paul was using the wrong approach? Of course not. My dad brought this to our attention one time while our family was studying Acts 17. When Paul preached on Mars Hill, he received three responses from his listeners. "And when they heard of the resurrection of the dead, some mocked: and others said, we will hear thee again of this matter ... Howbeit certain men clave unto him, and believed ... " (Acts 17:32-34).

Did you catch that? Some mocked, some weren't sure, and some believed. We should expect the same three reactions today. Understanding this concept has been very helpful to me. If we presume that everyone we talk with is

THE SOWER NEVER KNOWS WHERE THE SEED IS GOING TO LAND.

going to believe, we will become discouraged very quickly! Some people will reject the gospel no matter what. It does not necessarily mean we did a poor job presenting the message. And it does not mean that the Holy Spirit isn't working! A person may initially reject, but later God may bring to mind the truth we shared and soften his heart. Sometimes it is okay for us to simply walk away (Matthew 10:14).

Truth to Remember: There will always be three responses to the gospel: some will mock, some will be curious, and some will believe.

SCENARIO 2: I FEEL LIKE PUNCHING YOU.

Jeff used to attend our church, but now he is the director of a homeless shelter in New York. One day a troubled, homeless man named Markel showed up at the mission. Markel expressed his sentiments right off the bat: "I'm a Muslim. I don't like Jesus, I don't like this Jesus stuff, but I got nowhere to go."

Jeff welcomed him into the shelter and told him the requirements—one of which was to attend chapel every night.

I think I'm going to preach on the resurrection of Jesus Christ tonight, Jeff thought. *That will be a good topic for Markel!*

While Jeff preached, Markel sat there uncomfortably, with no choice but to listen. Jeff boldly pointed out, "Jesus is alive, but Muhammad is dead. Confucius? He's dead! Buddha? Dead. Jesus is alive!"

Well, Markel did not like the message very much. He got right up off his seat and marched to the front, shaking a fist at Jeff.

"I just want to punch you in the face," he told Jeff.

"Good!" Jeff replied.

"What do you mean 'good'?" Markel asked.

"That means the Holy Spirit is fighting for your soul—that's what that means. There's conviction. If what I say isn't true, then it would mean as much as Santa Claus—and you don't want to punch me over that, do you? I'm encouraged by this, and I'm gonna' step up the prayer!" Jeff told him.

Jeff prayed and the Holy Spirit continued to work. In fact, an amazing transformation was about to take place in Markel's life.

One day after studying the story of the Philippian jailor in Bible study, Markel came into Jeff's office saying, "You know, I am a bitter, angry man, but I want that kind of joy. I need that."

After another week of studying the Bible, Markel burst into Jeff's office in tears.

"I know how to be saved!" Markel exclaimed.

"I don't want to hear that," Jeff replied.

"What?" Markel asked.

"I don't want to hear that you know *how* to be saved; I want to hear that you *are* saved," Jeff explained. "You *know how* and you are just standing there?"

Markel, who had wanted to punch Jeff in the face, gave his life to the Lord and became the biggest evangelist in the mission—telling every single guy about the Lord Jesus Christ. He became one of the most joyful guys there, with a smile you couldn't wipe off his face.

Three weeks later, Markel died in his sleep. Jeff preached at the funeral to many of Markel's Muslim friends. Looking across at all those Muslims in the audience, Jeff had the opportunity to explain how Markel had no hope until he found Jesus. The real Jesus, that is—the Jesus of the Bible—God in the flesh.

Markel's initial reaction of anger was an indication of the Spirit at work in his heart. Jeff's willingness to boldly speak the truth infuriated Markel for a time, but it ended up bringing the greatest blessing of his life.

DISCOMFORT IS OKAY

Great. I probably offended him, and now maybe his heart is going to be closed to the gospel all because of me, I thought.

A homeschool conference was ending and everyone was packing up. I had just spoken briefly with an employee at the convention center who was rolling up table skirts. I asked him, "Do you think eternal life is a free gift or something you have to earn?"

"Earn," he replied.

I shared Romans 6:23 with him, explaining that Scripture calls it a *gift*. Unfortunately, this good news didn't seem very "good" to him, and he returned a sort of cold response. I approached him again later and offered him a tract, which he refused. The whole encounter discouraged me and I concluded that I must have mishandled something. I expressed my discouragement to my brother later that evening. But Stephen reminded me, "Sometimes people are going to be offended when you quote the Word of God to them. I think you did the right thing—you quoted a Bible verse! Scripture sometimes makes people feel very uncomfortable. He was probably convicted."

Stephen's words encouraged me. A negative response doesn't mean we did something wrong. It could mean that we just did something *right*—we were bold with the gospel and it pricked their conscience. The point is, we need a burden for souls, not simply a desire to keep everyone happy. If people seem uncomfortable, it may mean they are feeling convicted of their sin, and that's exactly what we want them to feel. True conviction of sin leads people to Jesus. In fact, if no one is ever offended by what we say, chances are not many people are being convicted either. But remember, it must be the Word of God that offends them—not our attitudes or behavior. In other words, the gospel is offensive, but *we* shouldn't be! We must always speak the truth in love (Ephesians 4:15).

Truth to Remember: When someone is unfriendly, it may mean he is feeling convicted—and that is a good thing (John 15:22).

SCENARIO 3: YOU'VE MADE ME FEEL TERRIBLE.

Seeing four junior high kids sitting on couches in a hotel lobby, my friend Nickie and I decided to go and witness to them. We asked them if they'd like to do our little questionnaire, and they happily said they would. They agreed that they had broken God's Law, and I pointed out that God requires perfection for Heaven.

"How do you *know* that?" one girl asked bluntly.

I was a little surprised by the sharp manner in which she asked, but I quoted Romans 3:23 and explained that the consequence of sin is death.

"How do you know what you are telling me is accurate?" she demanded. "I think you are off—you are out of line!"

"On what point?" I asked.

"On saying that God won't let sinners go to Heaven! My mother ran off with a guy at sixteen, but now she's the most forgiving and good person ... "

"No," I clarified, "I'm not saying that at all. I haven't come to my main point yet. You see— "

"Where did you get your information?" she asked critically. "Have you been trained somewhere? I could call my dad right now, and he's the deacon at my church, and he'd tell you that you are wrong."

"Look, I don't want to argue with you," I told her, "but I think you may be misunderstanding what I'm trying to tell you."

"No, I think *you're* misunderstanding what the truth is!" she retorted.

"What I'm actually trying to say," I explained, "is that this is about Jesus Christ. When He died on the cross, He was taking our penalty. If we repent and ask for forgiveness we can be saved." I shared John 3:16 and Romans 6:23 with her.

"Wow," she angrily replied, "I thought this was a survey. I didn't know you were going to preach at me! You've just made me feel like the worst, most terrible person ever, and I think you are all wrong. You know what I think? You are not talking about this stuff in an adult way!"

"I really didn't mean to come across that way," I explained. "I'm not talking to you guys because I just feel like chatting, but because I believe this is so important—for each of us to know where we'll be for all eternity."

"Okay," she said sulkily.

Nickie and I talked with them for about 20 minutes. We didn't want to leave on a bad note, so we tried again to explain our motives, repeating that we weren't trying to offend her.

As we were getting ready to leave, something interesting happened. A boy in the group, who looked about twelve and had barely spoken the whole time, piped up. "So, how do you become forgiven?" he asked. He seemed eager to know the answer. Touched by his sincerity, Nickie and I shared the gospel with him again.

Wow. So while the girl had been rejecting our words, *he* had been soaking them up with interest the entire time. In reality, he probably learned a lot more than he would have, had she not been arguing. He heard the gospel clarified several times as we gave answers to her many arguments.

If someone is rude to you, there is something significant that can be gained. When we respond with graciousness, giving soft answers and overcoming evil with good, all the others who are listening will notice, and it is a testimony to them. In fact, a humble reaction to unkind words may speak louder than anything else we say.

Our objective in evangelism is not to conquer by winning debates, but to conquer by laying our lives down—to go out as sheep, as Jesus sent out His disciples. "I send you forth as sheep in the midst of wolves: be ye therefore wise as serpents, and harmless as doves" (Matthew 10:16).

Although we can expect some people to be uncomfortable when we share the gospel with them, offending people is certainly not our goal! It can often be prevented if we demonstrate humility, tact, and wisdom. Sometimes Christians feel they are suffering for Jesus, when actually they are suffering because of their own pride, lack of sensitivity, or lack of discretion. Maybe they forgot about the meekness part of 1 Peter 3:15. "Be ready always to give an answer ... with **meekness** and fear ...."

Meekness is not weakness—it is strength under control. It is giving soft answers in humility. It is saying no to the temptation to argue just to prove the other person wrong. It is being kind and gentle, controlling our tongue, and leaving all results in God's hands. "A soft answer turneth away wrath: but grievous words stir up anger. The tongue of the wise useth knowledge aright" (Proverbs 15:1-2). (Also see Matthew 11:29 and Galatians 6:1.)

It is more difficult to show meekness than it is to win an argument. It demonstrates more strength. "He that is slow to anger is better than the mighty; and he that ruleth his spirit than he that taketh a city" (Proverbs 16:32).

WHY IS SHE BLAMING ME?

Why is she blaming me for every bad encounter with a Christian she's ever had? Mrs. Naas wondered as she tried to reach out to her unsaved friend, Gloria. They would see each other weekly at the YMCA, and Gloria seemed to constantly be making comments about how she did not like Christians. She complained that they are all the "same": they are exclusive, they want to preach their agenda, and they think they are better than everyone else.

Week after week, month after month, Mrs. Naas responded with kindness. "Lord, just help me to be her friend!" she prayed. Many times she would reply to her, "Gloria, I am so sorry that you have been hurt by other Christians. I can't help what they have done, but I am really sorry that they have made you feel that way."

As Mrs. Naas was telling me this story, we discussed how sometimes when we are witnessing we *do* make mistakes. Although Mrs. Naas did not know if the previous Christians in Gloria's life had mishandled things or not, she knew what *her* goal was—to extend grace. If you are talking with someone who appears to have been offended by a Christian in the past, remember to be humble and take any blame you can. Sometimes we can apologize for other Christians, even if we do not know all the details. We are all on the same team. We are not perfect, but we are all working toward the same goal. We should try to cover for each other when we can.

The months that Mrs. Naas persevered in returning good for evil were well worth it. God used her patience and humility to soften Gloria's heart. One day, after a personal family crisis, Gloria finally came to place her faith in Christ! She started coming to Mrs. Naas's Bible study luncheon and began to grow in the Lord.

Truth to Remember: Arguers are useful because all the other listeners will learn from your answers. But no matter how we are treated, we must always respond with meekness (1 Peter 3:14-15).

SCENARIO 4: %$*!&# #%$@&#

"Hey, would you like a free DVD?" I asked a guy as I was helping with an evangelism mass giveaway.

"I don't want your DVD or any of your %$$&# &#$&&# teaching," he said in a very irritated tone of voice.

"Oh, what's your view?" I asked him.

That was all it took. He blew up. Thankfully, I was only one part of a team, so he wasn't exactly yelling at me, but at all of us.

Using lots of profanity, he angrily told Dan, one of the guys on our team, how stupid he considered our views to be. He kept repeating how offended he was by the materials we were handing out. He wasn't open to reasoning or willing to listen—he was just mad. The interesting thing was that many of the bystanders turned to our side and began to defend us—even though we were in a liberal environment and most people there were unbelievers who wouldn't have otherwise sided with us.

The crowd was growing and an increasing number of people were getting fed up with this angry guy. One bystander exclaimed, "Just because I don't agree with them [Christians] doesn't mean I have a problem with them being here!"

"Yeah, why can't he just walk away?" another lady questioned. She couldn't understand why he was so upset. Another lady even began to cry and mentioned contacting the police.

These "nice," but unsaved bystanders did not comprehend what was actually happening. They didn't understand how offensive the gospel of Jesus Christ is to some people. Unlike the dead religions of this world, the message of the cross has power and may produce strong reactions from those who love darkness rather than light.

The Christians on our evangelism team were just grateful for the extra exposure. In fact, Dan took advantage of the growing crowd by preaching to everyone about how Jesus is coming back one day. We had our own little "open-air preaching service" erupt, all because of one angry person.

Why weren't we troubled by this angry man? Isn't it a little unnerving to have someone yelling at you? We were not upset because we understood what was actually happening. He wasn't really fighting against us—he didn't even know us! He was fighting against Jesus Christ.

Jesus gave us instructions about what to do when we are rejected: "Blessed are ye, when men shall hate you, and when they shall separate you from their company, and shall reproach you, and cast out your name as evil, for the Son of Man's sake. Rejoice ye in that day, and leap for joy: for, behold, your reward is great in Heaven: for in the like manner did their fathers unto the prophets" (Luke 6:22-23).

In the situation of the man yelling at us, we didn't suffer any real harm. It actually turned out for our benefit, because through it a whole crowd heard a message about Christ. However, there are times when Christians suffer rejection or persecution and it is painful and difficult. Yet believers who look at life from an eternal perspective are not as bothered by a little hardship here (2 Corinthians 4:8-9). In fact, they look at it as gain! "If ye be reproached for the name of Christ, happy are ye; for the spirit of glory and of God resteth upon you: on their part He is evil spoken of, but on your part He is glorified" (1 Peter 4:14).

One who experiences rejection for Jesus is in great company. The prophets,

EXPECT THE CROSS TO OFFEND   GAL. 5:11

apostles and Jesus Himself were also rejected. Paul desired to suffer with Christ so he could experience a closer fellowship with Jesus through it. He said, "That I may know Him ... and the fellowship of His sufferings" (Philippians 3:10).

Sometimes the things we fear are actually the means of God's greatest blessings in our lives. Imagine the pleasant surprise that awaited Shadrach, Meshach and Abednego when they were thrown into the fiery furnace. Instead of feeling the flames, they found themselves in the presence of the Son of God! What incredible joy they must have felt. Talk about fellowship with Christ through suffering. They were literally thrown into Jesus' presence! When King Nebuchadnezzar called them out, I wonder if they thought, *Aww ... do we have to come out so soon?*

"For our light affliction, which is but for a moment, worketh for us a far more exceeding and eternal weight of glory; While we look not at the things which are seen, but at the things which are not seen: for the things which are seen are temporal; but the things which are not seen are eternal" (2 Corinthians 4:17-18).

"For I reckon that the sufferings of this present time are not worthy to be compared with the glory which shall be revealed in us" (Romans 8:18).

Truth to Remember: People will reject us because they have already rejected Jesus and we have aligned ourselves with Him. When this happens, it is a cause for great joy (John 15:18-27; 1 John 3:13; Luke 6:22-23).

SCENARIO 5: "GOOD LUCK IN FINDING PEOPLE WHO WANT TO TALK!"

I went to the park on a busy Saturday to witness. *Who should I talk to first?* Usually the first conversation is the hardest. I sat down on a bench, and a lady and her teenage son came and sat next to me. I told them I was doing a little questionnaire and they agreed to take it. They thought you had to earn your salvation, so I asked, "Then how can you be sure you are going to Heaven?"

"You can't," they said, nonchalantly.

I told them that the Bible makes it clear that there *is* a way we can be sure we are going to Heaven—but it isn't by our good works.

It was apparent that the lady was getting annoyed. "I ran into this all the time where I used to live," she told me with an attitude of *I know exactly what you're doing ...*

"Good luck in finding people who want to talk," she told me a little sarcastically as I left.

Next, I approached a young couple on a bench to see if they wanted to talk.

"No," the lady said abruptly. "I've had people come to my door about this

… Jehovah's Witnesses and all that … " she said with raised eyebrows, "and I am *not* interested."

"Well, I'm not a Jehovah's Witness or Mormon," I explained. "I don't agree with them either." Still, she didn't want to talk, and I didn't want to push it, so I began looking for someone else. I sat down next to a young mother.

"Hey, I'm working on a little project trying to learn what people believe will happen when they die. Would you be willing to tell me your view?"

"No."

"Okay, no problem!" I said and left.

Am I using a wrong approach? This is getting discouraging! I thought.

I saw another lady sitting on a picnic bench. Walking up to her, I greeted her and said, "Can I ask you an interesting question?"

"Sure, go ahead!"

"Okay, you'll probably be surprised when you hear it," I said, warning her, "but it's an important question. What do you think happens when we die?"

"So is this what you are doing? You are just going around the park asking people this?" she asked.

Uh oh. Is this "strike #4?" I wondered.

"Well, yes, I've been trying to get into conversations with people," I answered.

"That's wonderful!" she exclaimed. "I'm a believer too. It's so great you are

WITNESSING DISCLAIMER

doing this. What a great way to spend your Saturday!"

Whew!

"So what would you say is the way to get to Heaven?" I asked her. (Even when I think someone is a Christian, I usually keep asking questions, because not everyone is a believer who claims to be.)

She gave me a solid gospel answer, and I told her how refreshing it was to meet her after all the other people who didn't want to talk.

"But that's not your fault," she reminded me. "You are just here to present the message and let God take it from there." She told me a story of how the Lord had been faithful to help her recently, and she promised to pray for me.

Thank you, Lord! I prayed as I bounced away with new energy and boldness.

The afternoon skyrocketed from there. I had a great talk with three responsive girls by the volleyball court. Following that, a half-hour discussion with a high-school girl who was open and friendly. Then a long talk with a teen girl who was watching some kids on the merry-go-round—with whom I've continued to have follow-up opportunities. Next, I talked with a young mom who started crying as she told me about difficult things she was going through. After that, I heard someone calling my name. It was a lady I had witnessed to at a coffee shop on the other side of town only two days before! Then guess what happened? Remember the lady who had originally not wanted to talk to me because she thought I was a Jehovah's Witness? She was still there, after all that time, so I thought I'd try once more with her. I had a DVD with me about creation and the gospel, so I greeted her again, saying, "You guys are still here! Hey, I don't want to bother you, but I just wanted to offer you this if you want it. It's a neat DVD about the existence of God."

"Actually, I'll take that," she said, more pleasantly than last time.

"Your kids will like it too," I told her.

Her husband especially seemed to appreciate it, thanking me as I left.

I was so glad I did not quit witnessing after the first three unfriendly encounters. There is an enemy who tries to discourage us from doing the Lord's work. It's easy to get discouraged and become tempted to give up or go home—or worse yet, not to start in the first place. We all have the tendency to doubt that we are actually accomplishing anything when we don't see "results." But God clearly assures us in His Word that work done for Jesus is never in vain.

Truth to Remember: "Therefore, my beloved brethren, be ye steadfast, unmovable, always abounding in the work of the Lord, forasmuch as ye know that your labor is **not in vain in the Lord**" (1 Corinthians 15:58).

NO DISCOURAGEMENT ALLOWED

Sometimes we feel discouraged not only because the message was rejected, but because we wonder if it was our fault. We know we could have done a better job and we wonder if things could have been different. It is actually kind of a good thing to feel this way, because it means we are taking our responsibility seriously. After all, since we have been entrusted with the gospel, we should desire to be wise and faithful stewards of it. "But as we were allowed of God to be put **in trust** with the gospel, even so we speak; not as pleasing men, but God, which trieth our hearts" (1 Thessalonians 2:4). We have a huge responsibility—having been entrusted by God with this infinitely important message to tell the world. It should cause us to tremble and beg for His help.

If you are worried that you said the wrong thing to someone, evaluate the situation and think of it as a teaching tool that God allowed in your life. Think, *What should I have said? What Scripture could I have used? What questions could I have asked?* If you were with a friend, get their opinion. Have them critique you. Sometimes we learn more from our mistakes than from anything else. If you missed an opportunity, make a special effort to pray for that person. Remember, God can even use our mistakes for good (Romans 8:28). If you think you mishandled something, just be encouraged that at least you were out there trying!

"It is not the critic who counts: not the man who points out how the strong man stumbles or where the doer of deeds could have done better. The credit belongs to the man who is actually in the arena, whose face is marred by dust and sweat and blood, who strives valiantly, who errs and comes up short again and again, because there is no effort without error or shortcoming, but who knows the great enthusiasms, the great devotions, who spends himself for a worthy cause; ... who, at the worst, if he fails, at least he fails while daring greatly, so that his place shall never be with those cold and timid souls who knew neither victory nor defeat." —Theodore Roosevelt

We all make mistakes. We can always think of things we could have done differently. The key is learning to fall *well*, just as one learns in horseback riding or other sports. We should look back just enough to learn from our mistake and correct it if possible—but we should not let the mistake keep us from running forward with full force. "For a just man falleth seven times, and riseth up again" (Proverbs 24:16).

We are supposed to be running, "looking unto Jesus" (Hebrews 12:2), rather than continually dwelling on our mistakes. In other words, instead of looking at our stumbling feet, we should be looking at the One who can keep us from stumbling. It is our love for Jesus that should motivate us to get up again quickly—for His sake—and keep going. There is much to do, and this is all about His glory, not ours.

SO BE ENCOURAGED!

If Satan can get a believer down through discouragement, he has won a big victory. We combat discouragement in a similar way to how we deal with fear. We place our faith in the promises of God. God's Word does not return void (Isaiah 55:11); God is the One who produces good results (1 Corinthians 3:6-9); God is more concerned about the unsaved than we are (2 Peter 3:9); our work in the Lord is never in vain (1 Corinthians 15:58); we *will* see results of our labor one day (Galatians 6:9); God works things out for good (Romans 8:28); God is not unrighteous to forget our work (Hebrews 6:10); we can do all things through Christ who strengthens us (Philippians 4:13); God is powerful to save (Isaiah 59:1)!

So what should we do when people "aren't so friendly"? We should not be surprised or discouraged. We should simply evaluate anything we can do differently and press on, always speaking in love, always remembering the promises of God, always placing our eyes on Jesus Christ—our ever victorious King.

Laughter and smiles filled the room as we ate pizza and told stories from the week. We had just concluded a week of Bright Lights conferences[1] and the small group leaders were sharing stories of ways we had seen the Lord work. The enthusiasm was contagious as everyone listened and rejoiced together in what God had done. An unsaved college student happened to be with our group of staff that night. Afterwards she commented to a friend, "I have a headache. I think it's from all the happiness!"

Unbelievers are not used to being around the kind of joy that Christians have. They simply do not understand it. In fact, they do not even know that this kind of joy is possible.

Why is joy relevant to a book on witnessing? Three main reasons:

1. Joy makes an **impact**. Without it, we cannot be an accurate representation of Jesus.
2. Our need for joy keeps us going to the **Source**.
3. Joy gives us **strength** when we feel we can't go on.

Let's discuss the impact, source, and strength of joy, and never underestimate the importance of the biblical command to "rejoice in the Lord!"

THE IMPACT OF JOY

Have you ever thought about how much you can learn about a person simply by his countenance? With so many sad, grumpy, and guilty people walking around in this world, think of what a contrast we can be if we are radiant and joyful! It catches people's attention and makes them curious. It is a major part of our witness because our joy tells people that God is good, and that He has made us glad. If someone sees a newlywed couple and the bride is radiating with joy, people assume that she must be married to a really great guy. Similarly, the Lord is our heavenly Prince, and we can show the world that He is wonderful by our joy. This brings Him glory and speaks loudly to those around us. The joy in our life confirms the message we speak. It also opens doors to share the gospel!

Maybe I could give a tract to someone in here, I thought as I entered a drugstore to pick up some vitamin C. As I walked down the aisle, I passed a girl who looked about my age (I was about thirteen), so I smiled and said hi.

"What makes you so happy?" she asked me.

Surprised by her question, I told her it was because of Jesus.

"How did you come to know Jesus?" she asked.

(The dream-come-true question for someone trying to witness, right?)

She called her sister over, and I was excited to have the opportunity not only to give a tract, but also to share my testimony.

JOY MARKS FOLLOWERS OF JESUS

Have you ever thought to yourself, "That person looks like a Christian"? This happened to me just recently. I met an international student from China. He was with a group of about 10 other students—most of whom I had never met before. But something about him was different. Sure enough, as we were getting acquainted, he told me that he had become a Christian two years earlier.

My friend Jeni has a waitressing job that can be somewhat stressful at times. However, Jeni has faithfully represented Christ and her joy has not gone unnoticed. Recently, another waitress asked, "Jeni, why are you always so happy? You've got to be one of the happiest people I know!" The waitress agreed to come to an event at Jeni's church, and Jeni has had continuing opportunities to share with her.

People are surprised by joy. It captures their interest and awakens their curiosity. It is beautiful. It is powerful. We cannot accurately represent Jesus Christ without it.

One day I had an interesting, yet somewhat frustrating, conversation with a public school teacher who was trying to convince me that believing the Bible was ridiculous. As soon as he left, a big African-American man who had been standing nearby commented, "You're not getting anywhere with that guy—I heard you!"

I smiled. I didn't know anyone else had been listening. But now that I had someone else to witness to, I decided to get straight to the point.

"So if you stood before God and He asked you why He should let you into Heaven, what would you say?" I asked the big, friendly man.

"Romans 4:8," he said confidently.

Wow, he's answering me with a Bible verse?

I grabbed a Bible and looked up the verse. Romans 4:8 explains how happy the man is whom the Lord will never charge with sin.

"That's me. I'm the happy man!" he said with a big smile. He explained that for years he had not been walking with the Lord, but had now surrendered to Jesus. There was such a contrast between him and the unbelieving school teacher. The joy of Christians is so refreshing.

Joy is a fruit of the Spirit—a natural result of walking with the Lord. It brings glory to Christ and gets the attention of a dying world. Not only is it an essential part of our witness, it is—for lack of a better phrase—so much fun! (Proverbs 15:15).

Do you remember the first proclamation about Christ after His birth? We find it in Luke 2:10-11. "The angel said unto them, Fear not: for, behold, I bring you good tidings of **great joy** which shall be to all people. For unto you is born … a Savior … "

The shepherds did not know very much as they went and proclaimed the news, but they knew that it was a message of joy. If it was great joy for them, how much greater joy should it be for us who have a much fuller understanding of the message? If we want to communicate the "good tidings of great joy" accurately, we'd better deliver these words with … joy!

THE SOURCE OF JOY

1. BEING WITH JESUS

We serve a God who is full of joy (Zephaniah 3:17; Hebrews 1:9). Jesus prayed that we would have His joy fulfilled in us (John 17:13). Psalm 16:11 says, "In Thy presence is **fullness** of joy; at Thy right hand there are pleasures for evermore." Fullness of joy—you can't have more joy than that! The closer we draw to Jesus, the Author of joy, the more joy we will have. The more joy we have, the brighter our light will shine.

Joy is a choice. We know this because God commands it. If we had no control over our emotions, why would God command us over and over in Scripture to rejoice? Philippians 4:4 tells us to rejoice in the Lord always. How is this possible? What if something horrible happens to us? The answer is found in the words *in the Lord.*

Look at this passage in Habakkuk: "Although the fig tree shall not blossom, neither shall fruit be in the vines; the labour of the olive shall fail, and the fields shall yield no meat; the flock shall be cut off from the fold, and there shall be no herd in the stalls: **Yet I will rejoice in the LORD**, I will joy in the God of my salvation (Habakkuk 3:17-19).

When our joy is rooted in the Lord, it is impossible for it to be erased, because it is not dependent on anything in this world. True joy comes only from Jesus Christ. It is the joy for which we were made—the joy that caused Job to fall on the ground and worship in response to his trials (Job 1:20). You see, Job's greatest treasure had still not been taken away. He talks about it later: "For I know that my Redeemer liveth, and that He shall stand … upon the earth: And though … worms destroy this body, yet in my flesh shall I see God: Whom I shall see for myself, and mine eyes shall behold, and not another (Job 19:25-27).

No matter what happens to us on earth, we can have joy because Jesus, our Treasure, can never, ever be taken from us. If joy depended on circumstances it would be impossible to have continual joy, because we know that we *will* face hard times in life. But when God is our joy, our joy is *secure*. And guess what? Facing trials is actually a reason to rejoice even more! James 1:2-3 says, "My brethren, count it all joy when ye fall into divers temptations; Knowing this, that the trying of your faith worketh patience."

What if we just made a big mistake? We can still rejoice in what we have *in the Lord*. In Jesus we find forgiveness and healing because of what He accomplished on the cross. We can rejoice that when we confess our sins, "He is faithful and just to forgive us our sins, and to cleanse us from all unrighteousness" (1 John 1:9).

Remember, joy does not mean the absence of sorrow. There is a time for godly sorrow (2 Corinthians 7:10). But in the midst of sorrow, there still can and *should* be joy. It is a joy that rests in the promises of God and is much deeper than our temporary problems—a joy that overrides earthly trouble because it stems from a relationship with Jesus Christ. "These things have I spoken unto you, that My joy might remain in you, and that your joy might be full" (John 15:11). What are the "these things" He was referring to? Abiding and obedience. Read it in John 15.

FRIDGE FULL OF HOT DOGS

Maybe it's not very nutritious, but it's cheap, and it's fast, a friend of mine concluded as he decided on his food plan for college. You see, he didn't have the money to buy a pass to the cafeteria, so he stocked up on hot dogs. He determined that electrocuting his hot dogs was the fastest way to cook them, so he also bought a hot dog zapper. I know that some single guys may not be that concerned about nutrition, but it doesn't get much worse than this!

After a semester of eating electrocuted hot dogs, guess what he learned? His scholarship included room and board with a meal plan at the cafeteria. He could have been eating there all that time.

How often, in our Christian lives, do we settle for a "snack"—something quick—instead of feasting on all we have in Jesus? Are we looking into the Word, considering all we have been given, gazing at the cross in gratefulness? Jesus didn't just set us free from bondage—He gave us an inheritance. He didn't simply pay our debt—He gave us His bank account of righteousness. He didn't merely release us from Satan's grip—He asked us to be His bride. He takes us from dungeon to palace. Ashes to beauty. Rejected to cherished. Starving to feasting.

Our response to what we have been given in Christ will not affect only *us*. Our joy, or lack thereof, will impact everyone with whom we come into contact.

2. OBEYING JESUS

Sometimes we think that if *we* could be in control of our lives, we would be happy. The truth, however, is that it is in submission to the Lord that our joy overflows (John 15:10-11). Witnessing may be tough at times, but what do we receive from doing it? Joy. Confessing hidden sin is painful and humbling, but what is the result in our heart? Joy. Surrendering areas of our life that we want to hold on to can be a deep struggle, but what is the outcome? Joy. Serving others when we'd prefer to relax is challenging, but what reward do we receive? Joy. The list goes on. Joy comes when we raise the white flag of surrender to our Master. Joy comes from obedience.

The world says, "Make yourself happy." Jesus says, "It is more blessed to give" (Acts 20:35). The world says, "Pursue your dreams." Jesus says, "Lose your life" (Matthew 10:39). The world says, "Reward yourself." Jesus says, "Take up your cross" (Matthew 16:24).

It is in denying ourselves and serving others that we, in turn, receive the most joy. "He laid down His life for us: and we ought to lay down our lives for the brethren" (1 John 3:16).

Let's illustrate this on a very practical level. When we walk into a room of people, perhaps at a party or church gathering, we naturally tend to think thoughts such as, *Am I making the right impression? Who is going to talk to me? Am I saying the right thing? Am I wearing the right thing?* Yet when we are wrapped up in ourselves, we usually end up disappointed, frustrated or with "empty gratification"—but not with true joy. My mom used to frequently tell me, "Grace, just remember to be a giver." Often in a group of people there is someone who is left out, less popular, or difficult to be around. Sometimes we ignore these people without even realizing it. But if we make it a habit to reach out to them, not only will we be demonstrating the character of Christ (who spent time with the unpopular and hurting), but we will have a new mission everywhere we go. Maintaining a ministry mindset in this way will also bring us a new level of confidence. No longer will we be worrying about ourselves and wondering what everyone is thinking of us. Instead we will be thinking, *Who can I encourage today? Who can I include in the group? Who needs someone to listen to them?*

When I was about ten, an older girl reached out to me at a graduation party. She invited me upstairs to the room where all the big kids were hanging out and made me feel welcome and comfortable. It meant so much to me that I still remember it 13 years later. We may never know the impact it makes when we reach out in kindness. More than that, those acts of kindness often open doors to share the gospel.

The principle in Proverbs 11:25 holds true: "He that watereth shall be watered also himself." In addition, Isaiah 58:10-12 says, "If thou [pour thyself out for] the hungry, and satisfy the afflicted soul; then shall thy light rise ... and thy darkness be as the noon day: And the LORD shall guide thee continually, and satisfy thy soul in drought, ... and thou shalt be like a watered garden, and like a spring of water, whose waters fail not."

WHAT'S WRONG WITH ME?

Sometimes we are dealing with struggles in our own lives and the last thing we feel like doing is reaching out to others, let alone doing it joyfully. One December afternoon I was going door-to-door in the neighborhood around our church, giving away Christmas gospel packets and getting to know neighbors. I was trying to be cheerful and loving, but I just didn't feel like it. *What's wrong with me?* I wondered. My emotional energy was running low, and on top of that, I was bothered with myself for not feeling more genuine love for these lost people. But then I had an encouraging thought. *Good thing my sufficiency is in Christ and not in myself!* (2 Corinthians 3:5, 9:8). Sure, I didn't feel like witnessing that day. But that didn't matter; it's not about how I *feel*. Love is not primarily a feeling—it is an action. Joy is not primarily a feeling—it is a choice. In reality, I was loving those neighbors because I was taking action to reach out to them. In reality, I *was* choosing to rejoice in the Lord whose strength is made perfect in weakness (2 Corinthians 12:9).

By God's grace we had some good talks that afternoon, and I was reminded again that the Lord gives grace in the moment—just as we need it. Sometimes

LITTLE KNOWN FACT: LUKE ALWAYS DREW HIS SMILEY FACES WITH BEARDS.

we don't feel like giving to others, and we simply must ignore our feelings and obey anyway. When we do, God supplies the strength we need. As we choose to obey, the emotions will follow.

THE STRENGTH OF JOY

Think of all the times Scripture commands us to rejoice. We are commanded to count it all joy, abound in gratefulness, delight, sing praises, be glad in the Lord, rejoice always, make a joyful noise to the Lord, offer the sacrifice of praise to God continually, and give thanks in everything, to name a few. It is impossible to come to the conclusion that this is unimportant. Why does God want us to rejoice? We have already talked about how it glorifies God and makes an impact on others, but it doesn't stop there. Joy also strengthens *us* to persevere in this race. " … for the joy of the LORD is your strength" (Nehemiah 8:10).

Those who "tap in" to the one true Source of joy find a strength and motivation that is unearthly—because it is truly not of this world.

Just as Jesus, "for the joy that was set before Him endured the cross"

(Hebrews 12:2), so we, looking to Him, are motivated to run this race, keeping our eyes on the goal. Jesus is the Rewarder and the Reward of those who seek Him. The awesome motivation of standing before Him one day very soon drives us on with perseverance, because we long to please Him. "Though now ye see Him not, yet believing, ye rejoice with joy unspeakable and full of glory" (1 Peter 1:8).

DON'T LET SATAN STEAL YOUR JOY!

In light of all this, would it not be obvious that Satan would want to sap joy from God's people? What tactics does he use? Many Christians seem to have lost their joy in the Lord. How does this happen? Maybe the Christian life has become a "duty," rather than a fulfilling walk with Jesus Christ. Maybe they have refused to forgive, and bitterness has swallowed them up in a miserable trap. Maybe they have set their focus on themselves and allowed self-pity, ingratitude and discontentment to overtake their hearts. Maybe they have yielded to temptation and are not willing to confess and forsake their sin— thus, their fellowship with the Lord is hindered. Maybe they are looking to other things to fulfill them, rather than to Christ.

Satan wants us to take our eyes off the true Joy-giver, so that we will seek other sources of happiness. Yet earthly things will eventually disappoint and leave us in emptiness and despair. Psalm 16:4 tells us, "Their sorrows shall be multiplied that hasten after another god." Another "god" could be a certain form of entertainment, a friendship, food, possessions, outward appearance or anything else that is receiving more of our affections than Jesus. Don't believe Satan's lie that if you fully surrender to the Lord, He will take the fun out of your life. Exactly the opposite is true. Surrender to Jesus is where joy begins!

God created us with deep needs so that He Himself could satisfy those needs! God knows all about our desires—He made us! Wouldn't He be able to completely satisfy us? He knows us better than we know ourselves. We should thank God for His gifts, but find our greatest joy in the Giver.

You see, the world has only circumstances to make them happy. We have God. We left the world for God because the world was empty. Why go back?

"For my people have committed two evils; they have forsaken Me the fountain of living waters, and hewed them out cisterns, broken cisterns, that can hold no water" (Jeremiah 2:13).

When our delight is in the right place—in Jesus—we run with strong motivation. When our delight is in the wrong place, we are hindered in the journey and slow our pace. We are distracted. We face continual disappointment. We are weakened. We may not even realize what is happening—that we have taken our eyes off the true Joy-giver and placed them on lesser things.

STRAIGHT DOWN OR STRAIGHT UP?

"Please come with me, I want to show you a new room I just decorated," a Muslim lady in Saudi Arabia told her visiting friend. This friend, a Christian lady, agreed and followed her to the room. What she found in the room came as a big surprise. The room was filled with people—about 80 of them—and they were waiting ... for her!

What is going on? she wondered.

Her Muslim hostess explained that these were all close relatives and friends, and they wanted to hear about Jesus.

"How can this be?" the Christian visitor wanted to know.

Then the story began to come out. "My housemaid from the Philippines was always singing and humming with a smile on her face. One day I asked her what she was singing about, and she explained that she was singing about Jesus and all He had done for her."

This lady continued to explain that, through her housemaid's words, both she and her husband had become followers of Jesus. They had begun witnessing to their friends, some of whom had also come to Christ. Now many had gathered to hear more about Jesus.

Do you think this housemaid would have imagined what would come from her simple joy in the Lord as she swept the house of her Muslim employer? This Filipino maid probably did not have an easy life. But she chose joy and it led many to Jesus.

Sometimes in life, what seems like straight down is actually straight up. Look at the cross, for example. To the disciples, it seemed that everything was falling apart—that nothing would ever be the same. But we know that the worst tragedy was actually the greatest triumph. In the same way, sometimes the things in life that hurt the most are tools God is using to do amazing things in and through us.

Think about the situation of Paul and Silas in prison. Here they were trying to spread the gospel, but instead they were severely flogged (Acts 16:23). With fresh wounds, their feet were fastened in stocks in the inner prison. Yet Paul and Silas responded to their situation with joy. At midnight, in pain and with no idea of what their future would be, Paul and Silas prayed and sang praises to God. Their joy was certainly not found in earthly circumstances! What was the result? The jailor fell down before them asking, "What must I do to be saved?"

Paul and Silas's joy in the midst of a trial spoke so powerfully about their God, it led the jailor and his whole family to the Lord. This brings us right back to where we started—the impact of joy.

It is during the hard times in our lives—the times when it would seem most unlikely to have joy—that our joy shines most brightly. When people see earthly things taken away, yet our joy remaining unaltered, it prompts questions!

Consider Peter's words: "If ye suffer for righteousness' sake, happy are ye: and be not afraid of their terror, neither be troubled; But sanctify the Lord God in your hearts: and be ready always to give an answer to every man that asketh you a reason of the hope that is in you with meekness and fear" (1 Peter 3:14-15).

Let me try to summarize his words. *If you suffer: be happy, be dedicated to the Lord, and get ready—because the questions will be coming!* People are surprised by joy, but they are even more surprised by joy in trial. It points them to the awesome God that we have. Paul and Silas didn't waste their trial; they used it to glorify God, and many came to Christ through it.

We do not know what the future holds. But we don't need to worry about it (Matthew 6:34). Our responsibility is to rejoice today, knowing that God will give us grace to rejoice tomorrow. One thing we do know: our lives pass quickly—like a breath—and we don't want to look back on a life where we failed to rejoice. When we stand before the Lord, our trials will no longer matter ... but the way we responded to them will.

So, for your own sake, for dying sinners who need to see Jesus, for the encouragement of our brothers and sisters in Christ, and, most of all, for the glory of God, let us choose to "rejoice in the Lord!"

The Cherubim Theme

The flaming swords of the cherubim continuously reaffirmed the most horrible truth the world had yet known: man was now separated from his Creator and denied access to the tree of life. You know the story: "Therefore the LORD God sent him forth from the garden of Eden ... He drove out the man; and He placed at the east of the garden of Eden cherubim, and a flaming sword which turned every way, to keep the way of the tree of life" (Genesis 3:23-24).

Yet God still desired to live with man, and His plan of reconciliation was already in place. He chose to unfold His plan by using a man of faith, Abraham, and his descendants. He told the children of Israel to build a tent for Him in the middle of their camp. Still, there was separation because of man's sin—the innermost part of God's tent was closed off with a thick curtain. No one was allowed to enter except for a qualified representative who went into the Holy of Holies—and he only once a year. It is very interesting to notice what God instructed to be embroidered on the curtain of separation: cherubim! (Exodus 26:31; 2 Chronicles 3:14). We don't know what they looked like, but maybe they were holding flaming swords.

Do you remember what happened when Jesus cried, "It is finished" on the cross? That veil—with the cherubim embroidered on it—was ripped from the top to the bottom. God definitely knows how to make a statement! This announced with unmistakable clarity the best truth the world had yet known—man could now have open access into His presence. Jesus' death provided Eden-like fellowship once again. And more than that: our relationship to Jesus Christ is even deeper than the relationship Adam and Eve had before they sinned. Not only are we blameless before Him as Adam and Eve were, we are His blood-bought bride.

CHAPTER 12

WHO? WHERE? HOW?

It feels overwhelming. People everywhere need the gospel! How will we possibly witness to everyone?

I expressed my frustration to my dad as we were driving one rainy morning. After a few moments of silence, he stated, "Yet, there is still a peace that God gives." His simple response stuck with me.

Yes, the needs *are* overwhelming. But our God is greater than the needs, and He is a giver of peace. Jesus said, "These things I have spoken unto you, that in Me ye might have peace. In the world ye shall have tribulation: but be of good cheer; I have overcome the world" (John 16:33). When Jesus sent out His disciples in John 20:21, He said, "Peace be unto you: as My Father hath sent Me, even so send I you." Second Thessalonians 3:16 says, "Now the Lord of peace Himself give you peace always by all means." There is no question: God wants us to have peace as we work for Him.

WHO?

Imagine you are at a county fair wanting to witness to someone. There are hundreds of people all around you. You want to share the gospel with one of them. Who are you going to pick?

There certainly are New Testament examples of times when God clearly and specifically directed the disciples to talk with particular people. But more often, it appears that they operated by the "Acts 17:17 approach"—they simply went somewhere and talked with those who happened to be there.

God never promised to give us signs in the sky or mystical clues to show us with whom we should speak. He simply said, "Go … and preach to every creature" (Mark 16:15). If we are always expecting God to direct us in a crystal-clear way, or if we rely too much on our feelings, we will most likely become confused. Feelings can be misleading. Instead, we should make choices based on the knowledge we already have of God's ways. Often it is not clear to me to whom I should witness, so I simply pick someone who doesn't seem too busy. Then many times I am able to look back and see plainly that the Lord was directing my steps, though it wasn't obvious to me at the time. "A man's heart deviseth his way: but the LORD directeth his steps" (Proverbs 16:9).

God's invisible hand of leading was especially evident to Sarah one day after she talked with a young couple, Jerry and Marissa, in the mall. Jerry told her, "I think this is a sign that you're talking with us. I mean, we haven't come to this mall in months … I really believe this is a sign."

"That's neat," Sarah said. "I haven't been to this mall in a long time either."

"You know, we've been talking about going to church again," Marissa said to Jerry, "and now we have a daughter, and we want to raise her in church. I think this is something we should do."

"Thank you so much for this conversation," Jerry told Sarah. "We really appreciate it!"

We were encouraged when Sarah shared this story with us. But how did Sarah know to talk to *them* out of all the people in the mall? Well, she didn't. She didn't hear any voice from Heaven or feel a mysterious urge to approach that table. She was simply at the mall seeking opportunities to talk with people about Jesus.

DID I MISS MY CUE?

Here's the point: Though God may sometimes direct us in an obvious or vivid way, He doesn't promise to do this. What He *does* promise, however, is to guide us through His Word. Therefore, instead of waiting for some kind of cue to witness to someone, let's dig into His Word so we begin to think like He thinks, and operate out of wisdom. Let's follow the clear command He has *already* given us: "Ye shall be [My] witnesses … unto the uttermost part of the earth" (Acts 1:8). God is more than able to orchestrate the people in our paths and the circumstances in our lives. "The steps of a good man are ordered by the LORD: and He delighteth in his way" (Psalm 37:23).

In whatever we do or wherever we go, we have the same basic instructions: don't be anxious (Philippians 4:6); ask God for wisdom (James 1:5); walk by faith (2 Corinthians 5:7); let His peace rule in our hearts (Colossians 3:15); overflow with gratitude (Colossians 2:7), etc.

It was about 5:00 a.m. as I walked into the waiting area to board my plane at the Los Angeles airport. I was very surprised to bump into someone I knew! He was waiting to board the same plane. To make the situation even more interesting, it appeared he was already in the middle of a witnessing conversation. He introduced me to a lady from Iraq whom he had just met. I'll call her Jawna. She was also waiting to board. We all talked for a few minutes.

As I boarded the plane, I wondered who God would place me next to. I was pretty surprised when I found my seat—right next to Jawna! She was even more surprised than I was, claiming that it must have been God's doing.

If even she says this is of God, I'm not going to disagree!

Jawna was an interpreter for the US Army in Iraq. She claimed to be a Christian, but I didn't think she understood the gospel. She was eager to get acquainted, and we talked most of the way from L.A. to Minneapolis, covering a wide variety of topics: her background, current difficulties in her life, spiritual beliefs, and the basics of Christianity. We stayed in touch via e-mail a little after that.

Another time, while wandering around in a mall food court, my friend Amy and I couldn't figure out who we should witness to first. Finally, we decided to talk to a young mom who was cutting up a piece of pizza for her little boy. Right away she began to open up to us about some struggles in her life. After a very good conversation, she told us, "This is so not a coincidence you came to talk to me. I saw you guys walking around, and just the fact that you came to me out of all the thousands of people in this mall ... I know God is trying to get my attention."

We left her with a book that explained more about the Bible and knowing Christ, and she exclaimed, "Oh, wow, I've been looking for reading material about this! Okay, now I have to give you a hug ... "

We had no clue whom to approach first! But God knew. "Man's goings are of the LORD; how can a man then understand his own way?" (Proverbs 20:24).

If we truly have faith in God, we will take initiative, trusting Him to guide. It is not hard for the Lord to direct our steps—as long as we are moving, that is! When we take the first step, He shows us the next step. However, if we are just standing still, waiting for a telegraph from Heaven, we might be standing and looking into the sky for a very looong time.

PRACTICAL SUGGESTIONS ABOUT "WHO":

In summary, although God doesn't always give explicit direction, He does give us wisdom. Here are some principles I have found helpful when choosing whom to witness to. Of course, these are not rules—just suggestions.

Gender: In general, I don't initiate conversations with guys if it is a one-on-one situation. I used to think it was a lot easier to witness to guys, because I thought they reasoned more logically (well, which is still true sometimes *[smile]*) and that they were often more open to discussion. But I've come to realize that sometimes a guy will misread a girl's motive for initiating a conversation with him. Generally, guys with guys and girls with girls is best, but each situation simply calls for discretion.

Safety: Young ladies especially need to remember to not place themselves in unsafe situations. Going in pairs brings extra protection. Do not go into questionable areas alone to witness. Ask your parents and follow their guidance. Don't go inside other people's homes unless you are sure the situation is safe. Be careful about giving out your contact information. In general, don't witness to men alone. Some guys in this world are not good characters. They need Jesus, but that doesn't mean it's our responsibility to be the evangelist.

Age: We can and should witness to people of any age. However, if I am in a crowd and have an option, my preference is to initiate conversations with people my age or younger. Young people are typically more "cool" with the idea of talking about their spiritual beliefs with a stranger. Also, when I am talking with someone my age or younger, I feel that I can be more authoritative and straightforward in my approach.

WHERE?

Although there are many places we can go specifically to witness, let's not forget about all the people we meet as we go about our daily lives. Paul told Timothy that there were only two times he should preach the Word: in season and out of season (2 Timothy 4:2).

One busy December day as I was checking out at Walmart, I realized that I had no cash in my wallet. My mind went blank and I couldn't remember my debit card pin number. The Walmart cashier had already scanned all my items.

Oh great.

"Forty dollars and eighty cents will be your total," she told me.

After a few seconds of frustration, I confessed, "I am so sorry—I can't remember my pin number and I don't have any cash! Could you hold it while I find my mom?"

"Uh ... sure," she agreed.

I began searching for my mom, but finding someone in a crowded Super Walmart is *not* easy, especially in December—and I didn't have a cell phone with me. Thankfully, after a minute or two I spotted my mom in another check-out line.

"Mom!" I exclaimed with relief.

"Grace, I can't talk to you right now. I need you to leave. I'm buying your Christmas gift."

"But, Mom, I need money—and the cashier is waiting—and there are people behind me in line—and—"

"Grace, just go stand over there and I'll talk to you when I'm done."

"But Mom—"

This is crazy! I thought.

After several minutes, my mom finished checking out and I rushed over to her. Now she had run into an old friend and was busy chatting.

"Mom," I interrupted, "I really need a check—or some cash—or something. I'll pay you back."

Returning to the cashier, I found that she, and the people behind me in line, had simply been waiting this whole time.

Great. Now they are probably all going to be mad at me.

Surprisingly, they didn't seem to be upset. I handed the cashier the two twenties and a dime.

"It's actually forty dollars and eighty cents," the cashier responded.

Uh oh. I had remembered the total wrong. I was still $.70 short.

The second search for my mom began. I didn't see her anywhere. *I can't believe this is happening. She was just here a minute ago! Why do embarrassing things always have to happen to me?*

After running around through several crowded check-out lines, I eventually found my mom sitting on a bench by the door.

After getting the change and paying the cashier, I apologized for the inconvenience and gave her a Christmas tract. Then I turned to the lady behind me in line and apologized for making her wait all that time. Thankfully, she didn't seem bothered at all—just amused.

At least I didn't try to swipe my driver's license instead of my debit card ... but that's another story.

A few weeks later I was at Walmart again, and I noticed someone waving at me. It was the same cashier girl. She was all smiles. She told me she still had the Christmas tract I had given her, and she pulled it out to show me. We became "friends" and from then on, whenever I went to Walmart, I would purposely try to go through her line. Sometimes even the most unique circumstances can be turned into opportunities to witness.

PRACTICAL SUGGESTIONS ABOUT "WHERE":

Location Ideas: Parks, town festivals, parades, farmer's markets, door to door, tailgating at sporting events, shopping areas, college campuses, your school, town squares, bus stops, rest areas, concerts, sports events, public sidewalks, county fairs, and your neighborhood are all good places for witnessing.

Private Property: We don't want to break the rules that authorities have set (1 Peter 2:13). Passing out tracts in mass quantities, for example, should be done on public property. However, if we are simply *talking* with people, that should be fine no matter where we are. Think about it this way: if something is newsworthy, it's reasonable to talk about it. If the president was coming to town, it would make sense to begin a conversation with a stranger at the store about it. If the area was under a tornado watch, it would definitely make sense to talk about it!

Make a Plan: Think about a goal you could set. Not something "over the top," but something you think you will be able to keep doing consistently. Maybe purpose with a friend to witness together once a week. Don't wait for opportunities; make them!

Think of the example of Philip. At first glance, one might conclude that the Lord always directed Philip to specific people in miraculous ways, just as He did with the Ethiopian official. But when we look at Philip's life more closely, we see that his approach to ministry was not random, haphazard or mysterious. Scripture tells us he worked his way up the coast all the way from Azotus to Caesarea (which was approximately one hundred miles) and "preached in all the cities" (Acts 8:40). It appears that he simply went town by town. Most likely, his amazing encounter with the Ethiopian official and God's specific instruction at that time were not the norm, but a special situation. The rest of the time, Philip simply obeyed the command Jesus had already given him to go and preach the gospel to every creature. It was simple, but it was … a *plan*.

HOW?

It was a quiet Sunday afternoon as I walked down to the park with my Bible and journal. Right away I noticed four teens sitting by the basketball hoop listening to their iPods. I decided to try to initiate a conversation by asking if they'd take my questionnaire.

"You talked to my friend on the Fourth of July," one of the guys blurted out. He looked about fourteen and seemed kind of rebellious.

"Really? Oh, I remember—there were about six of you in a circle," I said, recalling his group of friends wearing Gothic-style clothing. "And then you all left as I was talking with your friend."

"Yup," he said.

"Did your friend tell you anything about the discussion?" I asked.

"Yeah. I laughed at him," he replied.

"So would you all like to try my survey?" I asked.

"What's it about?" one of the girls replied.

"Well, it's about God, Heaven and Hell, and how to know where you are going when you die," I said.

They began laughing and making sarcastic comments.

"We think life is about dying and going six feet under. That's all it's about," the guy said.

"I'm an atheist, so I'm not interested," one girl said.

"If there's a God," the guy continued, "then He would have probably killed me by now because I've already broken probably every single one of His rules."

"Well, He's being merciful to you in keeping you alive!" I told him.

"If there's a God, why do I have so many problems in my family?" he said, and went on to list some sad things that had happened to some of his family members.

"I know, it's hard to understand why those things happen," I replied. "God didn't create evil, but He allows it. It's not God's fault there is evil in the world—He made everything perfect (see fuller answer on page 117) ... Yet sometimes God uses suffering to bring about a greater good."

I wanted to talk with them more, but I wasn't quite sure how to continue the discussion, so after a few minutes I decided to leave.

"Well, thanks for talking and I'm sorry for intruding on your afternoon here in the park," I said. As I was walking away, one of the girls called out, "Have a good afternoon!"

"Thank you!" I replied.

Wow, I think that was the only friendly thing they said to me that whole time, I thought.

I sat down under a tree with my Bible and journal about 50 yards away. As I sat there, I wondered if I should have said more. I wondered if I should go back. I decided to pray that God would cause *them* to continue the conversation somehow.

A few minutes later, two of the kids moved to a picnic table near me and called out, "You look bored! Do you have any million dollar bills?"

"How did you know I—?" I smiled and walked over to them, wondering how they knew I had million dollar bill tracts. *They must have seen me passing them out on the Fourth of July,* I figured.

I didn't have any "millions" with me, but I handed them an IQ card. The guy, Adam, tried it and figured out the optical illusion right away.

"Wow, not many people figure it out as fast as you did," I told him. Adam seemed to really appreciate that comment. The girl with him didn't catch on *at all*, and Adam thought that was really funny. Now they were both laughing.

"Here, do you want to try the quiz on the back?" I asked.

"Sure," Adam said.

I turned the card over and began reading the questions off the back. "Okay, the first question is: Is there a God?"

"Um ... I don't know ... maybe," he said with a smile. "Does it have to be a yes or no answer?"

"Yes," I replied.

"Okay. Yes," he said.

"Okay, the next question is, does God care about right and wrong?" I asked, continuing to read the questions off the back of the card.

"Yes," he replied.

"Are God's standards the same as ours?" I asked.

"No," he replied.

"Will God punish sin?" I continued.

"No."

"Is there a Hell?"

"Yes."

"Do you avoid Hell by living a good life?" I asked.

"No," he said.

"Okay, you were right on all of them, except one. We know that God *will* punish sin. Otherwise, why would there be a Hell?" I asked.

"Ah ... true ... " he agreed.

"I think I know what I am," he told me. "I learned the word once. It, like, starts with an 'A' or something."

"Agnostic?" I asked.

"Yeah! That's it!" he said.

"Like, where you don't really know what you believe?" I said.

"Yeah," he agreed.

"Okay, well, just because you haven't found the truth yet doesn't mean that what's true isn't true," I told him.

"That's true. Touché," he replied.

"So if you were standing before God and he said, 'Adam, why should I let you into Heaven?' what would you say?"

"I don't know," he said.

"So do you guys live around here?" I asked.

They did.

"You guys are a lot nicer than I thought you were," I told them.

They laughed. "Yeah, I felt bad about how my friends were acting over there," Adam said.

We continued to have a pretty good conversation about the gospel, but then Adam looked past me and got an expression of warning on his face.

"Oh no ... " he said.

His other two friends, the sarcastic ones, were coming to join our group.

That's okay, I thought. *This time they **have** to listen because they voluntarily came and joined us.* And they did listen. Then guess what happened? Two *more* friends of theirs came strolling through the park, and Adam called them over to join the discussion.

Wow—this group is getting big! I was thinking.

"Hi, I'm Grace," I told them, trying to confidently introduce myself to avoid awkwardness.

"Here—" Adam said to Emily, one of the girls who just arrived, "try the IQ test."

I guess he is helping me witness now.

Emily tried the quiz and answered the questions on the back. As I talked with her, she disagreed with practically everything I said, continuously asking, "But how do you know?"

What Emily didn't realize was that she was actually helping me witness by asking all of those questions. She was providing an opportunity for me to explain to the rest of them many of the reasons I believe in God and the Bible. When I mentioned that God answers prayer, Emily asked for an example.

"Tell us a story," she said.

"Okay," I agreed and shared the story of how I was born. My parents were told that having another child was a medical impossibility—but my dad cried out to the Lord for "grace" and God answered his prayer.

Emily listened, but then started arguing again. "You need to be open-minded," she stated.

"What do you hope to accomplish by being open-minded?" I asked her.

"Well, maybe if I had the chance to talk with everyone all over the world and learn everything there was to learn, and read all of the holy texts, then eventually I'd be able to find the truth," she explained.

"So you *are* looking for truth?" I asked.

She didn't exactly answer that. I guess if she *was* looking for truth, she didn't want to admit it.

Often people are very conscious of what others in the group are thinking of them. This may cause them to act silly or uninterested, but it doesn't mean they aren't responding inwardly to what we are saying.

Throughout this whole talk, Adam was listening attentively. After another 30 minutes or so, two more friends of theirs came walking through the park.

More people? I was thinking. *This is crazy!*

The group grew from seven to nine. Again, to minimize awkwardness, I told them upfront what was going on. "Hi, I'm Grace, and we're having a conversation about God, Heaven and Hell."

"Cool," one of them said and sat down.

Now I sort of felt like I was teaching a Sunday school class in our little park pavilion. I immediately noticed the necklace one of the guys was wearing—it was a crooked star.

"What does your necklace mean?" I asked.

He hesitated.

"I'm a Satanist," he said.

"This is gonna' be good," Emily exclaimed with a laugh.

"So, why are you a Satanist?" I asked.

"Because of the music I listen to," he said.

"Why do you listen to that kind of music?"

"Because I'm into it," he replied.

He told me that all the evil in the world caused him to believe that Satan was real. I asked him if all the good in the world caused him to believe that God was real. He didn't seem to be very interested in discussing the topic, but he was still pretty friendly and took a tract.

After hanging out with these kids, I reflected on what happened. No one prayed to accept Christ; no one admitted to a dramatically changed way of thinking. But they definitely seemed genuinely intrigued to have a talk about God with a Christian their age. Many unbelievers have thoughts, questions, and doubts floating around in their minds about God and religion, but they don't get the opportunity to talk about their questions with a Christian in a context where they feel comfortable enough to express them. We, as young followers of Jesus in their generation, must be willing to risk a little awkwardness and step out and converse with them.

THERE ARE NO ATHEISTS DURING FINAL EXAMS.

PRACTICAL SUGGESTIONS ABOUT "HOW":

Give Eye Contact: Look people in the eyes when you talk to them. This is very important. It demonstrates that you are not embarrassed or ashamed about what you are saying. It shows you are genuine.

Open a Bible: It makes an impact to actually show people verses from the pages of Scripture and have them read the words for themselves. When I was twelve, I heard the recommendation of buying a small Bible to make your "witnessing Bible." The suggestion was to note some key gospel verses, such as the "Romans Road" (Romans 3:10, 23; 5:8; 6:23; 10:9-10, 13), as this would provide a systematic plan to use when explaining the gospel. I remember the new level of confidence I received from doing this.

Draw Illustrations: Kristen, a girl I met on a bench at the mall, seemed to be very interested in what I was telling her. When I got to the core of the gospel message, I wanted to be sure it was clear, so I pulled out my post-it note pad. As I drew the bridge diagram,[1] I emphasized that the moment the little stick-figure-man takes his first step onto the bridge, he is placing his full trust in that bridge. I explained that it's the same for us when we put our full trust in Jesus.

It seemed to click for Kristen right at that moment. The next day Kristen and I texted back and forth for a good part of the afternoon. She had many questions. Near the end of our texting conversation she told me she was planning to start reading the Bible for a half hour every day!

Seeing a drawing that illustrates the point helps a person remember what you said. If you don't have anything to draw on, just grab a paper napkin!

Use Analogies: Hearing an analogy often has the same effect as seeing a sketch—it helps the message "click."

While talking with a teen girl on a swing at the park, I realized that she didn't seem to understand *justice.* I thought an analogy would help, so I said, "Let's say someone came into your house and beat up your mom."

She cringed at the thought.

"I know—" I said, "I'd feel the same way. This is just a scenario to make a point, okay?"

"Okay."

"Alright, and let's say the judge let the criminal go free and didn't punish him. He would not be a good judge, would he?"

She agreed with me.

"In the same way, God is good—so He doesn't overlook sin! And we all have sin inside of us."

It didn't take her long to get my point!

Be Personable: Asking casual "get-to-know-you" questions while we witness makes conversations more relaxed and enjoyable. If we are comfortable and confident in the way we approach people, they will feel more comfortable as well. People are more open to express their thoughts if they trust us and feel relaxed—if they feel they are in a "safe environment." Also, learning people's names and using them can mean a lot. Remember, people are not projects; they are people!

Use Technology: When concluding witnessing conversations, I often say something like this: "Hey, it's been great talking with you. There is a website that I like to give people that has some great information about what we've been talking about. If you give me your e-mail address, I'll send you a link."[2] This gives me the opportunity to have continued contact.

Another idea is to upload some short gospel video clips onto a tablet, phone, or portable device. You can show it to people while you are talking with them in order to help communicate a point. See recommended video clips at *www.willourgenerationspeak.com.*

Texting can also be a tool for witnessing. Maisie, a good friend who comes witnessing with me, points back to *texting* as the main tool her friend used to witness to her before she was saved. Her friend would text thought-provoking questions such as, "What do you think life is really about?" and "Why did God make us?"

We live in changing times. We have countless new avenues of social media by which we can share the gospel. No other generation had the tools we now have to communicate with people all around the globe instantly. But remember, technology can do more harm than good if we're not careful! As you know, it's easy to get sucked in and waste a lot of time—or worse, be defiled by the ungodliness. Instead of being "enslaved" by these things as many are,[3] let's make these tools *our* servants to help us serve Jesus.[4] Let's take advantage of technology for God's glory.

Keep in mind, however, that nothing beats face to face conversations. Our countenance, tone of voice, eye contact, and facial expressions communicate so much!

Use Your Testimony: Your testimony illustrates how the gospel works in *action*—not just in concept. It shows humility. Paul frequently shared his testimony. It is recounted three times in the book of Acts! And there are many other New Testament examples of people using their testimonies. The blind man said, "One thing I know … I was blind, now I see" (John 9:25). The

woman at the well said, "Come see a man that told me all things that ever I did" (John 4:29). After Jesus cured the leper in Mark 1, the grateful man "went out and began to publish it much and to blaze abroad the matter" (Mark 1:45).

You see, one of our best tools for witnessing is to share what Jesus has done for us personally. Even sharing a very brief version of our testimony gives us the chance to communicate the main points of the gospel. I often start by saying, "When I was six, I realized that even though I grew up in a Christian home, that didn't make me a Christian. I began to think about Heaven and Hell and I was scared I would go to Hell. I talked to my mom about it and she explained … "

Keep It Simple: Essentially, people need to know three things:
1) Their sickness and its consequence (sin and death)
2) The cure (Christ's death and resurrection)
3) How to take the cure (repent and believe)

There's no need to make it complicated. Jesus said, "Except ye be converted, and become as little children, ye shall not enter into the kingdom of Heaven" (Matthew 18:3).

Go in Pairs: Peter and John went witnessing together. So did Paul and Silas. Jesus sent out the disciples two by two. It's a scriptural pattern. What are some of the benefits of witnessing in pairs? You will learn from listening to each other. You can critique each other afterwards. One can pray while the other talks. Your friend may notice things about the individual you are witnessing to that you don't notice. Having two of you often makes situations feel more natural. One can jump in when the other doesn't know what to say. You can keep each other accountable to witness regularly. *If you want to go fast, go alone. If you want to go far, go together."*—African Proverb

Aim to Disciple: "I've never had anyone explain it to me like that before," Julian told me with appreciation after my friend Abby and I talked through the gospel with him and his friends. We had noticed them at a park, hanging out by their car, and had started a conversation. They responded with such hunger for truth that not only did we have a lengthy talk at the park, but we also scheduled to meet again at a coffee shop the following week. This time I brought my brother Stephen along.

"Have you thought more about our conversation from last week?" I asked them after ordering our drinks at the café.

"It's really weird, but we were talking about it all night and all week, actually … It just really stuck with us and we haven't been able to get it out of our minds," Terrance said.

"Really? Wow, well, that's good!" we replied.

"We don't think it was an accident you ran into us last week," Terrance continued. "We were bored that day and our talk with you was, like, the most entertaining part of our day … I'm sure if you had run into us in the past we probably wouldn't have been interested, but the timing and everything was amazing."

Our conversation that evening covered a wide range of topics from the first sin in the garden, to Jesus' identity, to the lessons God taught through animal sacrifices. We kept explaining more and more because they were soaking everything up like sponges.

"So here's another question," I said, trying to ask questions to keep the conversation progressing. "How could the death of one man save the world?"

We talked about how it was because Jesus was perfect, and explained the picture God gave the Jews in ancient Israel. They were required to sacrifice a lamb without spot or blemish. This was a picture of Jesus—the perfect Lamb of God. Jesus is *our* Sacrifice.

"If Jesus hadn't been perfect, He would have had to die for His own sin," Stephen said. "But because He was perfect, He was the only One who could die for the sins of the world."

"And," I added, "He was the only One who could fully absorb God's wrath for sin. He is our *Savior*. This is something other religions don't have."

"That means we can have confidence about our salvation," Stephen continued. "Muslims, for example, never know if they've been good enough—but we know that the price has *already* been paid."

"We already know that we're *not* good enough," I told them. "That's why we need a Savior."

My dad had suggested to me beforehand that we explain the concepts of *Sacrifice, Savior,* and *Substitute.* So, next, we explained how Jesus became our Substitute when He died in our place.

Julian, Terrance, and Courtney looked like typical teens, but they definitely did not *act* like typical teens. Their interest in spiritual things was rare and encouraging.

"It was really refreshing coming here and talking to you guys about this," Julian said. They all agreed and thanked us numerous times. We gave them each a Bible and invited them to our home for a Bible study the following week. They came. Julian had started reading Genesis on his own and seemed thirsty to know the Lord. We talked through John 1, showed a 30-minute Christian video, served cookies and popcorn, and then just talked for a long time about all kinds of things. They stayed until midnight.

"Well, should we do John 2 next time?" Stephen asked them.

They seemed eager. I was ecstatic about how well this was going, and I hoped to continue on a regular basis. But now comes the sad part of the story.

It was very hard to schedule the next get-together. There was one evening when it might have worked, but I suggested that we postpone it because it didn't seem like a good evening to me. I regret that decision now because that "next time" never came. You see, on the day we had rescheduled the Bible study, the boyfriend and girlfriend had a big fight. Then they broke up, and later the other guy went off to college. Now I've lost contact with all three of them.

I believe there was a huge spiritual battle raging in that situation. When people are that eager—that close—Satan often puts up a huge fight.

I tell this story in hopes of preventing others from making the same mistake I made. Discipling people is hard work. It is draining at times. It takes a lot of prayer. It takes perseverance. But it is what Jesus has called us to do! Sharing the gospel with someone the first time is merely the start. Our goal is to make disciples. This means teaching "all things" that Jesus has commanded us (Matthew 28:19-20).

And for all of you who have just read this story, maybe you could take 30 seconds right now and pray for these three young people with whom I dropped the ball. I know that God is strong, even though we fail, and He can continue the work He started in people's lives.

CHAPTER 13

SEVENTEEN WAYS TO START CONVERSATIONS

I couldn't think of anything to say. I wanted to witness to the hotel receptionist because he didn't seem too busy.

If only I could think of a way to start a conversation.

I kept going out to the lobby to get glasses of complimentary lemonade, hoping I would think of something to say while I was out there. However, after four glasses of lemonade and no conversation, I decided that my method wasn't working. Now I needed another excuse to go to the lobby.

Hearing me complain about my predicament, Stephen offered, "You could go get *me* some lemonade." So I headed to the lobby again. *[smile]*

"Anyone else want lemonade?" I asked my family after I returned with Stephen's glass.

Okay, this is silly. I just need to say something! I realized.

Finally, I asked the receptionist if he had a family, and I gave him the book that Sarah, Stephen and I wrote about 10 years ago on making your brothers and sisters your best friends. In the morning, he was still working his shift. It sounded like he had been reading the book for a good part of the night. He thanked us warmly and told us about his five kids. He also said he would be going to my blog which he had seen listed in the back of the book.

Getting conversations started is one of the hardest parts of witnessing. Once we take the first step—say those first words—it's often smooth-sailing from there. In this chapter we are going to look at 17 ideas of ways to begin conversations about the Lord. No matter what your personality, I think you will find the ideas in this chapter useful. They have been helpful for me. Hopefully this list of initial ideas will stimulate more creativity. I wonder how many thousands of ways Christians have started conversations about Jesus over the past 2,000 years!

1. TAKE A QUESTIONNAIRE

"Hi! I am doing a little questionnaire at the park today, asking people about what they believe. Do you have time to answer a few questions?"

Starting conversations this way brought me to a new level of confidence in witnessing. Approaching strangers felt less awkward, and the questionnaire would often springboard into a longer discussion. We have also found that younger girls who come witnessing with us are more confident to initiate conversations on their own when they have a questionnaire to follow—a simple half sheet of paper with four or five questions on it.

Initially, I didn't think the younger girls would want to come witnessing with us. But I was wrong! These girls got excited about the conversations we were having, and soon they began asking me, "Grace, when are we going out witnessing again?" Now they don't want to just come with us and listen as we witness to people. *They* want to do the talking. Questionnaires were one of the things that helped them grow in confidence.

2. HAND THEM SOMETHING

"Hello! Here's something for you to read when you have a chance."

On a flight home from New Orleans, I was seated next to a teenage guy. As he sat down, he put his earphones in and began reading a book—without even looking at me or saying hi. He seemed like the type of guy who felt awkward just *sitting* next to a girl, so I was wondering how in the world I would get him to actually have a discussion with me! *Of all the types of people God could have given me, this is about the hardest!* I thought. However, since I had prayed in advance for the person who would be sitting next to me, I decided I needed to at least try *something*. I concluded that God was simply stretching me out of my comfort zone—again! I prayed that the Lord would open a door. After a while, Sean took his earphones out and I knew I'd better seize the opportunity. I casually handed him a dinosaur booklet tract and told him what it was about. I explained that we can trust the Bible and that science doesn't contradict it as some people say. He nodded in agreement and read the first few pages right away.

"So, what do you think?" I asked.

He said that it made some interesting points about presuppositions which he had never thought of before. He told me he was planning to read the rest later.

"Do you have any kind of church background?" I asked him.

He had gone to church some, but he told me that there were some things he didn't really understand or agree with. Apparently, he had been taught that both faith and works were required for salvation. I shared the gospel briefly, explaining that we can have peace with God *only* through trusting in Jesus and the work He accomplished on the cross. Just before He died, Jesus said, "It is finished," which means *paid in full.* Romans 3:28 states: "A man is justified by faith without the deeds of the law."

The more we talked about this, the more interested Sean became.

"Yeah, that makes sense," he told me. "I don't get to talk about this stuff very often."

I gave him a tract about evidence for the resurrection of Christ. Sean turned to the gospel part on the back and seemed anxious to understand it.

"So, basically, you just repent?" he asked.

It was encouraging to see his thirst for answers. I gave him a book that had further answers to his questions.

He told me, "My mom (sitting a few rows ahead) has a ton of food with her if you're hungry."

I thanked him and laughed.

"I just sort of feel like I owe you for the book," he explained.

Sean seemed close to becoming a believer, and I was grateful for that dinosaur booklet which helped me begin a conversation in a seemingly awkward situation!

3. TAKE INITIATIVE IN CASUAL CONVERSATIONS

"How has your day been? Have you heard about the blizzard in Minnesota?"

- **"Where are you headed?"**
  This is a good question to ask in gas stations or airports. People will often return the question, and this gives us an opportunity to tell them where we are going and why. If we include a reference to Christian activities in our answer, it can generate a discussion in that direction.

- **"What's next for you?"**
  What are your plans after you finish school? Do you have any life goals?

- **"What do you think of 'such and such' an issue?"**
  Asking someone his view shows respect. It shows that you value his opinion. If he returns the question, you have an opportunity to witness.

- "I like your hat!"
  Taking a friendly interest in others often leads to more opportunities.

- **"Do you have any Christmas traditions?"**
  Holidays provide an expanded array of conversational topics. We can ask people if they have special plans, what family traditions they enjoy, or what the holiday means to them. We can ask questions such as, "Do you know what Emmanuel means?" See more holiday ideas at *www.willourgenerationspeak.com.*

4. DROP HINTS

"I'm on my way to a Bible study. We're studying Revelation tonight."

Mentioning Christian activities in which you are involved gives others the opportunity to ask questions. It's like setting out bait to see if they bite.

"Nice shirt," the guy selling popcorn told my friend Lizzy as she got a refill of Pepsi.

"Thanks, it's from camp," she said.

"It's from a *Christian Bible* camp that people at our church go to sometimes," I inserted.

"Oh, you're Christians? What church do you go to?" the guy asked.

"Just a Bible-believing church—it's not a specific denomination," I said. "What about you?"

He didn't claim to be anything.

"So what do you think about life after death? What happens when we die?" I asked.

"Well, what do *you* believe?" he asked me.

Perfect! Now I had the opportunity to share my faith with him—he was asking me for it!

"Well, I believe in a Creator ... " I started, and went on to share about the Lord.

5. LEARN FROM THEM

"So, you're a school teacher. What do you think is the biggest need of kids these days?"

"You're from Denmark? What would you say are some of the biggest differences between Denmark and America?"

While shopping for groceries one afternoon, I noticed a Muslim lady in my aisle. She was wearing a pretty black coat, and I told her I liked it.

"Thank you," she said and kept shopping.

Okay, that didn't go too far.

She seemed shy.

Is there something else I could say? I wondered. *(Think, Grace, think!)*

I kept an eye on which aisle she was in. Finally, I decided to try the "learn from them" approach, even though I knew it may come across a little random.

"Can I ask you a question?" I said.

She agreed.

I asked her to explain how relationships worked in her Muslim culture. (Was she married and, if so, how did she and her husband get to know each other?) She told me she was married and gave me a brief synopsis of how the courtship process works in their culture. We had a short but nice conversation, and I learned her name was [Izza]. When I commented on her cart full of baby food jars, she explained that she was stocking up because she was leaving the country to teach in Saudi Arabia.

About 30 minutes later, as I was leaving the store, I noticed that my new friend Izza was checking out.

I realized, *This is my last chance to say something to her.* I decided to go for it.

"Can I ask you another question?" I said, walking up to her after she checked out.

"Sure."

"Have you ever read the Injeel?" I asked. (The Injeel is the Arabic term for the New Testament gospels—which the Qur'an actually tells Muslims to read.)

"You mean the Bible?" Izza replied.

"Yeah."

"No, I haven't," she said.

"Oh. Okay,"

Now what do I say? Nothing came to mind, so I simply told her, "Well, it was nice meeting you!" and left.

Izza was very nice and we left on friendly terms.

Well, I tried. Maybe somehow God would use that encounter in Izza's life, I thought.

I decided that I could at least pray for Izza—that she would remember what I asked and become curious about the Bible.

Many times when witnessing, it feels like "nothing happened." We think, *That didn't go anywhere.* But we need to remember that for every "extraordinary" story, there are dozens of ordinary stories—simple attempts to witness with no known results. Yet, in God's eyes, I think often the ordinary is extraordinary. Here's why. It takes more faith to persevere when we don't see results. God controls the results. What He wants from us is *faith*. "Without faith it is impossible to please Him" (Hebrews 11:6). And how do we know that the ordinary is ordinary? We shouldn't think of those "mediocre" encounters as second-rate. Maybe God is doing something amazing behind the scenes. We just don't see the whole picture yet.

6. USE CURRENT EVENTS

"It's pretty unbelievable about the earthquake in _____. Have you been watching the news? Do you ever wonder why God allows things like that to happen?"

Even Jesus used this approach—He used a current event in the news to turn people's attention to their own need to repent (Luke 13:1-5).

7. WEAR AN ILLUSTRATION

"I'm glad you asked. There is actually a special reason why I wear this ... "

Curt, a friend of mine, wears one white shoe and one black shoe. Whenever people ask, "What's up with your shoes?" he explains that his black shoe represents his old life (living in sin and darkness), and his white shoe represents his new life in Christ.

Another friend, Mirren, wears a pin that says "IF?" on it. When people ask about it, she tells them what it stands for: "If you died today, would you go to Heaven?"

While driving through Illinois, my dad was a little frustrated because he couldn't find the entrance ramp to the highway he was trying to get on.

"Hey, look—there's an ice cream shop!" I said. (See how helpful I am.)

A few minutes later Dad made a U-turn and said, "Hmmm, I think I need to stop and ask for directions."

"The ice cream shop would be a good place to ask for directions," I pointed out.

We both went in. Dad got directions; I got ice cream. Since it was late at night and the employees weren't busy, they gathered to see who their customers were.

"Hey, you have an awesome tie!" one girl said to my dad. His tie had a picture of a Behemoth on it and a Bible verse from Job (40:15).

"I love dinosaurs," she said. "What's the name of that one? Oh, duh, it says right there—Behemoth."

"Yes," my dad answered, "because that's the name the Bible uses for dinosaurs. Did you know that the word 'dinosaur' wasn't invented until the 1800s?"

More employees had now gathered and my dad shared some interesting facts about dinosaurs living in the not-so-distant past, and about creation and evolution.

We went out to the car and brought in several dinosaur booklets to give them. The booklet takes something that intrigues people—dinosaurs—and springboards from there into the reliability of Scripture and the gospel. They thanked us warmly.

8. ASK ABOUT THEIR JEWELRY, PIERCINGS, OR TATTOOS

"Is there a special meaning to the necklace you are wearing?"

While checking out, I asked the cashier if there was any meaning behind the jewelry she was wearing. (It was very unique.)

She was happy to explain her views about diversity to me, and said that her piercings were her way of expressing herself. After I had listened for awhile, she asked me, "And what do you believe?"

Perfect. That was my chance to briefly explain about Jesus and the Bible.

Piercings or tattoos often have special meanings to people. Without condoning them, we can still take an interest in the person by asking about their meaning. You may be surprised by how naturally it opens doors for further discussion.

9. ASK ABOUT THEIR CULTURE OR RELIGION

"Where are you from? What is the primary religion of your country back home? Do you have any religious beliefs?"

We passed the Indiana welcome sign. *Two more states to drive through and we're home.* We were traveling with our team of Bright Lights leaders after running some conferences. Traveling with that many girls means rest stops take much longer *[smile].* During one of these stops, I noticed a Muslim lady with her little son, and I wondered if there would be an opportunity to talk with her. As we were getting ready to leave the travel station, I noticed her again—standing by the door.

I wanted to say *something,* so I smiled and greeted her. "Hey, are you doing Ramadan?" I asked. (Ramadan is the month when Muslims fast. Christians globally make a special effort to pray for Muslims during this time, and our team of Bright Lights leaders had chosen to make Muslims a prayer focus on the trip.)

"Yes!" the Muslim lady replied.

What she said next totally took me by surprise. "Are you from Cedar Rapids? Haven't we met before?"

"Oh!" I said, as it all came rushing back into my mind. She was the Muslim girl I had talked to at Walmart with all the baby food in her cart—six months earlier!

"You're Izza!" I exclaimed. "We met at Walmart, right? I thought you were in Saudi Arabia."

She explained that she had only been overseas for a few months. Her husband was standing outside, so I introduced them both to my dad.

"So you are from Cedar Rapids too!" her husband said. "Where are you coming from?"

I briefly told them about the Bright Lights ministry, explaining that we had been traveling with a team of young ladies leading conferences for girls—teaching about purity and being strong for the Lord in your youth.

"That's great—good morals!" he replied.

"Maybe we'll see you on the road home," Dad said as we left. "We have a big van and trailer."

"Well, I have a bad tendency of getting where I want to go a little faster than I should," he remarked.

We all laughed.

"God be with you," he said as we parted.

First we met in an aisle in Walmart in Iowa. Then, six months later, we met at a gas station seven hours from home in Indiana. We were only there for a few minutes, and Izza and her husband were only there for a few minutes, but God had it timed perfectly. Now, with increased faith in God's ability to bring two paths together any time He chooses, I am praying that I will meet Izza a third time and will have the opportunity to share the gospel with her.

10. USE THE MEANING OF THEIR NAME

"I like your name. Do you know what it means?"

"Hey, I'm Grace. Do you live here in the neighborhood?" I asked as I sat down on a swing next to a girl who was swinging by herself.

She nodded and said she had just moved in.

"So what's your name?" I asked.

"Rachel," she said.

"Oh, do you know what the name Rachel means?" I asked her.

"I think I used to, but I don't remember," she said.

"It means 'little lamb,'" I told her as I pulled out my pocket-sized "name meanings" booklet.

"Would you like to hear the Bible verse that goes along with it?"

She did.

I read her the corresponding verse for the name Rachel: Isaiah 40:11. "He shall feed His flock like a shepherd: He shall gather the lambs with His arm, and carry them in His bosom ... "

Her face lit up. "Cool!" she said.

"Do you have a Bible at home?" I asked.

"Yeah."

Rachel and I talked for awhile about God and what will happen when we die. Eventually, her mom came to the park looking for her. I asked where they lived, and learned that their family had recently moved in right across the street from us! I had already been planning to go over and meet them.

Rachel, her mom, and her sister agreed to come over for a weekly Bible study, and my mom and I have been studying the book of John with them ever since.

11. ANSWER ORDINARY QUESTIONS IN A NON-ORDINARY WAY

"Thanks for asking. I don't know yet where I am going to college, but my main goal in life is ... "

"School is going well. One thing I've learned recently is ... "

"Our family is doing well. God answered prayer for us in a really encouraging way recently ... "

Every question we are asked is an opportunity to seize.

12. WITNESS IN THIRD PERSON

"Can I tell you about a really interesting conversation I just had?"

While walking home from the park one afternoon, I was feeling very encouraged by the opportunity the Lord had just given me. I had talked with four teens who were sitting at a picnic table, and one of the boys seemed extremely close to putting his faith in Christ.

As I walked up our street to come home, I saw our neighbor, an elderly man, sweeping his driveway. I stopped to talk and told him what had just happened at the park. He seemed very interested in my story. I recounted the conversation in as much detail as I could remember—emphasizing the main points about the gospel. I had been wanting to witness to this neighbor and was grateful for this opportunity.

Talking in the "third person" is a natural, non-offensive way to present biblical truths. By telling an unbeliever about a recent witnessing conversation you had, you are teaching him the gospel in an indirect way. Sometimes there is wisdom in treating another person as if he is a believer, even if you don't know if he actually is. He will be learning from you without a barrier of pride being put up. For example, if you say, "The problem with this nation is that so many have forgotten God," people will often agree with you. Then you have an open door to explain the solution.

I am not saying that we shouldn't be bold and upfront with people. I'm merely saying that sometimes we can use tact instead of being "preachy"— especially if we are talking to someone older than we are and want to make sure we come across respectfully. Sometimes it is wise to gently teach concepts one by one, as they can receive them. Other times, it's better to be straightforward, as in the examples below.

13. ASK DIRECTLY IF THEY WOULD LIKE TO HEAR THE GOSPEL

"Hey, we are out here sharing the gospel with people today. Would you like to hear it?"

"Have you ever heard the gospel before?" Ryan, a friend of mine, asked a young teenage guy outside an apartment complex.

"No," the boy replied.

"Never?"

"No."

"Would you mind if I shared it with you?" Ryan asked.

The guy listened with interest, and Ryan was surprised to receive a phone call from him a few days later—at 5:00 a.m.! This guy's sincerity and interest in the gospel was evident, and he was anxious to ask more questions. He appreciated having a new friend who would answer them.

Ryan and a number of his friends often use this "starter question," and have had many fruitful discussions at that apartment complex. If people say no and aren't interested, they simply move on to others who want to talk.

People appreciate it when we are honest about who we are and what we are doing. There's no need to sound like a salesman, coax people into hearing the gospel, or beat around the bush. We are not ashamed of this message! Paul said, "I am not ashamed of the gospel of Christ: for it is the power of God unto salvation to every one that believeth" (Romans 1:16).

One time a friend and I walked up to a group of teens sitting at a table. My friend started the conversation by saying, "Hey guys, we want to talk to you about Jesus Christ."

Wow, that was a pretty bold introduction, I thought.

But they responded with interest, and we ended up having a great two-hour conversation with them.

People respect it when you are willing to be upfront with them. Even if they say they don't want to talk, or are unwilling to hear the gospel, at least they have now *met someone* who was bold with it! That short encounter alone will be a testimony to them. (Maybe, looking back, they'll regret that they turned down the opportunity to hear what you had to say!)

14. GO DOOR TO DOOR

"Hi! My friend and I live here in the neighborhood and we are doing a little project. We are asking people three questions ... "

"Hi! My brother and I decided to take on the summer project of sharing the gospel with everyone on 36th and 37th Street. Have you heard the gospel before?"

"Hi! My sister and I are making an effort to pray for our neighborhood. Is there anything you would like us to pray about?"

15. CAPTURE INTEREST THROUGH OBJECTS

"Would you like to try an IQ test? Have you seen the rope trick? Would you like a color bracelet? Let me explain what it means."

Little objects make it easier to generate discussions. IQ quizzes, evangecubes, wordless books, pressed pennies with the Ten Commandments, and color bracelets are a few I'd suggest.[1] These tools capture people's attention (especially kids) and make it easy to begin discussions.

The "rope trick," for example, is where you take three ropes of different lengths and make them look as if they are all the same length. It illustrates that no matter who we are, each one of us is a sinner needing salvation. I didn't think I had the right "personality" to do illusions like this. It seemed more like the type of thing an older man at church would do. Recently, however, I have come to realize what a great tool this little illusion can be. It is a natural and appealing way to suddenly gain a captive audience! Kids stick around waiting to see the end of the "trick." While they listen to you share the accompanying gospel message, the visual illustration helps drive the point home. For further information, go to *www.willourgenerationspeak.com.*

16. SIMPLY SAY, "CAN I ASK YOU AN INTERESTING QUESTION?"

"What do you think happens when someone dies? Do you think peace with God is a free gift or something you have to earn? Do you have any spiritual beliefs?"

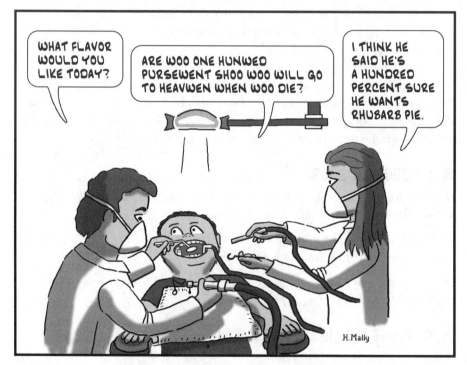

WITNESSING AT THE DENTIST

A couple at my church asked their waitress, "If you died today, do you know where you would go?"

The waitress sat down across from them, looked them in the eye, and replied, "Honestly, if I died right now, I think I'd go to Hell." She was anxious to hear whatever they had to say.

Hearing this story emboldened me to try harder to initiate conversations with waitresses. Five days later, six girls and I were sitting at a table at Cracker Barrel after a conference. I had prayed in advance that I would be able to witness to our server. After we ordered, I told my friends, "When our waitress comes back, I'm going to throw out a question to see if we can get a witnessing conversation going."

Everyone seemed to like that idea. So, the next time she came by, I said, "Hey, I have an interesting question for you."

"Okay!" she replied.

"Do you think going to Heaven is a free gift or something you have to earn?" I asked.

She said she believed that one gets reincarnated several times and then eventually ends up in Heaven. She was really friendly and willing to talk, so I asked some questions about her beliefs.

"When you finally get to Heaven, are you in your 'human form' again?" I asked.

"Hmm … good question. I guess I've never thought about that," she said.

"Well, some people believe that in the Karmic circle you eventually become 'one with the universe.' Is that what you believe?" I asked.

"Yeah, I think that's more what I believe. Eventually, I'll just become 'energy'," she replied.

"Interesting," I said.

"My relatives and I debate this all the time," she said, "but no one really knows, so we always keep going in circles."

"Well, it's important stuff to talk about," I commented.

"So what do you believe? I'm curious now!" she asked me.

"Well, I'd like to tell you, but I also know you are on the job, and I don't want to take your time," I replied.

"I'll tell you what," she said, "I only have one other table. I'll go take care of them and then come back!"

After a few minutes she came back, eager to hear what I had to say.

"Well, first of all, I think this world was *designed*. I think it's obvious when we see the beauty and complexity around us." I gave her a few examples of this. She definitely agreed with that point.

"So the big question is: Who made us and why?" I continued.

She agreed.

"Well, I've come to the conclusion that there are a lot of reasons to believe the Bible," I explained, and began to list some of them.

"Oh, I've read the Bible, but I just don't think I completely agree with it," she said, bringing up some problems she had with Christianity, such as hypocrisy in the church.

"But just because people make mistakes doesn't mean that what God told us in the Bible isn't true," I told her.

She nodded.

I mentioned that God has to punish evil because He is just and good. Therefore, we all need God's mercy because we have all broken God's law.

"Yeah, and that's what makes me tend to believe more in the reincarnation thing," she said, "because I know I mess up, and with reincarnation you have the chance to start over and keep trying."

What she did not yet understand is that it is actually in *Christianity* that we truly have the chance to start over with a clean slate, having been cleansed by the blood of Christ. I didn't think of saying that at the moment, but I shared the gospel and explained that it is in the cross we see God's love and justice together. He punished sin—yet He didn't punish us. He punished His Son so He could show mercy to us.

After talking for awhile, I asked her if she liked to read.

"I LOVE to read," she replied. I gave her a book that clearly explains the gospel and answers many of the questions unbelievers have.

As we were leaving she told me, "My friend in the kitchen was looking at the book you gave me and she wants to read it. So now I'm going to have to *share* it," she complained, jokingly. She gave me a hug and said, "You made my night!"

I know it can be difficult to witness to waiters or waitresses. One idea is to ask your server, "Hey, we are just about to pray for our meal. Is there anything we could pray for you about?" If you are unable to get a conversation going, another idea is to write a short personal thank-you note (even if it's just on a paper napkin), expressing gratefulness for the good service. Include a Bible verse on the note, and tip well in order to be a good Christian testimony.

17. MEET NEEDS

"Can I help you with that?"

"Don't worry about paying for your coffee—I took care of it."

When we get involved in people's lives by helping neighbors, giving unexpected gifts, bringing people meals, and looking for creative ways to meet needs, it prompts questions and strengthens relationships. It speaks louder than a thousand words. And, very often, it opens doors for the gospel.

We've covered 17 ideas, but there are hundreds of other possible ways to begin conversations about Jesus. God is creative, and we should be too. I'd like to hear *your* ideas!

CHAPTER 14

IF THE FOUNDATIONS ARE DESTROYED ...

"If the foundations be destroyed, what can the righteous do?" (Psalm 11:3).

While eating spicy goat meat with naan bread at a Pakistani restaurant in town, Sarah and I asked our two new Nepalese friends (local college students) about the religious beliefs in Nepal.

"How many gods do you actually have?" I inquired.

"Thirty-three million," Sunita and Rajan replied.

"Thirty-three *million?*" we asked in surprise.

"Yes," Rajan said, motioning toward his water glass. "We believe water is god ... there is a god of almost everything. But there are six main gods ... " he continued, describing their characteristics.

"So if I went to Nepal and spoke to someone about God, which god would they think of?" I asked.

With puzzled expressions, Sunita and Rajan replied, "Well, probably whatever god they respected the most."

WHICH GOD?

All right, let's think about this. If I traveled to Nepal, got off the airplane, and started witnessing to someone using John 3:16, it wouldn't make much sense to my listener. If I said, "For God so loved the world that He gave His only begotten Son ... " they would think, *"Really? Which God? What is love? How does God have a Son?"*

Therefore, it would be a better plan to start by laying the foundational understanding of one Creator God, beginning with Genesis.

As Sarah and I continued eating at the restaurant with our Nepalese friends, Sunita referred to a college class she had taken on basic Christianity. "It was so confusing," she complained.

I offered to give her an explanation of the true essence of Christianity. Starting at the very beginning, I shared the creation story and gradually led up to the cross. She and Rajan listened with interest and told me that they had not known all of this before.

"I don't really know why I believe what I believe," Sunita replied. "I think most people simply believe what their parents believe, but don't really stop to think about it."

"Can we get together again to talk about this stuff more?" Rajan asked.

This dinner conversation just happened recently, and we are excited about meeting up with Sunita and Rajan again.

Most of you reading this book don't live in Nepal. You probably live in America. But did you know that America is becoming more and more like Nepal every day? We are becoming biblically illiterate. We may not believe in 33 million gods, but many people, especially in our younger generation, know very little about what the Bible teaches.

WHO ARE ADAM AND EVE?

I like to hang out in our town square sometimes with the teens who congregate there. On one of these occasions I met Julia and Samantha, junior high girls, who were sitting on a picnic table eating Doritos. They were silly and playful, but beneath the surface laughter there was pain and confusion.

Julia told me, "When my parents got a divorce a few years ago, it made me think there wasn't a God."

We began discussing why God allows bad things to happen, and I explained that the sorrow we see around us is a result of sin.

"Do you know who the first two people were?" I asked.

"No," they replied.

"You don't know who the first two people God created were?" I asked, surprised.

They shook their heads.

"Marsha?" they guessed hesitantly.

I finally told them: "Adam and Eve."

"Oh, yeah! That sounds more right than Marsha," they replied.

Given the high percentage of Christians in America, how is it that these girls didn't even know the very basics? What is wrong with this picture? It's understandable that some Nepalese don't know much about the Bible since less than 3% of the population in Nepal is Christian. But here in America?

"All right, well, God made Adam and Eve and put them in a beautiful garden," I explained to Samantha and Julia, feeling like I was a missionary in a remote tribal area, even though I was in the square of my own home town. "He told them they could eat of any of the trees in the garden except one ... "

I continued to teach the account from Genesis and then explained, "Today, our sin still separates us from God."

I needed to illustrate this, so I took one girl's drink to represent God and one girl's empty Dorito bag to represent us. I separated them and put my purse (representing sin) in the middle. This illustration could definitely have been improved [smile], but it was the best I could come up with at the moment.

"Now, there is an answer for how we can get right again with God," I said. "But I'm not going to tell you unless you want to hear."

"I want to hear!" Julia said.

"I'm scared to die, actually," Samantha said.

These girls had real questions and wanted real answers. But those answers, the gospel, would not have made sense to them if I had not first laid some foundations about our Creator and how sin entered the world.

DON'T ASSUME THEY KNOW WHAT YOU MEAN!

"I think we go to Heaven and then we are reincarnated," a teenage girl told me.

"Yeah, so do I," her friend agreed.

"What's that mean?" a third friend asked.

They answered her, "It's where you, like, become someone else and keep on living ... "

"So, where did you get your information from?" I asked them.

"I don't know, it's just something I've heard ... like on TV and stuff I guess," one girl said.

"What 'percent chance' do you think there is that there's a God?" I asked.

"I'm gonna' go with 40%," one replied.

"80%," said another.

"10%," the third answered.

"Okay," I nodded, "well, would you like to know why I think—er—*know* there is a God?"

"Sure."

"Well," I began, "if you look at a painting, you know there's a painter, right? And if you look at a book, you know there's an author, right? Books don't just come out of nowhere. If you see a book, you know someone wrote it. When we look at nature around us, and our own bodies—and how complicated they are—we know there was a Designer. There's no way it could have all come from nothing."

After I said this, they all seemed to automatically agree with me that there is a God. So I moved on.

"How do you know what happens when you die?" I asked them.

"There's no way to really know," one girl replied.

"Actually, there is a way to know," I explained. "God has spelled it all out for us in the Bible."

As I began to share that God actually chose to die for us, one of the girls interrupted me.

"Wait a minute," she said, "I thought *Jesus* died on the cross."

"Jesus *is* God," I clarified.

Their jaws dropped.

"Jesus is *God?*" they exclaimed.

"I never knew that!" one of them said.

This new piece of information seemed to arouse some excitement, and we continued to have an encouraging discussion.

Young people in our generation need someone to teach them basic biblical history and concepts. They don't simply need "preaching"—they need teaching. How could these girls have understood the gospel without understanding Jesus' identity? Laying foundations is not merely helpful—it's *necessary*.

CHRISTIAN LINGO: THEY DON'T GET IT!

A hundred years ago most Americans understood basic Christian terminology, but that's not the case anymore. Not in *our* generation, at least. We often need to start from scratch.

Take the word *love* for example. We assume people know what that means. But do they? The world's version of love is very, very different from God's love. In fact, it's sometimes the opposite. It often means, "I want you in order to satisfy my own desires." God's love means, "I am laying down my life for your benefit."

Faith. People recognize this as a religious word, but that doesn't mean they understand it. Faith is putting all of your trust in something or someone.

Saved. While talking with a Lutheran girl at a local college, I asked if there was a specific time in her life when she asked God to save her. She proceeded to describe a time when she survived a car accident. I realized that she did *not* understand what I was asking!

Heaven. "What is Heaven?" I asked a mom and daughter as I was talking with them at the mall. "Peaceful, no stress, relaxing" was about all they came up with. I've had other people tell me, "I think Heaven is whatever you want it to be," or, "I believe everyone has their own personal Heaven," or even, "I think your spirit will have a choice of where it wants to go when you die."

The essence of Heaven is the *presence of God*. If people miss that, they are missing everything. The Bible does not speak of a place where people sit on clouds playing miniature harps. It speaks of being blameless in the presence of the God of the Universe—who is Himself the source and essence of good. *He* is what makes Heaven *Heaven*. The reason Hell is so horrible is that God's goodness is withdrawn. People are there because they have rejected God who is the only source of good. Defining Heaven and Hell in this way gives people a new dimension of understanding and makes a difference in our witnessing conversations. It creates a new starting point—an increased understanding of the nature of God.

In fact, in order to be as clear as possible, sometimes instead of using the word "Heaven" we can refer to "having a restored relationship with God" or "eternal life."

Clarifying terms is important, but it's simply an introduction to this chapter. Laying foundations means much more than making sure they understand the meaning of our words. It means teaching history from the Bible, communicating what God has done in the world up to this point, and explaining the concepts on which the gospel is built. In our biblically illiterate generation, witnessing often needs to start with Genesis 1:1.

FIRESIDE MUSINGS: WHERE DID WE COME FROM?

HOW WOULD PAUL WITNESS IN MODERN AMERICA?

Did you know that Paul encountered beliefs similar to the ones we combat today? The Epicurean and Stoic philosophers mentioned in Acts 17 were similar to the atheists, new age evolutionists, and humanists of present day America. They were curious about Paul's "strange doctrine" and asked him to explain it.

Now, if Paul would have stood up and quoted John 3:16, their response may have been similar to the response from a person in Nepal: *Who is God? What is love? Who is His Son?*

But Paul knew better. He had already been looking around and conversing with them, and he had a pretty good understanding of their erroneous views. Therefore, Paul laid a *foundation* before presenting Jesus. Starting at the very beginning, he explained the nature of the one true God who created the world. He taught them that all nations are "one blood." He explained about God's power and loving character. Then Paul spoke of Christ's resurrection, our sin, and the coming judgment. All of this in one little sermon!

In contrast, when Peter presented the gospel in Acts 2 to the Jewish people, his main theme was, "You missed it! Don't you see? This Jesus, whom you crucified, was the Messiah!" Peter didn't need to lay the same foundations that Paul laid because the Jewish people already knew about their Creator, His Law, and their problem of sin. Maybe they were comparable to people in America a hundred years ago when the culture had a basic knowledge of Christianity and the biblical God.

FIRST THINGS FIRST

"Do you believe we were created by God or through evolutionary processes?" I asked four high school girls outside a hotel in New Hampshire.

"Evolution," they all answered.

"So, do you think there is a God?" I asked.

"No," they answered, without hesitation.

"Oh, okay."

Now what do I say? Where do I go from here? How do I start witnessing to them if we do not even have a place to start? I guess I wasn't expecting them to be so adamant in their reply.

"So, obviously you guys don't know for *sure* that there is no God—I mean, you can't *prove* there's not, so what 'percent chance' do you think there is?" I asked.

They decided on "fifty-fifty."

Interesting. They just went from believing there is no God to acknowledging there is a 50% chance He exists.

"What are some of the reasons that make you doubt God's existence?" I asked.

"Science," was their reply.

Science. God made science, yet people use it as a reason to reject Him. We'll come back to this story.

IT TAKES MORE FAITH TO BELIEVE IN EVOLUTION

As I approached a couple sitting at a picnic table, I asked if they would answer a few questions for me about what they believed. They happily agreed. Naomi and Sam looked like they were in their early 30s.

"What do you think happens when someone dies?" I asked.

"Nothing—you just go into the ground," they said.

"Okay. So did you grow up with any certain faith or religion?" I asked.

Sam had not. Naomi had grown up in a Unitarian church.

"The next question is, if you had one problem with Christianity, what would it be?"

"Just *one* problem with Christianity?" Naomi asked.

I smiled. "No, you can give more than one," I said.

"Well, I guess it would be that I don't agree with Christians who say the Bible is 100% literal and has to be taken as fact. I think it's more metaphorical," she said.

"What about you?" I asked Sam.

"I don't have a problem with Christianity," he said. "In fact, a Christian friend just helped me out with something recently. Actually, I hope there is a God."

"So why don't you believe the Bible?" I asked.

"Because I believe in evolution," Sam said.

There we go again. Science. (Well, what he thinks is science.)

Let's pause the story for a second. Did you know that there are two main reasons people believe in evolution?

1) It is a way for them to "get God out of the picture." If there is no God, then there is no ultimate standard for right and wrong. People can live any way they want without being accountable to a Creator.

2) They have been taught evolution all their lives and they simply trust their teachers. They don't realize the fallacies of evolution, and they don't know that the evidence is actually on the side of the Bible.

Now let's go back to Naomi and Sam. Naomi stated that *they* believe in science and that *I* just take the Bible by faith.

"But it takes faith to believe in evolution too," I told them, "because it's a story of something that happened in the past."

They couldn't disagree.

"Yeah, I wasn't there [when it happened]," Sam said.

Exactly.

"Both creation and evolution are stories of something that happened in the past and they have to be believed by faith," I explained. "But I would say it takes a whole lot more faith to believe evolution."

"So really, you don't see any problem between Christianity and science?" Sam asked.

"No, not at all!" I replied.

"I really hope there is a God," he said again. "The idea of a Creator and afterlife is so much nicer than just going into the ground to become worm food."

I would have to agree with that. [smile]

Then he asked, "What actually *is* God?"

Although Sam was an intelligent adult, living in one of the most "Christianized" countries in the world, he hardly knew anything about God or the Bible. When I mentioned Jesus' identity, it completely took him by surprise.

"Jesus is God?" he asked. He couldn't believe he hadn't known that before, but he seemed intrigued by the idea and took the booklets that I gave him.

FIRESIDE MUSINGS: WHY ARE WE HERE?

"FOR THE FIRST TIME, I REALIZED I COULD TRUST THE BIBLE"

Responding to the skeptical questions of evolutionists is often not as hard as one may imagine. In fact, in only five minutes we can make some points that really cause them to think. Let me share the story of Rich, a good friend of ours, who has been a part of our church for years. When Rich was in junior high, evolution was one of his favorite topics. He was so enthralled with it that he'd write extra papers on the topic to earn more credits.

When Rich was in his early 30s, he began watching a Christian TV show by Dr. D. James Kennedy because he liked its political views. One time the show focused on the topic of creation science. Dr. Kennedy put a pocket watch in a lunch bag and pounded it with a hammer. Then he began to shake the bag and asked, "How many years of shaking this bag do you think it will take before it becomes a pocket watch again?" He proceeded to share that God's Word has the answer to origins.

"It was then that I realized for the first time that the Bible could be true," Rich recalled. He put his faith in Christ to save him that very night.

Evolution truly is a "fairy tale for grownups." Just as it takes faith for us to believe Genesis 1:1, so it takes faith (only much more of it) to believe the story that goes something like this: *"Billions of years ago the universe began in a tiny, infinitely hot and dense point that exploded and rapidly expanded. Then pockets of expanding material somehow collapsed into galaxies, stars and planets. When earth cooled, single celled organisms began to form and evolved into all the life we see today."*

If even a watch could not construct itself, no matter how many billions of years you give it, how could a cell? The simplest cell is far more complex than man's most complicated machine, let alone a watch! Actually, there is no such thing as a simple cell.

Evolutionists are people of great faith. Do you know what their faith is in? It's in *time*.[1] They conclude, *Given enough time, anything can happen.* But if you take away time, their belief collapses.

Did you know Paul warned Timothy that counterfeit science would be one of the reasons people would reject the Christian faith? He said, "O Timothy, keep that which is committed to thy trust, avoiding profane and vain babblings, and oppositions of **science falsely so called**: Which some professing have erred concerning the faith" (1 Timothy 6:20-21).

Evolution fits the category of which Paul spoke. It isn't actually science at all. It is a belief system. It is an alternative view of origins under the pretense of science.

Before we go any further, it is important to understand that there are two kinds of science.

1. Operational science (which is observable, repeatable, and testable)
2. Historical science (the study of non-repeatable events that happened in the past)

It is through *operational* science that people create spaceships, heart monitors and computers. But beliefs about origins fall into the second category—*historical* science. To understand the term historical science, let's think of a detective. He can't say, "Come back to life so we can kill you again and see how it happened." No, he can only look at clues and then come to a conclusion (which may or may not be correct).

In the same way, evolution is merely an idea of what happened in the past. I think Sam, the guy who didn't want to become worm food, stated it best: "I wasn't there." None of us were. But God was, and He told us how it happened in the book of Genesis.

It is also significant to note that when "evolutionary processes" are tested using *operational* science, they fail. (For example, after thousands of generations, fruit flies and bacteria are still fruit flies and bacteria).

I am not saying that evolutionists are bad scientists. Many of them are brilliant in their fields—which is evidenced in the amazing inventions modern science has provided. The problem arises when those scientists who are evolutionists do not differentiate between operational and historical science, using the *same authority* to discuss (or teach) both.

WHAT IS YOUR STARTING POINT?

How do intelligent scientists, who have created amazing inventions through operational science, come to such flawed conclusions about origins? It's because they are looking at the world through the wrong lenses—the wrong presuppositions. They *start* with the conclusion. They begin by concluding that there is no God and everything happened by chance over millions of years. Then they work backwards and produce an argument to make their case. They base their science on their conclusion, rather than their conclusion on their science.

Creationists have presuppositions too. We start with the Word of God. In fact, the Bible is our starting point for everything we know. God's Word is infallible, inerrant and perfect. Science textbooks change all the time. We need to start with the Bible and use the Bible to understand the world around us. Prevailing science standards may come and go, but true operational science will never invalidate the truth of the Bible.

SHAKING THE FAITH OF AN EVOLUTIONIST

For all of us who aren't scientists, we don't have to pretend we know all the answers. We don't need to spend the rest of our lives studying carbon dating and researching fossils in order to prove evolutionists wrong. Yet, I believe we *should* be able to discuss this topic with a basic degree of knowledge, because there are many "Rich's" in this world who simply need someone to help them see that science actually supports the Bible, not evolution.

Though science is not one of my strong points, I've learned that I don't need to be intimidated when talking with people who are more educated than I am in this area. I simply have to learn to ask good questions.

- How did life begin?
- If everything evolved from random chance processes, why do we find so much intelligence and beauty in the world around us?
- Where did the original matter come from?
- Why don't we find transitional fossils (missing links)?
- What about the second law of thermodynamics? (For example, everything is wearing out, not getting better.)

- What is the main reason you believe in evolution?
- What evidence do you have to support the idea that God does not exist?
- Why does evil bother you?
- Suppose God made a perfect world and then man broke it. What should God do?

When asked with the right attitude, questions show respect to the person with whom we are talking. Questions help us avoid coming across as arrogant or as if we are pretending to be an expert in something that is not our field—while still challenging others' thinking. Our goal is not to get into an argument, but to lead them to evaluate their own evolutionary foundation. It may only take one question they can't answer to cause them to walk away with new doubts about their faith in evolution. They will not likely admit that to us, but that's okay. It takes time.

A POSITIVE TERM GIVES CREDENCE TO A LIE.

Remember the story I said I'd come back to of the four girls in New Hampshire who didn't believe in God (pages 218-219)? Throughout the conversation, they brought up many scientific arguments. I didn't do a very good job answering all of their questions, but I explained that creationists and evolutionists look at the same evidence, yet come to different conclusions because they have different presuppositions. I referred to canyons, explaining that some people say the Grand Canyon was carved with a little water over a very long period of time. But *we* say it was carved with a lot of water in just a *little* time. We believe that it was the flood of Noah's day that formed the rock layers we see today.

For an example of this, we can look at the huge canyon that was formed at Mount St. Helens on March 19, 1982, after its crater lake catastrophically drained. This canyon has rock layers and steep sided walls—very similar to what we see in the Grand Canyon! We know exactly how long it took for that 140-foot-deep canyon at Mount St. Helens to be cut—and it wasn't millions of years. It took only hours.

Evolutionists say the Grand Canyon was formed by slow erosion over millions of years. But slow erosion leaves merely rounded hills. Only catastrophes cut steep-sided canyon walls.

I didn't explain all of this to the girls, but I shared the main points and they listened politely, with interest. Although they had initially expressed strong beliefs in evolution, they seemed willing to at least consider another way of looking at it.

"What do you guys think?" I asked, not wanting to do all the talking myself.

"You really know a lot about this stuff," one girl said.

Her answer surprised me. I felt I had done a very poor job articulating my positions. But apparently I had said enough to show them that I had at least thought about this before, and that *Christians had answers.*

ON THE WINNING SIDE

Some Christians are afraid of the issue of science, not wanting to "go there" in their conversations. Maybe they don't realize that the scientific evidence strongly argues for the truth of the Bible! Remember, God made the world that scientists investigate. Of course He can "get it right" in the book He wrote for us!

We do not judge Scripture by science as if science were the standard. Rather, God's Word is the standard that judges both history and science. If science and the Bible *were* in conflict, we would side with the Bible. But we do not need to make that decision because they are in harmony.

If you are not already familiar with the clear ways that science lines up perfectly with the record given in Genesis, I'd encourage you to research answers so you can share them with others.

Evolution is one of the "giants" our generation is facing. Like Goliath, evolutionary thinking defies and mocks the living God. It prevents many from trusting His Word. We need to be "Davids" and stand against this myth— for God's glory. Remember, David was only a young person. He wasn't a professional. He didn't have all the world's credentials. But he hated seeing God mocked, and he did something about it. He didn't wait for someone more "qualified." He took responsibility, exercised faith, and ran boldly to fight Goliath (1 Samuel 17:48). Though the world around us says God's Word is a joke, let us be "Davids," standing firm upon every verse.

"If I profess with the loudest voice and clearest exposition every portion of the Word of God except precisely that little point which the world and the devil are at that moment attacking, I am not confessing Christ, however boldly I may be professing Him ... Where the battle rages there the loyalty of the soldier is proved; and to be steady on all the battle front besides is mere flight and disgrace if he flinches at that point."—commonly attributed to Martin Luther

The evidence is on our side. The Creator is on our side. The cause couldn't be greater—God's glory and lost souls. Let's take the offense in this battle and rescue people from false ideas, "casting down imaginations, and every high thing that exalteth itself against the knowledge of God, and bringing into captivity every thought to the obedience of Christ" (2 Corinthians 10:5).

THE GOSPEL REMAINS PRIMARY

Our chief goal is not merely to combat error, but to establish truth. To win someone to Christ, we do not need to knock down their evolutionary views first. Once they come to Christ, everything else will begin to come into focus as God changes their thinking (Romans 12:1-2). As useful as creation science is in witnessing, people don't come to Jesus through scientific debates. Rather, "faith cometh by hearing, and hearing by the Word of God" (Romans 10:17). Creation science is a useful tool to lay the foundational concepts that there is a Creator and the Creator's Word is trustworthy, but our main focus should always be on the Creator Himself—Jesus Christ. I have found that if I begin talking with people about how design points to a Designer, it usually doesn't take long for them to agree with me that God exists. Then we move on to the gospel, not getting bogged down in debate.

So how much should we talk about creation science when we are witnessing? Honestly, I do not frequently find myself debating science at length with unbelievers, nor do I think it accomplishes very much on its own. It varies from case to case, and I have a lot to learn, but here's what I typically do: Once I establish the fact that God exists, I usually move on to discuss the problem of sin and the solution found in Christ. However, if they continue to use evolution as a reason for not believing the Bible, then I'll explain a few of the ways that science is consistent with the Bible, not with evolution. Often they have not thought of these things. Or sometimes I'll say, "I know you aren't completely sure that there is a God, but could we just assume there is for the sake of the conversation?" And then, as we go on to talk about sin, guess what? Their own conscience is another testimony to the reality of the existence of God. Let me illustrate.

"I BELIEVE WE CAME FROM THE APES ... "

"I believe we came from the apes," a teen girl at the park told me, "and when we die, that's it."

Her friend, who looked about seventeen, explained that all the evil in the world makes him think there isn't a God. He described a tragic assault situation and asked, "Why wouldn't God have just stopped that and not let it happen? I feel sorry for anyone who has to live in this world."

"The thing is, guys," I told them, "you have to ask yourself, *'Why does evil bother me so much?'* Why does it make you so upset to hear about such horrible injustice? *That* in itself is evidence that there is a God, and that He made us in His image. Those things happen in the animal world all the time and it doesn't bother *them!*"

"That's a good point," the girl who claimed to believe the ape theory replied.

You see, even if people deny God's existence, they still have a conscience—and this is another strong evidence of a Creator. Instead of debating science, we can aim to "bypass the intellect," so to speak, and talk directly to their conscience. Romans 2:15 explains that unbelievers have "the law written in their hearts, their conscience also bearing witness." Their own conscience is proof that they were created in the image of God. Watch how this plays out in the next story.

THEIR OWN CONSCIENCE IS PROOF OF A CREATOR!

"Evolution is pretty much a proven fact," a college student, Carter, told Sarah. He and his friend, both atheists, were sitting on a bench studying together.

"How do you believe life started?" Sarah asked.

"Well, one theory I have is that the big bang loops and continues."

"But how did it *start?*" Sarah asked again.

"It's eternal," Carter replied.

Notice that Carter believed, by faith, that matter is eternal. And Sarah believes, by faith, that God is eternal. Sarah pointed this out to him: "So both of our beliefs are based on faith. Neither of us can actually 'prove' it to the other."

He agreed.

Having laid this foundational point, Sarah decided to switch topics and address the issue of sin, speaking to his conscience. She took Carter through the "good person test" (the Ten Commandments). They talked about lying, stealing, blasphemy, and anger.

"Do you know what God did for you so that you don't have to go to Hell?" Sarah asked.

With disdain in his voice, he said, "Yeah, Jesus died on the cross."

(Carter and his friend both said they had bad experiences in their Catholic/Lutheran high schools.)

"But did you know that it was actually a legal transaction that was taking place?" Sarah said. "Jesus died in our place. The fine has been paid; now we can go free!"

Then Sarah noticed something that surprised her: Carter had started shaking very visibly. He noticed too and seemed embarrassed.

"Sorry, I'm cold," he said.

However, he had just been studying outside and he wasn't shaking before! Though Carter claimed he didn't even believe in God, hearing the Law of God still had a profound effect on him. In fact, it caused him to become *more* interested in what Sarah was saying. Instead of "reasoning with his intellect," Sarah had spoken directly to his heart through his conscience.

"How bad could someone be and still be saved?" Carter wanted to know next. *Interesting question for someone who doesn't believe in God, don't you think?*

Sarah explained that the blood of Jesus covers everything, but if one is truly saved, his faith will be evident by his life. She continued, "The only reason we are out here today is because we care about where people spend eternity. If we truly believe Heaven and Hell are real and don't share the truth, we would be extremely selfish."

As they ended the conversation, Carter reached out and shook Sarah's hand. "Thank you for a good talk. I appreciate your willingness to discuss these things in a rational way," he said warmly.

"I was going to say the exact same thing to you," Sarah replied.

How many students are there like Carter who, if challenged by a loving Christian who has answers, would begin to question their own belief system? How many, when confronted with truth, would choose to embrace it? What do we have to lose by at least *trying* to speak with them?

May we be grieved for their condition, and may this embolden our generation to speak, as Paul was stirred up to witness in the city of Athens. "Now while Paul waited for them at Athens, his spirit was stirred in him, when he saw the city wholly given to idolatry. Therefore disputed he in the synagogue with the Jews, and with the devout persons, and in the market daily with them that met with him" (Acts 17:16-17).

CHAPTER 15

HOW WE KNOW THAT WE KNOW

Meet Kyle. He's a fictitious character representing a young man in our generation. He's a junior in high school. A smart guy. Likable. Into sports. And lost. His parents are divorced and there is a lot of tension in his home—but, even so, he considers his family to be better than most. He goes to church occasionally when he's living with his mom.

The main thing I want you to understand about Kyle is that he has been brainwashed. That sounds extreme, but it's true. Kyle has literally been *indoctrinated* with humanistic thinking and anti-God ideas. As he sits in school, watches TV, interacts with friends online, and listens to music, he doesn't even realize that the philosophies of this world are molding his thinking. He has been saturated in an ungodly culture that calls evil good and good evil. Though he doesn't realize it, all of this has left him very confused. The subtle (and not-so-subtle) messages of the world have conditioned him into believing the idea that it's up to him to decide what is right.

Before discussing more about the life of Kyle, let's talk about the epidemic from which he is suffering—the idea that man creates truth.

I was sitting in a hotel lobby in Atlanta, Georgia, waiting for my family to be ready to leave. A man sitting nearby saw the Bible in my lap and asked, "Are you part of a Bible study group?"

"Oh, I just like to read my Bible," I replied with a smile.

"What denomination are you?" he asked.

"Not really a specific denomination—I just believe the Bible. What about you?"

"I grew up in church," he said, explaining a little about his childhood.

"So do you think Heaven is a free gift or something you have to earn?" I asked.

"The church I grew up in would say you have to earn it," he said.

"But what do you think?" I asked.

"You have to earn it," he replied.

"So, if you have to earn it, your faith is in yourself, right?" I asked.

"Well, I suppose … " he agreed, but then he mentioned that everyone's standards are different. "It's not fair to judge others by your own standard," he explained, "because maybe they have had a different background than you."

"Well," Sarah (who had just joined our conversation) replied, "maybe *God* has a standard and, although we can't judge each other by our own standards, God can judge us by His perfect standard."

"Well, that *could* be," he agreed, "but I think that you have to think about everyone's different background. What is true for one person might not be true for another."

"So do you believe there is any kind of absolute truth?" Sarah asked.

"No, I don't think there is," he said, after a moment of thought.

"So you believe everything is relative?" Sarah asked.

"Yeah, pretty much," he replied.

"Are you sure about that?" Sarah asked.

"No, I'm not really sure, but I heard some people on TV talking about how all of God's Word is subject to man's interpretation," he said, "and everyone has a different interpretation."

"It's true that there are many people who are trying to discredit the Word of God," Sarah replied, "but I've never heard any piece of evidence that contradicts the Bible."

"Well, there are theologians that will back me up," he said.

"Yes, and there are also theologians that will back me up," Sarah replied playfully.

"And that just goes to prove that everything is relative," he said.

"No, that just goes to prove that some people are right and some people are wrong," Sarah said with a laugh.

He scratched his head, glanced out the window, and complained that this was too heavy of a conversation to have at ten in the morning. Just then his ride came. He shook our hands, asked our names, and took the booklet we gave him.

This man is similar to Kyle in his thinking. He is believing a wrong concept that our culture is teaching. Let's think about his statement: "What is true for one person might not be true for another." Is this a correct way to think? Well, if you are talking about your favorite color, maybe. But if you are talking about historical fact, of course it's not. What happened, happened! Caesar Augustus ruled the Roman Empire. Someone may doubt that Caesar Augustus existed, but we have evidence which confirms that he did. Someone may doubt that Jesus Christ was raised from the dead, but we have irrefutable evidence to support the fact that He did. The truth is the truth whether you believe it or not.

DID MAN REALLY GO TO THE MOON?

Last fall as we were roofing our house, my dad began a conversation with the man who was delivering the dumpster. They began talking about how the world is changing. The delivery man told my dad that his boys came to him, saying, "Dad, did you know that we never actually sent anyone to the moon?"

Shocked by their absurd claim, he replied, "What do you mean, 'We never sent anyone to the moon'?"

"We didn't land on the moon," they repeated. "It was all a hoax."

"Where did you hear this?" he asked.

"The Internet," they replied.

"We are going to talk to your uncle about this," he told his boys. "Your uncle worked on that project."

This father explained to my dad that he actually had to have his boys call their uncle to get the real story.

Now, most people don't doubt the reality that men walked on the moon. Instead, they doubt realities that are even more obvious: they doubt that the beauty and complexity we see around us has a Designer. They doubt that truth

THEORY MEETS REALITY

even exists. This leaves them without ground to stand on when it comes to determining what is good and what is evil.

IF YOU CAN'T BE WRONG, YOU CAN'T BE RIGHT

An unsaved friend and I rode the gravel trail through the woods near my house. The bike ride was calm and peaceful, but in my mind I was wrestling. *How can I transition into a spiritual discussion with her?* I wondered. I knew that my friend and I had completely different worldviews, and it was hard to find common ground. I was glad when the conversation turned to the history she'd been studying in school.

"What is your basis for defining right and wrong?" I asked her.

My friend didn't believe in God or the Bible, so she claimed that morality was shaped by culture and the laws of the land.

But consider the implications of that belief. What if your culture was Germany in the 1940s, and the new "law of the land" was to exterminate a certain people group? Does that make it right?

My friend and I both agreed that the Holocaust was a terrible thing, but she had no foundation upon which to base such a conclusion.

In an atheistic world there would be no evil—because there would be no standard of good. We distinguish evil by comparing it with good, just as we distinguish a crooked stick by comparing it with a straight one. But if there is no God, then there is no standard of good. "Good" could be whatever you want it to be. "Good" could be ridding the world of "inferior" people, or torturing someone, or killing unborn babies. In a world without God, one would be forced to say, "If that's what you think good is, then on what basis can I tell you it's wrong? Even though *I* don't think it's good to kill babies, what makes my opinion better than yours?"

So, how do we really know that we know anything? How do we know for *sure* what is right and what is wrong? We need a standard—a "perfectly straight stick" to which we can compare everything.

Jesus is the truth. HE is the standard by which all else is measured. He is the Designer and the Creator.

People who are opposed to God want to eliminate the idea of an absolute standard of "good" by which their actions will be measured. That's why the idea that "everything is relative" is saturating our generation. According to the Barna Group, nearly two thirds of Americans deny that absolute truth exists.[1] In other words, two thirds of Americans are saying, "No one can know anything for sure." The guy on the couch at the hotel who claimed that what was right for him might not be right for someone else was simply repeating what he had been taught. Our fictional character, Kyle, has been taught the same thing. When people do not think for themselves but simply accept the beliefs of the culture, they are brainwashed. When they deny that truth exists, they feel the liberty to make up their own "truth" instead. That's comparable to writing a fantasy story and labeling it "true," just because you believe it!

This reminds me of a conversation I once had with a lady who introduced herself as a local pastor. I asked her, "Let's say a friend of yours was stabbed and had only three minutes to live. They knew they were going to Hell, but they wanted to know how to go to Heaven. What would you say to them?"

"I would just comfort them," she said.

"But they are going to Hell!" I repeated.

"I don't believe in Hell," she said.

"Really? So you don't believe the Bible?" I asked, surprised.

"I believe that we need to interpret what the Bible says by how it fits into today's culture—and to understand that at the time the Bible was written things were very different than they are today … such as the roles of men and women … "

"Well, Jesus talked about Hell, so He obviously wanted us to know about it," I said.

The lady pastor continued to explain that the Bible is subject to man's interpretation. She stated, "*My* God would never send people to Hell. He is full of mercy … "

I tried to express (respectfully) that our personal opinions do not matter. "What matters is what is true," I told her. "But you have a position of leadership and a large influence. If you are telling everyone that there is no Hell—"

"I don't tell them that," she interrupted. "I tell them about a God who loves them unconditionally, who will continue to give them second chances over and over again, who cares for them, who is full of grace … "

"Then you are creating a god who doesn't exist. It doesn't matter what god you'd *like* to believe in—"

"Or what *you* would like to believe in," she inserted.

"Sure," I agreed, "what matters is who God really *is!* No one stands in the middle of the highway and says, 'I don't believe in semi trucks.' If you don't tell people about Hell, it's like not telling a person who has cancer about his situation. Yes—God's grace is the cure, but people don't want a cure unless they know they are in danger!"

At this point she needed to go.

This lady was putting her intellect above God's Word, making herself the one who determines its true meaning for today. When people do this, they can twist and stretch it any way they want. And who knows where it will end?

"I GET TO PICK WHAT IS TRUE"

My dad and I brought our laptops to a coffee shop, hoping to get away from distractions and get some writing done. Well, that was the idea at least. It worked for the first five minutes until I noticed the words "World Religions" on a thick, yellow textbook sitting on the table next to ours. I pointed it out to my dad.

"How do you like your book on world religions?" my dad asked the guy who sat down at that table with his drink a few minutes later.

"It's great," he said. "I'm learning a lot and I think it's really going to improve my life."

"They're a lot different, aren't they!" I commented.

"Yeah," he replied, "but it's amazing how compatible they are—except for a few extremists."

"Well, the key issue is *who is God*," my dad said.

"Or *what* is God," Scott replied.

"So, one has to determine whether God is a person, or some kind of force," my dad responded.

"Well, you don't have to decide; it doesn't matter," Scott said.

"What's your definition of truth?" I asked.

He didn't seem to have one.

"Well, there are some basic underlying concepts that need to be identified and understood," my dad explained. "One is the identity of God. Another is eternity. Another is what God has revealed to us … "

Scott didn't seem very interested in hearing our thoughts. Instead, he shared the "fascinating" things he was learning about Buddhist priest traditions and other religions. It soon became evident that he was happy with all the religions *except* Christianity.

"So have you picked one?" my dad asked.

"You know, I'm happy with all of them," he said. "I don't feel like I have to pick one."

"That sounds similar to situational ethics," my dad said. "What you are saying is something like, 'Everyone should do what is right in his own eyes'" (Judges 21:25).

"Yeah, that's right," Scott said. "I think religion can really benefit people. It brings people together so that when bad things happen, people are there for you."

We made a few comments encouraging him to consider the importance of eternity—not simply our current life on earth.

"No offense to you guys or anything," Scott told us, "but Christians are

always trying to convert people and spread their beliefs."
Happy with all the religions ... except for one.

Scott didn't want anyone telling him the truth. He wanted the power to choose what was true for himself. The problem is, it doesn't work that way. What is true is true, whether you like it or not. Some laws apply to all of us, such as gravity. Even though one might claim he doesn't believe in gravity, he still cannot jump off a 100-story building and be okay.

No matter how much one may want to change the truth, he can't. I could believe that astronauts didn't go to the moon, but they did. I could believe there's not a Hell, but there is. I could believe that God is like a Santa Claus-figure who lets everyone into Heaven, but He's not. God is not whoever people desire or imagine Him to be. God told Moses, "I AM THAT I AM."

One day every knee will bow and every tongue confess that Jesus Christ is Lord. If only Scott would do that now!

REVEALING ERROR GENTLY

Many claim that there is no truth ("absolutes"), but Scripture says about these people that they are "ever learning, and never able to come to the knowledge of the truth" (2 Timothy 3:7).

When the man in the hotel lobby told Sarah and me that everything is relative, he was confused. You see, if everything were relative, then the statement, "everything is relative" would also be relative. It would be impossible to make a statement that was absolutely true. In other words, everything cannot possibly be relative. The very statement refutes itself.

A great way to help a person see the error of their relativistic thinking is to simply respond with good questions. Here are a few examples:

- "There is no truth." — Are you sure that's true?
- "You cannot know truth." —Then how do you know *that?*
- "There are no absolutes." — Are you absolutely sure?
- "What's true for me is not true for you." — Do you mean that statement to be true for just you, or true for everybody?
- "You shouldn't judge others." — If judging others is bad, then why did you just judge me?[2]

Sometimes it takes time for a person to recognize the error in his thinking and begin to search for truth. But when their search begins, we need to be ready to give an answer for the hope that is within us.

"I AM COMPLETELY CERTAIN THAT NO ONE CAN BE COMPLETELY CERTAIN."

PILATE'S QUESTION

All right, let's jump back to Kyle now. Whether he realizes it or not, he's bombarded 24/7 with relativistic thinking and humanistic agendas. What does he think about all of this? Well, to be honest, one of Kyle's problems is that he's *not* thinking about it. If he was, he would realize that he cannot be sure that everything is relative. In fact, he cannot be sure about anything, because he already believes that nothing is for sure.

You see, Kyle is only hearing what he *wants* to hear. Why is the idea of "relative truth" what he wants to hear? It's simple. He is a sinner. He knows he is guilty. He has lied, stolen and cheated in school. In Kyle's case, he is also struggling with some addictions (though he wouldn't call them that himself), and he knows he is not living up to God's standards. Rather than dealing with the sin, it is easier, for now, to simply believe there is no god. Because of this, the evolution he is taught in school is very appealing. It's a belief that allows him to justify his lifestyle.

As we look at Kyle's daily routine, we see that his life is constantly full of "noise." But in the very rare moments when all is quiet, thoughts about God, eternity, and his Christian grandma come into his mind. They make him feel very uncomfortable, so he turns on his music. He concludes, *Well, how could you ever know which religion is true anyway?*

Good question! At least Kyle has admitted to the possibility of "true" and "untrue." He is asking, "What is truth?" That's exactly what Pilate asked Jesus. The problem is, Pilate didn't listen for an answer. Hopefully, Kyle will.

WHAT ABOUT ALL THE OTHER RELIGIONS?

Let's consider Kyle's question: "How can one know that Christianity is true and all the other religions are false?" Kyle has heard people claim that all the religions are very similar and it doesn't matter what you believe, as long as you don't hurt anybody.

What he does not yet understand is that, although the various world religions have similarities at some points, Christianity falls into a completely different category. In fact, it isn't a religion at all—it's a relationship. A *religion* is a system of ritual, belief and self-effort. Christianity is a personal relationship with our Creator, Jesus Christ.

No other individual in the universe is more spectacular or desirable than God. A personal relationship with *Him* is the best thing imaginable. Only He could make such a relationship possible—and He has!

Jesus has credentials that make all the religions crumble to ashes. Let's talk about what Kyle would find if he took the time to investigate who Jesus is.

Jesus Conquered Death. Muhammad, Buddha, Confucius, Joseph Smith, and the other religious leaders are dead. Jesus *conquered* death! Jesus is alive.

Jesus Fulfilled Prophecy. Jesus fulfilled hundreds of specific predictions which even His *critics* concede predate Him by hundreds of years.

Jesus Alone is Both God and Man. Therefore, He is qualified to be a mediator between both parties.

Jesus is Sinless. He is the only Man who perfectly fulfilled the Law of God. His record of righteousness is now stamped upon those who believe in Him.

Jesus is Our Savior. He does not merely teach, lead or help us. He *saves* us!

Jesus Offers Pardon. Because of His substitutionary death for us, He is the only One who is able to justly erase our criminal record.

Jesus Changes Hearts. Other religions may change people's behavior, but Jesus gives us a new heart.

Jesus Offers Assurance. Most people are always striving to pass the "good enough" mark, but they never know if they have. The truth is, they never could. However, because our trust is not in ourselves but in the finished and sufficient work of Christ, we as Christians have assurance of eternal life.

Jesus is unparalleled. Indescribable. He is the " ... theme to a million love songs, hero to a thousand stories ... the most talked about, preached about, debated about, lied about, fought about Man in history ... "[3] He created the universe and named the stars, yet He washed men's feet in the apparel of a slave. He sees the nations as a drop in the bucket, yet He sympathizes mercifully with our individual weaknesses and needs. He stumps the greatest scholars and baffles the wisest men, yet He associates with the lowly and values the praises of little children.

The most important question each man or woman must answer is, *How will I respond to Jesus Christ?* There is no middle ground. You are either on His side or you aren't (John 3:36).

THE "MANY PATHS" MYTH

When Jesus was on earth, He was clear and bold about His identity. In fact, the claims He made about Himself would be considered outrageous—except for the fact that they are true. He claimed to be the fulfillment of the law and the prophets, greater than Moses and Abraham, the Son of God, and Judge of all. He said that He Himself is THE way, the truth and the life. He said that no one comes to the Father *except* by Him (John 14:6). Extreme and narrow-minded? Absolutely! Yet think about it: if one could attain peace with God through Buddhism, Islam or another religion, then Jesus would not have had to die on the cross. If there was *any other way* our sins could have been forgiven, then Christ's death on the cross was unnecessary (Galatians 2:21).

Why do many of the religions of the world look nice on the surface? It's because that's exactly how the enemy wants them to look. He makes counterfeit paths to God seem attractive to divert people from the truth. Remember, Satan will often incorporate some truth into a lie to make the lie look good.

How much do we need to know about other religions in order to witness to those who follow them? We do not need to know every lie in the world in order to recognize error. There is no need to be highly educated in all their false ideas. If we are grounded in the truth, we will recognize lies.

However, it can be very beneficial to have a basic knowledge of what others believe. It may help us to know what questions to ask so we can steer the conversation in the right direction. It will also give us a better idea of what concepts to focus on. But even if we don't know much about the false religion of the person we are talking with, we can simply ask him to explain what he believes and why he believes it.

One thing makes it easy when witnessing to people of other religions. They all have a common denominator: self-effort. They are "do" religions. When it comes to Christianity, however, the theme word is "done." Christianity is not based on what we do, but on what Jesus has already done for us.

We don't have to knock down all of the errors of other religions before we present Jesus. No matter whom we are talking to, they need to hear the same message: God created us. Our sin separates us from Him. Jesus alone provides a way for us to be forgiven and reconciled to God.

THE "YOU SHALL NOT SURELY DIE" LIE

Though we don't have space in this book to discuss all the world religions, let's talk about one belief that is an increasingly "trendy" view that young people in our generation love to claim: reincarnation.

It was the Fourth of July—a perfect day to gather a team to witness to the thousands of bored people waiting for fireworks.

"I feel so tired," I told Sarah as we arrived at the location where the fireworks were being held. Neither of us felt like even getting out of the van. After some discussion, prayer, and dark chocolate, we still didn't feel like getting out of the van. But, here we were. *[smile]*

As I've mentioned before, the first conversation is usually the hardest! Once we got going, though, we had a great time—and looking back we see that the Lord definitely supplied the strength we needed that day.

I started out by walking up to three teens on a bench, asking them if they'd like to take my Fourth of July questionnaire.

"Why not?" they replied.

After I asked a couple of patriotic questions to break the ice, I told them, "The next question is, what do you think happens when you die?"

"I'm Buddhist and I believe in reincarnation," one of the girls, Shannon, replied.

"Oh, okay. Why are you Buddhist?" I asked.

"I was born into a Buddhist family."

"What were you in your last life?" I asked.

"I don't know. I don't think it's really possible to remember," she replied.

"What will you be in your next life?" I asked.

"Probably a dog—my dog and I are so much alike, it's amazing."

"Are you the one who gets to pick what new body you get when you die?"

"Um, no, not really ... " she said.

"So, there is some force or power out there who decides what you'll be?"

"Kind of, I guess," Shannon said.

"So, that 'force' or 'power' would have to know you really well—including all the thoughts and intents of your heart, right? Because 'it' would have to see everything you've done (as well as your motives for doing it) and then decide what kind of body you deserve."

"Yeah, I guess so," Shannon said, her tone of voice indicating that she had never thought of this before.

"And not only that, this 'power' would have to be all-powerful, because 'it' would have to be able to recreate you (and everyone else in the world) into something else."

She agreed.

"Also, this 'power' would need to have a perfect sense of morality in order to know who was truly good and who was evil, so 'it' could judge everything perfectly, right?"

Shannon told me she didn't understand how it worked; she simply believed that she would go into the ground and her spirit would then somehow become something else.

As you can see, for reincarnation to work, it would require an 'entity' who is omnipotent, omniscient and omnipresent—a righteous judge with a perfect standard. Does this description remind you of anyone? It describes the God of the Bible, and He has already told us of His intentions in dealing with man. (And I'm glad it isn't to be continually recreating them into other creatures!) God's plan is for us to *truly* start over and be "born again," not into another creature, but into His own family—to be His child forever!

Most world religions are actually rooted in the original lies Satan told Eve in the garden. For example, the lie behind reincarnation goes right back to the words, "You shall not surely die ... " (Genesis 3:4). Believing in reincarnation is a way to try to avoid the harsh reality of death. That is, at least for a little while—and only in your mind. But the Bible says, "It is appointed unto men once to die, but after this the judgment" (Hebrews 9:27).

Obviously, Shannon's beliefs about reincarnation and the message of the Bible cannot both be true, because they make opposite claims. There can only be one correct answer—and she wouldn't want to be wrong! But Shannon didn't want to reason. She just wanted to believe what she believed. That's okay, right? We can let people believe what they want to believe, can't we? I mean, if it works for them, it's fine. Right? Wrong! For us who know the truth, that's like seeing a blind person walk off a cliff and not shouting a warning to them.

Okay, back to Kyle. One day in the cafeteria, another guy in his class, Joel, sat down across the table from him. Kyle knew Joel was one of the football players, so he thought it was kind of cool to get acquainted. After discussing the last school football game, they began talking about the recent car wreck of a fellow student. This led into a conversation about why a good God allows bad things to happen. Joel mentioned that the suffering in this world isn't God's "fault," but rather a consequence of sin. He referred back to the first sin committed by Adam and Eve.

Adam and Eve? Kyle thought. *Joel actually believes in Adam and Eve?* Intrigued, he decided to voice his question.

"But how do you know the Bible is true?" Kyle asked. This question always gnawed at his mind when he heard stuff about God. He had heard a lot of arguments against the Bible: *Wasn't it just written by men? Doesn't it contradict itself? What about science? Hasn't the text been distorted over the years—like a game of telephone?*

Joel answered Kyle with a question that had never entered Kyle's mind before. He said, "If God can create the universe and sustain it through the ages, don't you think He can preserve His Book?"

Kyle had never thought of it that way.

Now, let me tell you something about Joel. Joel has five friends from his youth group who also go to the same high school. After praying for their school at a youth meeting one Friday night, they had a radical idea: "Let's try to talk to everyone in our class about Jesus this year." It would take a lot of time ... and courage ... but they decided to go for it. Sometimes they'd use questionnaires, sometimes plan events after school, sometimes just hang out with kids—and sometimes, during the lunch break, they'd sit with students they didn't know very well and get acquainted. Thus, Joel meets Kyle today.

Joel finds it convenient that most high schoolers voice the same arguments. He has already answered this question about trusting the Bible several dozen times. For this reason, he's studied it quite a bit and has many things to explain to Kyle. Actually, Joel loves it when people ask this question because there are so many good answers and it's such an important foundation to establish.

HOW DO WE KNOW THE BIBLE IS TRUE?

Satan's strategy, from the beginning, has been to attack God's Word. He asked Eve, "Yea, hath God said … ?" (Genesis 3:1). Throughout history, Satan has tried to destroy the Bible, produce counterfeits, and spread lies about God's Word. Yet he will never succeed, because the Bible is an indestructible book.

Despite what people claim, the Bible has not been passed down through the ages like a game of telephone. Translators have worked from reliable ancient Greek and Hebrew manuscripts.

The discovery of the Dead Sea Scrolls, found in a cave at Qumran in Israel in 1947, confirms without question the precision with which the texts of the Old Testament have been preserved. The scrolls (dated about 200 B.C.) were about 1,000 years older than any other Old Testament manuscript we had, yet they contained no significant differences.[4]

People don't seem to have trouble trusting the accuracy of other ancient books. They don't doubt the existence of Julius Caesar or the historical information in his book *Gallic Wars,* even though only ten ancient manuscripts remain. People generally accept the credibility of Plato, even though there are only seven remaining ancient copies of his writings. In contrast, do you know how many extant early manuscripts of the New Testament we have? Over 20,000 copies or fragments! Even more significant is the incredible consistency within these ancient manuscripts. They are considered to be 98.3% in agreement with each other, and the 1.7% represent only minor differences that do not affect doctrine.[5]

THE WITNESSES AGREE

God has given us an overwhelming amount of evidence to confirm that the historical facts recorded in Scripture are true (Acts 1:3). Some people may argue, "I only believe what can be proven scientifically," but remember, we don't prove historical fact by observational science. We don't prove by *science* that Jesus died and rose from the dead any more than we prove by science that Alexander the Great conquered the world. Rather, when confirming history, we look at recorded evidence. We look to witnesses—just like a jury does in court. If the testimonies of the witnesses agree, we trust their report.

The writers of the New Testament were eyewitnesses. They had known, talked and walked with Jesus, and they frequently remind their readers of this (Luke 1:2; 2 Peter 1:16; 1 John 1:1). Jesus had been well known in Israel. Thousands of people had listened to Him teach and observed His miracles. If the disciples had been teaching made-up stories about Christ, many people who knew the truth were still alive and could have easily refuted their claims.

Yet, thousands believed and within 50 years Christianity had spread across the whole Mediterranean world.

Speaking of consistency in witnesses, the Bible was written down by over 40 individuals, and their testimonies agree perfectly. Not only that, these writers lived over a span of about 1,500 years on three different continents and wrote in three different languages. Yet, the Bible fits together like a perfectly woven tapestry. How is this possible? It's simple—though there were 40 writers, there is only one Author: God.

HISTORICAL AND ARCHAEOLOGICAL EVIDENCE

Evidence found outside the Bible is also consistent with what the Bible describes. For example, Tacitus, a Roman historian, and Josephus, a Jewish historian, who both lived shortly after the time of Christ, wrote about Jesus. In addition, over 25,000 archaeological finds provide evidence confirming specific people and locations mentioned in the Bible. In fact, a renowned Jewish archaeologist, Nelson Glueck, stated, *"No archaeological discovery has ever controverted a biblical reference."* [6]

The combination of all of these facts shout a loud proclamation about the Bible's authenticity!

But that's not all. God has provided another piece of evidence that is simply mind boggling: fulfilled prophecy.

FULFILLED PROPHECY

The Old Testament contains hundreds of detailed prophecies that have been fulfilled down to the smallest detail.[7] No other religious book can even *begin* to make such a claim! A few of them are listed on the next page.

Foretold & Fulfilled

Date Spoken:	Prophecy:
1500 B.C. (Approximately)	He would come from the tribe of Judah (Genesis 49:10).
626-586 B.C.	He would be a descendant of King David (Jeremiah 23:5).
750-686 B.C.	He would be born in Bethlehem (Micah 5:2).
701-681 B.C.	The Messiah would be born of a virgin (Isaiah 7:14).
750-686 B.C.	He would go to Egypt (Hosea 11:1).
701-681 B.C.	He would perform miracles (Isaiah 35:4-6).
520-518 B.C.	He would enter Jerusalem on a donkey (Zechariah 9:9).
520-518 B.C.	He would be betrayed for 30 pieces of silver (Zechariah 11:12).
701-681 B.C.	He would be silent before His accusers (Isaiah 53:7).
701-681 B.C.	He would be numbered with the transgressors (Isaiah 53:12).
1,000 B.C.	He would be pierced through His hands and feet (Psalm 22:16).
701-681 B.C.	He would be buried in a rich man's tomb (Isaiah 53:9).
1,000 B.C.	He would rise from the dead (Psalm 16:10).

Yes, we can trust the Bible. If you want to say it in a nutshell, consider how author and speaker Voddie Baucham explains why he believes the Bible: *"I choose to believe the Bible because it is a reliable collection of historical documents written by eyewitnesses during the lifetime of other eyewitnesses. They record supernatural events that took place in fulfillment of specific prophecies and claimed that their writings were divine rather than human in origin."* [8]

MOST POPULAR BOOK, MOST HATED BOOK

One of the best ways to answer objections is to ask a question in return. We don't need to prove the Bible is true—we can let others try to prove it is not.

- Can you show me any errors in the Bible?
- Where did you hear that it wasn't true?
- If God created the world, isn't He able to preserve His book?
- Since the Bible is the best-selling book of all time, don't you think you should at least take a look at it?
- Have you ever read the Bible yourself? How much of it have you read? What part did you like the best?

Let me explain another reason why Kyle is confused about the Bible. At school Kyle is taught scientific "facts" about origins which directly contradict what the Bible says. As a kid in Sunday school he was taught the stories of Adam and Eve, the flood, and David and Goliath ... but now he wonders if any of that actually happened. You see, at church he just hears *stories*. At school he is learning proven *facts*. At least, that's what he thinks. No one at church is answering the dozens of questions accumulating in the back of his mind. *How did Noah fit the animals in the ark? Why would a loving God send anyone to Hell? Where did Cain get his wife? Doesn't carbon dating prove that the world is billions of years old? What about the dinosaurs? Why is there so much suffering in the world? What about all the people who have never heard about Jesus?*

As Kyle continues to hang out with Joel, he is amazed that Christians **do** have answers to each of these questions. Never before did Kyle realize that the Bible and science are consistent. Never before did he know that one could take the Bible at face value—from cover to cover.

Joel did something each one of us should be doing: he answered Kyle's questions. He gave a true, genuine defense for the Christian faith, as 1 Peter 3:15 tells us to do. Not only that, Joel shared with Kyle how Jesus Christ had radically changed his own life. Kyle can see the difference in Joel's life. He knows he doesn't have what Joel has, but he is beginning to want it more and more.

You see, yet another evidence for the truth of the Bible is our personal testimony of how much God's Word has changed our lives and continues to change us daily! Our testimony speaks powerfully to others—often even more loudly than apologetic facts. However, it should not be our only piece of evidence. A Mormon could tell you that the Book of Mormon changed his life, but that doesn't make the Book of Mormon the Word of God.

GENESIS 1:1 AND JOHN 3:16

While filling sandbags in the middle of the night to help our city of Cedar Rapids during the flood of 2008, I found myself in an interesting mix of people who had volunteered to help with the crisis. We began having a friendly debate on religious topics which continued as the hours passed. In the heat of the discussion (about 3:00 a.m.), a guy named Nick came over to help us load more sandbags onto the pallet, and wanted to know what we were talking about. I asked him, "Do you think the Bible is 100% accurate?"

"Well, I'd better believe that," he stated. "Otherwise, how would I know what was true and what wasn't?"

I was thinking, *Good answer!* And I was glad that the other sandbaggers heard his answer as well.

On another occasion I received a very different answer from a girl named Mackenzie—a biology major I met on a college campus. She told me, "I'm a Christian, but I don't completely trust the Bible. Like, how could Noah have fit all the animals into the ark?"

Mackenzie was putting greater faith in her teachers than in God's Word. But let's think about this: if Mackenzie can't trust Genesis, how can she trust the rest of the Bible? She claimed to believe that Jesus died for her sins. But if she doesn't believe what God said about Noah and the ark, how can she believe what God said about Jesus' death and resurrection? It's all part of the same book! In fact, Jesus Himself referred to Noah by name (Luke 17:27). Mackenzie is essentially basing her entire destiny on what she considers to be a "flawed" book!

If we are not standing firmly on the beginning of God's Word, neither can we stand firmly on the end. We don't get to pick and choose. It's all or none.

And for the record, how many animals were on the ark? There were probably about 16,000 land-dwelling animals—one pair of each "kind." In his book, *Noah's Ark: A Feasibility Study*, John Woodmorappe explains that "less than half the cumulative area of the Ark's three decks need to have been occupied by the animals and their enclosures."[9] This means the rest of the space could have been used for food, fresh water, and supplies.

THE LION DEFENDS ITSELF

Charles Spurgeon once said, "The Word of God is like a lion. You don't have to defend a lion. All you have to do is let the lion loose, and the lion will defend itself."

Although Scripture tells us to be *prepared* to give a defense for the gospel (Philippians 1:7; 1 Peter 3:15), there is something that is even more powerful than explaining evidence to people. It's when people encounter the Word of God for themselves. Most people choose to believe the Bible, not because of an intellectual debate on its credibility, but because they are confronted with its powerful words and the Holy Spirit uses it to bring conviction to their hearts. "For the word of God is quick [living], and powerful, and sharper than any two-edged sword, piercing even to the dividing asunder of soul and spirit, and of the joints and marrow, and is a discerner of the thoughts and intents of the heart" (Hebrews 4:12).

Yes—we should be able to defend the Bible's authenticity, but we don't have to prove the Bible is true before we use it. In fact, one of the best ways to prove it is to *use it* and watch the results! Remember, "faith cometh by hearing, and hearing by the word of God" (Romans 10:17).

"KYLES" ARE EVERYWHERE

I want to conclude this chapter by telling you a few more things about Kyle. Even though Kyle says he does not believe in God, he does. As Joel spends more time with him, he can see this plainly. For one thing, Kyle is angry with God. How can you be angry with someone you don't believe in?

Kyle has a godly grandma who loves Jesus and prays every day that he will be saved. Kyle doesn't seem very interested in listening to his grandma, so she has been praying that God will bring someone else along (maybe a young person in his generation) to share Christ with him. She doesn't know that God is already answering those prayers.

Kyle is merely a fictional character—but not without similarity to countless young people in our generation. May we look with the eyes of Jesus—eyes of compassion—and see the many Kyles in this world who are deceived and hurting, "having no hope, and without God in the world" (Ephesians 2:12). Maybe *you* are the "Joel" that God will use to answer a grandma's prayers.

EVIDENCE FOR THE RESURRECTION

HUNDREDS OF EYEWITNESSES.

"Christ died for our sins according to the Scriptures ... He was buried ... He rose again the third day ... He was seen of [Peter], then of the twelve: After that, He was seen of above 500 brethren at once; of whom the greater part remain unto this present, but some are fallen asleep" (1 Corinthians 15:3-6). These eyewitnesses were around for many decades to testify to the facts!

ENEMY EYEWITNESSES UNABLE TO REFUTE FACTS.

Jesus was *not* popular with the Jewish authorities of His day! They were extremely jealous. After finally finding a way to have Him executed, His resurrection must have been their worst nightmare! Obviously, they would have tried everything in their power to disprove the event and stop the news from spreading. But the tomb was empty for all to see and the authorities could not produce the dead body.

DID HIS FOLLOWERS STEAL THE BODY?

Because the Jewish leaders feared this very thing, they petitioned Pilate to have His tomb marked with a Roman seal and be protected by Roman guards, who were obligated to protect it under penalty of death. To imagine that a few of Jesus' followers could roll away a stone (which likely weighed two tons and required a lever system to put in place) in order to steal His body while Roman soldiers slept on duty, is absurd.

JESUS' FOLLOWERS WOULDN'T DIE FOR A KNOWN LIE!

Let's imagine for a moment that Jesus' followers really *had* conspired together to steal the body of Jesus (if that were possible) and produce a brilliant hoax to fool the world. History tells us that 10 out of the 12 were tortured and martyred because they would not deny the truth of their claim! Would these men suffer and die for something they knew to be a lie? Men may be sincerely deceived and die for what they believe to be the truth. But people just do not die for something they *know* is a lie! If anyone knew the true facts, His closest followers did. And these men went from being fearful cowards to suddenly having the boldness to preach Christ everywhere in spite of persecution!

MAYBE JESUS WASN'T REALLY DEAD?

The Roman army was one of the fiercest, most powerful armies in world history. If anyone knew how to be sure a criminal was dead, they did. Jesus was brutally flogged with Roman flagrums, had spikes driven through His hands and feet, hung on a cross bleeding for six hours, and was thrust through with a spear. After the Roman army proclaimed Him dead, He was embalmed with over 100 pounds of spices, wrapped in linen, and laid in a tomb for three days. It is ridiculous to imagine that He was still alive. Besides this, critics who say Jesus merely fainted and then revived have to explain how He regained strength to move the stone and get past the Roman guards.

CHAPTER 16

START AT HOME BUT AIM FOR THE WORLD

"I have a suggestion for Dad's birthday," Mom said. "Let's watch the home video from our trip to the Grand Canyon."

As soon as we started watching the video, it became apparent that operating a video camera was not a strong point for our family in 2001. The video camera was shaking all over the place and continually zooming in and out. At one point, my mom had been trying to tape us on a horse trail ride, but she had the camera zoomed in way too far. All we saw on the screen for the next several minutes was moving green blurs with an occasional half-second glimpse of a horse.

After watching this thriller movie for awhile, Sarah said, "I have a headache and I'm feeling sick. I can't watch this anymore." She laid down on the floor. A few minutes later both Mom and Dad realized how dizzy they were and turned off the video. Stephen and I also began complaining about our stomachaches. The dynamics of our birthday celebration had changed quite a bit, as we were now literally laying on the floor feeling nauseous. No one felt like eating the special dessert we had made for Dad's birthday.

Sometimes in our lives, the camera is zoomed in way too much. Our perspective is limited. We get so focused on our own little world—our needs, our struggles—that we forget to zoom out and see the lost world around us. So let's take a minute and zoom out.

- Today over 2.8 billion people live in unreached people groups. They have little, if any, opportunity to hear the gospel. They make up about 40% of the world's population.[1]

- 500,000 villages in India alone have never heard the gospel.[2]
- Turkey has 75 million people—with .008% evangelical Christian.[3]
- Yemen has 24 million people—with .0002% evangelical Christian.[4]
- Three out of every five people in the world live in Asia.[5] Approximately 70% of the people groups in Asia have not been reached with the gospel.[6]

When I was little, I knew there were countries on the other side of the world where people didn't know about Jesus. But I didn't think about it that much. I mean, after all, what could *I* do about it?

Recently, I have been increasingly impressed with the fact that this is no longer a mindset I can have. None of us can. God has given the commission to go to the "uttermost parts of the earth" not to some of us, but to all of us. It should not be that some Christians have a heart for missions and some don't. We should *all* have a heart for missions. It is God's heart! Some of us may never travel to another country, but if we are not seriously praying and taking action to help in any way we can, it reveals where our heart truly is in this matter of global evangelization.

We cannot ignore the truth that millions have not yet heard the gospel and it is God's heart that they be reached. Consider this message in Proverbs: "If thou forbear to deliver them that are drawn unto death, and those that are ready to be slain; If thou sayest, Behold, we knew it not; doth not He that pondereth the heart consider it? and He that keepeth thy soul, doth not He know it? and shall not He render to every man according to his works?" (Proverbs 24:11-12).

Jesus has already commanded each of us to "go." He has already given the call, and it applies to all of us who know Him. We can read it in Acts 1:8; Matthew 28:19-20; Mark 16:15; and Luke 24:44-49. The only question that is left is—where?

WHICH SIDE OF THE GLOBE?

Now that we have zoomed out and taken a quick look at the world, let's *zoom back in* and think about our present situation. Many of us would love to do mission work overseas one day. Yet, if we are not faithful to spread the gospel to those around us *here*, then we do not truly have a missionary heart. In North Korea, Laos, Iraq and many other countries, believers face prison, torture and death—yet they continue to speak out for Christ. Here in the States we are actually *protected* by the government as we share the gospel. If we are not faithful now, why should we expect God to entrust us with the responsibility of greater challenges? If we aren't making disciples here, what makes us think we'll be able to do it somewhere else?

When Hudson Taylor was seventeen (before he went to China as a missionary), he and his younger sister Amelia felt burdened to share the good news that had changed their lives.

"We do not well to hold our peace," they decided (quoting the lepers in 2 Kings 7:9).

Hudson was working long hours and had only a little free time each week. But he decided to spend these few hours in seeking to reach the lost in England. Week after week, he and Amelia ventured into the poorest parts of town to hand out tracts and share the gospel with those who would listen.[7]

Likewise, Amy Carmichael was a faithful missionary at home before heading to Japan and India. She started a weekly prayer meeting for schoolgirls, held meetings for neighborhood children, ministered to girls from the poor area of town, worked at a Christian organization which reached out to young people, and acted as a second mother to her younger siblings.[8]

When we consider how many have not yet heard the gospel, it seems evident that many of us *should* go overseas one day. But the precedent that we see in Scripture is to start where we are and then expand. When Jesus healed the demon-possessed man in Mark 5, the man begged Jesus to allow him to come with Him. But Jesus' first assignment for him was to go home. Jesus said, "Go home to thy friends, and tell them how great things the Lord hath done for thee, and hath had compassion on thee. And he departed, and began to publish in Decapolis how great things Jesus had done for him: and all men did marvel" (Mark 5:19-20).

USUALLY THE BEST PLACE TO START IS RIGHT IN FRONT OF YOU.

MISSIONARY TRAINING 101

The initiative in ministry that Hudson Taylor and Amy Carmichael took in their hometowns when they were young prepared them for their work overseas. In the same way, each of us has a "starter mission field" not far from our front door: our neighborhoods, towns, schools, colleges, workplaces, and relatives. If you have brothers and sisters, or friends from church, you already have a team. And just think—you already speak the language, know the culture and have many relationships in place. What a great head start! So, let's take a few minutes and discuss some practical ideas of things we can do right now.

NEIGHBORS

He is so cute! I thought as an affectionate black Lab showed up at our house. The puppy had lost both its home and its tag, so we weren't sure what to do. Then we had an idea: This would be a great way to meet more neighbors! I began knocking on doors, asking if anyone knew who owned the dog, and getting acquainted.

In an age where people are self-sufficient and often stay inside, it takes creativity to think of new ways to make contact with neighbors. One idea is to invite them to an event—such as a neighborhood dessert party in your driveway. This gives a good excuse to knock on all the doors and talk with them. Other ideas are Christmas caroling, helping with yard-work, bringing treats for holidays or birthdays, giving welcome baskets to new neighbors, and meeting various needs that arise.

Eric and Ambre, a young couple in our town, began eating watermelon in their driveway twice a week with some boys who were in foster care who lived across the street. Both of the boys and their foster mom came to Christ and started going to church with them. Eric and Ambre began a Bible study with this family, and Ambre told me with enthusiasm that since then eight more people have come to Christ and joined the study!

Often entire families can be reached through kids. My friend Haley and her family desired to reach their neighborhood for Christ—and they began taking action. The first Friday of every month they would welcome all the kids (and parents too) into their home for activities, Bible stories, Scripture memory, games and food. Let me tell you what happened. Two kids came to know the Lord. Subsequently, their parents were saved and began coming to church with them. Next, the four other children in this family, two of whom were already married, also got saved. Then, the spouses of those two came to the Lord as well. Talk about a domino effect! Haley's family had the whole clan of new believers over to their home for Easter, Christmas Eve and other occasions—studying the Bible with them and teaching them the ways of the Lord. How did this all start? They welcomed the neighborhood children into their home.

INTERNATIONAL STUDENTS

According to the US State Department there are over 700,000 international students in the United States.[9] Often these students are lonely, homesick, or in need of assistance as they adjust to life in the US. Many internationals never get to experience being in an American home, and would be grateful if they had the opportunity! Many of them would love to be friends with an American family. This is a tremendous foreign mission field right on our own turf that is often overlooked.

Our church invited some international students from nearby colleges to join us for a special meal and program the Sunday before Thanksgiving. During dinner I was talking with a student from Germany named Freddy.

"I was taught evolution, but I don't see a contradiction between evolution and the Bible," he told me. "I just take Genesis metaphorically."

I made a few comments about science and the Bible being consistent with each other. I referred to the Grand Canyon, explaining that present earth geology is a result of Noah's flood.

The surprised, skeptical look on his face told me these ideas were new to him. But he seemed intrigued that I held this view.

"So you really take the Bible *literally?*" he asked.

"Yeah!" I replied.

"I've *heard* that there were people like you in America, but I've never met one," he told me.

Okay, so what am I supposed to reply to that? [smile]

I didn't want to talk about origins the whole time, so I said, "Well, the most important thing to understand is the gospel—that Jesus died and rose again for our sins ... But how can one believe the end of the Bible if he can't believe the beginning?" I asked him.

"Yeah, I've wondered that before," he said, "like about the contradictions in Scripture."

I mentioned that it's true that people *claim* there are contradictions, but I've never been shown a true contradiction. There are always explanations.

As the 11 international students climbed back into the van to be dropped off at their school, they were very warm and grateful. Two girls from Vietnam didn't seem to want to leave (even after we arrived at the college) but stayed by the van, talking. Freddy seemed very eager to receive the book I gave him. They all appreciated the warmth of the people from my church and the opportunity to have an "American" experience. I was reminded again that holidays are a great time to show hospitality to internationals and teach about American culture, emphasizing the true spiritual messages behind the holidays.

Did you know that the Bible specifically tells us to reach out to internationals? Over 40 times in Scripture, the Lord mentions His concern for strangers, foreigners and sojourners. When we invest in internationals, we are actually investing in the country to which they will be returning. Reaching the "uttermost part of the earth" may not be as difficult as we imagine.

STARTLING BELIEFS

ASSISTED LIVING CENTERS

Most elderly care centers are *looking* for people to come in and visit with their residents—many of whom are still mentally capable of spiritual discussions. One time after my family gave a gospel presentation at an elderly care center, a lady approached my dad. "I've never understood eternal life before," she said, getting up out of her wheelchair to stress her point, "but now I finally understand." She added, "Please keep doing what you are doing."

HOSPITALITY

The Crock-Pot was simmering. Beds were prepared. Company would be arriving in just a few minutes. But there was something very unusual about this situation: the company was coming from the other side of the world. They were literally just getting off the plane. Some good friends of ours, the Skrnich family, had volunteered to host a refugee family from Bosnia who were being relocated to the United States. The refugee family, worn and grieved from the harsh conditions they had endured, were greeted by the Skrnich family with big hugs and warm hospitality. Day after day, the Skrnichs showed them the love of Jesus. Although there was a language barrier, they poured everything they had into caring for this family who lived with them for five months. They brought them to church, the store, and special events, and they included them in family activities. They shared about Jesus and the Bible, but never saw fruit from their labors ... until 12 years later. This Bosnian family, still living in the States, made contact with them again and reported that their whole family had been saved and baptized, and was now getting involved in a church. Can you imagine the joy in the Skrnich's house when they heard this news?

A Christ-honoring home is a powerful center for ministry. In a culture where families are crumbling all around us, a godly, close-knit family makes a huge impact. Home Bible studies are one of the most effective means of spreading the gospel. Many people may not be willing to step into a church building, but they would come to a home. "Let brotherly love continue. Be not forgetful to entertain strangers" (Hebrews 13:1-2).

JUST DO SOMETHING!

If you are a follower of Jesus, you are a part of the team—and we all have a role to play. If you aren't sure what to do, just pray and pick something! God can adjust your steps as necessary.

There is a biblical term for all these efforts: *good works*. Most of us are not called to run huge gospel crusades. God may raise up a few big-name evangelists, but mostly He uses individual "nobodies," who are simply faithful in doing good works and sharing the gospel on an individual, one-to-one basis. The theme of good works surges through the New Testament. It is a beautiful characteristic of God's people.

"Who gave Himself for us, that He might ... purify unto Himself a peculiar people, **zealous of good works**" (Titus 2:14).

"For we are His workmanship, created in Christ Jesus unto **good works** ... " (Ephesians 2:10).

"Let your light so shine before men, that they may see your **good works**, and glorify your Father ... " (Matthew 5:16).

"In like manner also, that women adorn themselves ... with **good works**" (1 Timothy 2:9-10).

Whether we are in America, Congo, China, or Sweden, most people come to the Lord the same way: through loving conversations with believers who reach out to them and share the good news. It happens *one by one*. What better way could we prepare for overseas mission work than by doing it here?

ZOOM IN MORE

Now let's zoom in further: past our towns, past our neighborhoods, and into the walls of our own home. Sometimes home is the very hardest place to obey God. Yet, it is a specially-designed training ground for us—a launching pad for the rest of our lives. We may not like everything about our current situation—whether it is struggles with family members, irritations, difficult circumstances or obstacles to overcome. Yet, God knows exactly what training, experiences and lessons we need in order to be prepared for future ministry. His lessons often come at unexpected times in unexpected locations. Brothers, sisters and parents are common "professors" in God's university. Each season of life prepares us for the next. How can we expect to be fruitful later if we are not learning the lessons He has prepared for us now?

A young man, Dennis, was visiting a Christian family's home for dinner. Right away he noticed that there was something very different about this family: the children were kind to each other and there was peace and harmony in the home. Dennis was curious about what made this family different, and they told him it was because of Jesus Christ. He gave his life to the Lord, and now he is the director of a Christian camp—and a friend of ours.

Do you think that those kids would have ever imagined that their love for each other would be the tool God would use to get someone's attention and lead him to salvation? When we are faithful to obey Jesus in the little, everyday things, *He* is able to cause our light to shine for many to see. God isn't concerned about what seems impressive to us. He is concerned that our hearts are faithful in the daily grind. The person we are when no one is watching is the person we truly are. The "smallest" things are sometimes the hardest things—mundane acts of service, the struggles of our hearts, efforts no one else sees, time spent in prayer, and consistency in our walk with Him. A true hero is one who is a conqueror daily in the little things.

It doesn't necessarily matter what side of the globe we are on. God cares more about *who* we are than *where* we are. What matters is that we are obedient to Jesus right here, right now. Jesus said that the one who is faithful in little is faithful in much (Luke 16:10).

KEEP ZOOMING IN

In light of this, let's zoom in even further—into the walls of our own hearts. 2 Chronicles 16:9 gives us a big clue about what God is looking for: "For the eyes of the LORD run to and fro throughout the whole earth, to shew Himself strong in the behalf of them whose heart is perfect toward Him." God isn't looking for those who see themselves as great, but those who see themselves as small. He isn't looking for the strong, but the "weak" (1 Corinthians 1:26-29).

He is not impressed with eloquence, intelligence or fame. He is looking for those whose hearts are set upon Him.

When I was fifteen, I read the biography of Vanya, a Christian soldier in the Soviet army in the 1970s. Vanya would not quit witnessing to his fellow soldiers and, consequently, he was put through many interrogations and tortures by the military authorities. It angered them that Vanya did not react to their punishments and cruelty. They could not take away his joy! In fact, the more they hated him, the more he loved them. Many other soldiers were putting their faith in Christ because of Vanya's words and example. In one final effort to break him, they handed him over to the KGB (Soviet Secret Police) where Vanya was put to death. In one of the officer's own words, "He died hard, but he died a Christian." Vanya was twenty years old.

Vanya knew that if he would quit sharing his faith, the persecution would stop. But he had a fire in his bones to share the gospel and he could not be quiet (Jeremiah 20:9). His heart burned with a love for Jesus, and he wanted others to experience a relationship with Him as well.

I remember finishing this book, deeply moved and convicted, thinking, *How can I have that kind of passion? How can I be that kind of person?* What impressed me most was not what Vanya *did*, but how much Vanya loved God. The book explained that one of Vanya's greatest challenges in the army was trying to find time to pray. He had been accustomed to spending hours in prayer. Vanya's passion was not merely to serve God, but to know Him. And, in the pursuit of knowing Him, his life bore incredible fruit. In fact, his life is still bearing fruit: his story is *still* influencing people today.[10]

FUELING THE FLAME

The way to be useful to God—the way to be on fire—is not to focus on doing, doing, doing, but to focus on abiding. We should concentrate on sinking our roots deep into the Word of God. As we deepen our walk with Christ, He broadens our ministry. Jesus said, "I am the vine, ye are the branches: He that abideth in Me, and I in him, the same bringeth forth much fruit: for without Me ye can do nothing" (John 15:5).

When Jesus told His disciples, "Ye are the light of the world," and instructed them not to hide their light under a bushel, but to let it shine for all in the house to see, what did they picture? Probably a little oil lamp, similar to the one on the cover of this book. It was a common household light in Israel at that time. Everyone knew what those lamps needed to keep burning: oil. In the same way, it is impossible for us to muster up the strength to keep burning brightly. Just as an oil lamp must regularly be refilled, so we must be refilled continually by the Lord. Our relationship with Him is always top priority.

FIRE LIGHTS FIRE

The way to reach the world for Jesus is to walk intimately with Him ourselves—right here, right now. We may not be able to change others, but we can make the decision to seek Him with all of our hearts ourselves. It is only then that we will reflect Him in an accurate way to those with whom we come in contact, be it many or few.

Sometimes we may feel alone, like we are the only one trying to share the gospel. However, with time and patience, one person's radical obedience lights a fire that spreads contagiously to other believers—lighting flame after flame. It produces a blazing fire that the darkness cannot overcome because it is a work of God's Holy Spirit. Let's pray for this reviving work to happen among the young people in our generation!

Now let's begin to zoom back out and consider the impact it will make on towns and nations when we join together—as a team—to proclaim the gospel.

TEAMWORK

The plan was arranged: "We'll meet at 6:30 p.m., pray, and then go to the town square to witness. Afterwards we'll come back for ice cream."

We had just completed some witnessing training, and we wanted to put it into practice. About six junior high girls came that evening and we had an encouraging time sharing the gospel.

I wonder how many people we witnessed to collectively tonight, I thought as we gathered for ice cream and began reporting stories. I know success isn't measured by numbers, but I thought it would encourage the girls to count how many people we had talked to. The number came to over 50 people. That's more unsaved people than step through the doors of many churches in an entire year!

Encouraged by this, we began to see that when you mobilize a team you are able to reach many more people. One of the biggest gifts the Lord has given us as we seek to reach this world for Christ is *each other*. The work load is huge, but we're in this together. There are so many benefits that accompany teamwork evangelism. For example, it helps us stay consistent. When we are scheduled to meet at 1:00 p.m. we can't back out! We are strengthened by the presence of our brothers and sisters in Christ working alongside us. It is easier to be bold. We learn from each other. We pray for each other.

We now have a small team of about six of us who frequently go out witnessing on Saturday afternoons. It is definitely a highlight in our week! (Though it is certainly not always *easy*.) We divide into pairs, look for people with whom we can begin conversations, and then come back together to share reports and pray. Later we often send out an e-mail to those on our team with the first names of the people with whom we spoke, so that we can keep praying for them.

Let's do a little math now. Usually, the total number of people our group witnesses to is somewhere between 10 and 30. But let's just pick 18 as an average number. Now, if we spoke with 18 people every week, our little team would share the gospel with 936 people in one year.

Looking at it from this perspective, what if ten little groups in our town (consisting of six people each) went out witnessing every week? They'd average 180 conversations a week, adding up to 9,360 gospel conversations in one year! Given a few years, they could have a one-on-one talk with everyone in their whole town about the Lord. And this is not taking into consideration the fact that some of those people will get saved and start witnessing themselves. It's not hard to understand how Christianity spread so rapidly in the early church. If people take Jesus' command to share the gospel seriously, growth can happen *really* fast.

It is not a huge stretch of the imagination to think of 10 small groups of young people in one town going out witnessing once a week! Often, with a little training and organization, momentum builds and people want to get on board.

WHAT MANY CHRISTIANS DON'T REALIZE

Think of what could happen in our country if our generation joined together with a purposeful resolve to communicate the gospel all over our towns and neighborhoods. Not only would many more people hear about Jesus, but Christians would be strengthened deeply in their faith. It is when you explain the gospel over and over again that you truly begin to understand and appreciate it more thoroughly yourself.

In addition, the fellowship that is generated by doing something difficult together as we serve the Lord is sweet, and it draws us closer as brothers and sisters in Christ. Many have not yet discovered that some of the best fellowship takes place in the context of witnessing. Whenever you do something difficult with another person, there is a bonding that takes place. You are pulling hard together and have to encourage each other. When you experience victory, you celebrate, share the joy, and make awesome memories together. Witnessing is made up of great struggles and great victories. Some of the very best fellowship happens as we witness side by side.

More importantly, witnessing takes our eyes off ourselves and centers our attention on our King and His purposes. It realigns our focus, showing us what is important in life and what is not. It severs pride and selfishness. Witnessing is an all-around cure for spiritual complacency! It strengthens new believers; it revives discouraged believers. It continually reminds us of the amazing hope of the gospel.

You may not be able to recruit 60 people to join you in sharing the gospel, but what about a couple of friends? What about your brother or sister? God simply desires faithful individuals who will respond to His call—who will join the host of men and women of God who have lost interest in the attractions of this world because they have caught sight of a calling so much higher, so much nobler, that they are willing to take up their cross and follow Him. Their goal is not merely to serve Him, but to know Him. That's where it all starts. And that's where it all ends: Following the Lord. "Follow Me," Jesus said, "and I will make you fishers of men" (Matthew 4:19).

AIM FOR THE WORLD!

Let's review the sequence: We should sink our roots deeply into Christ, be faithful at home, take initiative to do ministry in our own communities, and then aim for the world.

"The Spirit of Christ is the spirit of missions, and the nearer we get to Him the more intensely missionary we must become." —Henry Martyn

Though we should start right where we are, is that where we want to finish? Of course not! The lessons we learn as we witness now will help us all along the way— and who knows what extraordinary missions God has ahead for each one of us!

Don't forget that though it is easy for us to *plan* to be a missionary here at home, it is also easy to

MOM, JOEL SAID HE CAN'T GO WITNESSING TODAY. SO I GUESS I DON'T HAVE A TEAM.

WHAT ABOUT US?

H.Mally

get our priorities off and become distracted by living in this rich country of America. One advantage of going overseas is that at least it's not as easy to forget one's purpose for being there!

Let's pray big prayers, asking God to do amazing things through our generation—not just here, but globally. He already is. God is at work in many mighty ways in the world today. Our generation *is* speaking. The gospel *is* being proclaimed boldly. It is an exciting time to be alive! Operation World reports that evangelical Christianity is the fastest growing "religious" movement in the world today, spreading around the world in unprecedented numbers.[11] Non-western countries are sending out nearly as many (some sources say more) missionaries than western ones. In other words, it's no longer Christians from countries like the US going to countries like India—it's Christians from *everywhere* going *everywhere!* Let's consider a few encouraging examples of ways that the Lord is working in other nations.

- In Iran, massive numbers of Muslims are turning to Jesus Christ. Thirty years ago it is estimated that there were only 500 believers in Iran who had come from a Muslim background. Today a conservative estimate puts that number at over 100,000 and very possibly much higher.[12]

- The staggering growth of the church in China is a wonderful and amazing work of God. In the last 50 years, the church has grown from under 3 million evangelical Christians to 75 million (and possibly many more).[13] Our brothers and sisters in China are sending out missionaries to both unreached people groups in their own country, and to other nations which are closed to the gospel. They believe that God has used the many years of intense persecution to prepare them for the suffering they will face as they venture as missionaries into hostile areas. Operation World estimates that they have already sent out 100,000 missionaries![14]

- Many Filipino believers, due to unemployment and financial need, are forced to find work in other nations. Since many of these nations are closed toward Christianity, churches in the Philippines see this as a unique opportunity. They are training these workers in evangelism before they leave, and these believers are going forth with a special intent: to reach people with the gospel. An estimated 50,000 have already been sent out and hundreds of churches have been planted—many in countries that are most inaccessible to the gospel. The story I told in chapter 11 about the housemaid in Saudi Arabia is one amazing example of this.[15]

- Some of the largest prayer meetings in the world have been in Nigeria. The church is growing rapidly and has been sending out thousands of missionaries. They have a specific goal of sending out 50,000 missionaries by 2020.[16]

"Behold, the LORD's hand is not shortened, that it cannot save; neither His ear heavy, that it cannot hear" (Isaiah 59:1).

What can we do right now from home? We can research needs, ask the Lord to show us ways we can help missionaries, and begin adjusting our lifestyle in order to invest time and money into the needs we learn about. We can host missionary families on furlough, pick a particular country to study and pray for, and put reminders on our walls to pray for persecuted believers. We can remember that the missionaries who are already on the field need help. Sometimes they become weary and discouraged, and we can be a strong source of encouragement through correspondence, packages, financial support, and most of all, by letting them know that we are remembering them in prayer.

We tend to want to be "where the action is" because we like excitement. Did you know that the *most action* happens when we are on our knees before the throne of God? Prayer is the biggest way we can help missionaries, and we can do that from our bedroom.

A TALE OF TWO BROTHERS

Once upon a time, in the early-to-mid 1900s, there were two brothers. Both dreamed of being a missionary in a far-away land. They'd talk about their dreams as they worked side by side doing odd jobs around town in Portland, Oregon. The youngest was dynamic and energetic, vibrant and noticeable. The older was quieter, but had a joyful spirit, a ready smile, and—perhaps what some didn't realize—the same fire burning within. The younger would speak of the passion he had for missionary work, for the aching he had to be on the field preaching Jesus. The older would smile and nod, affirming his little brother. Together they would pray that God would send them.

The younger brother did not lose his passion nor zeal, but charged on with full steam until the day of his death—a death so cruel and surprising it shook the country and made worldwide news. Since the time of Jim Elliot's death, when he was speared by the Auca Indians of Ecuador in 1956, the Lord has used his story and journal entries to spark a flame in the hearts of Christians around the globe to live with the same kind of zeal.

What many do not know is that Jim had an older brother: Bert. Broken-hearted, yet faithful, Bert continued to serve God in the steamy jungles of Peru—planting churches and schools, counseling, making disciples and teaching the Word of God. Bert went home to be with the Lord just recently, in February, 2012. He had been serving the Lord as a missionary for all of those years! What a reunion—to meet his brother Jim again—and to finally be with Jesus. Jim Elliot served God with all his strength for the six years of service God gave him after college, but his brother Bert served God in Peru for over 60 years! Bert and his wife planted 150 churches.[17] He was not well known on earth, but he is well known in Heaven.

CHAPTER 17

THE ESTHER 4:14 PRINCIPLE

As Sarah turned off the engine, I heard a blood-curdling scream. It was my mom. Her fingers were stuck in the window. They got caught between the glass and the top of the door as Sarah rolled up the power window. As you might remember from chapter five, when my mom screams, it's loud. *Really* loud. Sarah quickly rolled the window down again and we looked at Mom's fingers. They had black indention lines on them, but Mom said she was okay. Sarah and I were pretty startled ourselves after that loud scream, and Sarah took my mom home to get ice.

I stayed at the park thinking, *This has never happened before, and when does it happen? Right when we arrive at the park to witness.*

Though this particular afternoon had a difficult start, it had an encouraging end. When Sarah returned, she began a conversation with a lady at a picnic table.

"What do you think happens after you die?" Sarah asked.

"I don't know, but I'm scared," the lady replied.

"Well, that's a good start. It's good to be concerned," Sarah said, explaining that we are all sinners and God is a righteous Judge.

"Now I'm really scared," she said.

Opening a tract, Sarah showed her two verses written on the inside: 1 John 1:9 and Ephesians 2:8-9. Sarah assured her that we do not have to be afraid to die if we trust in Christ. By the look in this lady's eyes, it seemed that she was taking this very seriously.

Another lady that afternoon asked Sarah, "Can I ask why you picked me to talk to of all the people at the park? I've noticed you before. You talked with my niece one time." Apparently, this lady had seen Sarah witnessing at the mall. It definitely seemed that God had prepared her for this encounter, and she responded with warmth.

Meanwhile, I had some interesting talks as well. When Sarah and I shared stories afterward, we were very encouraged by the conversations the Lord had arranged that day. We were reminded again of the importance of perseverance.

There are many obstacles we face when witnessing. Whether it's spiritual attack, discouragement from people, complications in scheduling, or simply our flesh not wanting to do something difficult, witnessing is rarely smooth sailing. Often it seems that there are distractions and obstacles at every step—bigger difficulties than getting your fingers caught in a window. We are in a spiritual battle. It won't last forever—but for now, we must persevere. Rest is sweeter when the work has been hard. When we are with the Lord one day, I don't want to look back on a life of ease as someone who never "enlisted" in the battle! Isaac Watts wrote, *"Must I be carried to the skies on flowery beds of ease, while others fought to win the prize, and sailed through bloody seas?"*

ESTHER 4:14

Sometimes it's overwhelming to consider all the needs in the world. In every country, we are seeing the sad consequences of people rejecting God. As we see godly foundations crumbling, it's easy to become discouraged or fearful about the future. But look at it this way: the Lord has chosen for each one of us to live at this time in history for a reason. We can be *excited* that He has placed us here in the twenty-first century. There is special work to do, and God is calling *us* to do it!

Imagine this. We are in Heaven, listening to amazing stories from missionaries throughout history who gave their lives for the gospel. They recount the spiritual battles they fought and the great adventures on which God took them. They explain about the struggles, the dilemmas, the victories—and the faithfulness of God through it all. I'm sure there will be countless thrilling stories to hear. But—what if, looking back, we realize that we totally missed the real spiritual work because we were blinded by distractions? What if we realize that, while others were fighting true battles, we were wasting time on ourselves?

The difficult tasks God gives us are not actually burdens, but blessings! Does God *need* us? Of course not. But He calls us to be "laborers together with Him." (See 2 Corinthians 6.) When a father allows his five-year-old son to help him change a tire, the main thing that happens is "bonding time" between father and son. In a similar way, we can obey God's call—or refuse and miss the blessing.

When Esther was faced with an enormous, daunting task, Mordecai told her, "If thou altogether holdest thy peace at this time, **then shall ... deliverance arise to the Jews from another place;** but thou and thy father's house shall be destroyed: and who knoweth whether thou art come to the kingdom for such a time as this?" (Esther 4:14).

Jesus said that He *will* build His church (Matthew 16:18). Obviously, Jesus can do it without us! If we "hold our peace" and do not speak out for the Lord, God will raise up someone else. But remember, being in the battle with Christ is the most thrilling adventure—the most rewarding journey—of which one could possibly dream! If we refuse, we are foregoing an extraordinary privilege, an invitation of amazing worth. **God will raise up someone else, but we will miss out.** It's the Esther 4:14 principle.

A.D.

H.Mally

ZEBEDEE WATCHES AS HIS SONS LEAVE THE BOAT AND FOLLOW JESUS.

THERE IS NO HIGHER CALLING THAN TO BE A FISHER OF MEN. MATTHEW 4:19-22

LIVING FOR THAT DAY

We are clearly told in Scripture that each individual who knows Jesus Christ will personally stand before Him. "For we shall all stand before the judgment seat of Christ ... So then every one of us shall give account of himself to God" (Romans 14:10-12).

I don't know what words could describe being face to face with Jesus, so we'll just use the words "terrifying joy." Jesus' discerning eyes will see through every situation with a thorough understanding. He will take into consideration not only our actions, but also the motivation behind those actions. Our only concern at that time will be what *Jesus* thought of how we lived our lives. Scripture describes what will happen on that day: "Every man's work shall be made manifest: for the day shall declare it, because it shall be revealed by fire; and the fire shall try every man's work of what sort it is. If any man's work abide which he hath built thereupon, he shall receive a reward. If any man's work shall be burned, he shall suffer loss: but he himself shall be saved; yet so as by fire" (1 Corinthians 3:13-15). (Also see 2 Corinthians 5:10.)

Maybe we will be ashamed of waste and loss, of times we failed to speak out for Christ, of times we sought our own glory instead of His. Jesus, in His mercy, will wipe the tears from our eyes and we will be assured that He has removed our sins as far as the east is from the west. We will be at peace—forgiven, and deeply loved.

But it won't stop there. We will also be able to see the fruit of our labors. All the things we had completely forgotten ... we will find that the Lord did not forget! Small acts of kindness, tears of struggle, surrendered dreams, steps of obedience. Can you imagine the joy of hearing the Lord express pleasure over your faithfulness to Him? It is somewhat beyond comprehension—but this is not fantasy.

As sobering as the thought of giving personal account to Jesus may be, it is a beautiful and wonderful truth. We should be looking forward to this day with confidence—actually *longing* for it. David said, "My soul thirsteth for God, for the living God: when shall I come and appear before God?" (Psalm 42:2).

HOW MUCH KINDNESS CAN THERE BE?

It is important that we have a correct understanding of the "judgment seat of Christ." The Greek word for *judgment seat* is the word *bema*, and it refers to a step or raised platform where an authority sits to give out awards at a race or competition. This "judgment" does not mean punishment. It is entirely different from the judgment unbelievers will face at the Great White Throne (Revelation 20:11-15).

Our punishment already happened—it was laid entirely on Jesus Christ on the cross. Because of His death, "there is therefore now no condemnation to them which are in Christ Jesus" (Romans 8:1). The judgment seat of Christ (the "judgment" of believers) is simply a matter of reward or loss of reward.

Isn't it enough that God has saved us from Hell? Isn't it enough that He loves us so much and shows such patience toward our shortcomings? And then, on top of that, He wants to reward us? What an amazing God. We don't deserve such kindness. But if God desires to reward us, He has the right to do as He wants! And He has told us that this is His plan. So, let's run for the prize!

"Know ye not that they which run in a race run all, but one receiveth the prize? So run, that ye may obtain. And every man that striveth for the mastery is temperate in all things. Now they do it to obtain a corruptible crown; but we an incorruptible" (1 Corinthians 9:24-25).

This is not a matter of running against each other: it's running *with* each other. In fact, one of the ways to win is to help others win! It's not about getting our own glory but rather striving to give Jesus as much glory as we can!

THE MONKEY IN SINGAPORE

The little monkey in Singapore stood on the fence and watched our group. We were in Southeast Asia, leading some Bright Lights youth discipleship conferences, and enjoying a free day at a park. The monkey relaxed in one position, leisurely watching us. He scratched his stomach. He yawned. He meandered closer to our group. We were busy talking and didn't take much notice of him. All of a sudden, the deceptive monkey dashed right into the center of our group, grabbed a plastic bag, and raced up a tree. The scheming little guy had been devising his plan all along, merely waiting for an opportune moment to make the dash.

The plastic bag did not contain anything to eat (as the monkey hoped), but only a pair of shoes. The disappointed monkey eventually dropped them out of the tree. I thought it was kind of funny how smart this monkey was and how sneaky he had been in stealing our stuff. I guess he had quite a bit of experience robbing tourists. After that, we watched our bags a lot more carefully!

Just like that monkey, thieves are subtle and deceptive. That is the way they work. They steal from you when you are least expecting it. Satan is the most dangerous thief of all; his strategy is to steal, kill and destroy (John 10:10; 1 Peter 5:8). One of the main resources that Satan wants to take from us is our time. Why our time? Because it is one of the most valuable treasures the Lord has given us. The enemy is subtle in his strategies. He distracts us with *good* things which are not the *best* things. He tempts us to waste minutes here and there, adding up to hours and days and years. He wants us to be consumed with things of lesser importance, so we will not have energy or time to put into those things of greatest importance. It's a deceptive plan. One day, however, it will be crystal clear what mattered and what didn't.

While driving with four other friends in the vehicle, a friend of mine posed a thought-provoking scenario: "What if we were in Heaven and we heard the Lord say, 'I need five courageous volunteers to stand in the gap for Me and proclaim My truth to a wicked and perverse generation'?"

Everyone in the vehicle listened as my friend continued, "And what if the five of us were the ones chosen to go? How would that affect the way we live our lives today? How would it affect our everyday decisions?"[1]

Total silence filled the SUV. This hypothetical situation definitely makes one think! And it is not a far-fetched scenario. Second Corinthians 5:20 says, "we are ambassadors for Christ."

"REMEMBER THE BEMA"

Many adults reach a point mid-life where they look back, evaluating their life, and confess with regret, "I wasted so many years."

God gives opportunities to redeem wasted time if we repent (Joel 2:25), but if you are a young person reading this book, you have a lot to be excited about! We still have most of our lives ahead of us, and we can choose *now* that we are going to invest our years wisely—making daily decisions based upon what will matter on the day we stand before Jesus.

A friend of mine shared that in college, he and his friends had a theme—a little motto by which they would operate: "Remember the Bema." (*Bema:* the Greek word used for the judgment seat of Christ.) Living with this perspective makes each moment of each day extremely significant!

The motivation of giving a personal account of our lives to Jesus releases us from so many burdens. It reminds us that the only thing that matters is what matters to Jesus. It doesn't matter if we please other people; it doesn't even matter if we please ourselves! We don't have to worry about getting what we think we want in this life. Our lives here are just a passing vapor anyway (James 4:14). A vapor! That's practically nothing. It's here and then it's gone. The only thing that should matter to us now is what will matter then.

Nate Saint, one of the five missionaries martyred in Ecuador in 1956, stated, *"People who do not know the Lord ask why in the world we waste our lives as missionaries. They forget that they too are expending their lives ... and when the bubble has burst, they will have nothing of eternal significance to show for the years they have wasted ... If God would grant us the vision, the word 'sacrifice' would disappear from our lips and thoughts; we would hate the things that seem now so dear to us; our lives would suddenly be too short; we would despise time-robbing distractions and charge the enemy with all our energies in the name of Christ."*

A RUNNER'S FEARS

It was the last lap of the men's 5,000 meter race at the NCAA Division 3 Indoor Track and Field Championship. My brother was one of the photojournalists covering the event. A specific scene stood out in his mind, and he told me about it later.

"On the last lap, everyone is pushing as hard as he can," Stephen said, describing the race to the finish line. "When they cross the finish line they're exhausted because they just ran 25 laps and they were running really hard to the end."

Stephen said that as the runners pass the line, one by one, they bend over in exhaustion or collapse on the track. Once all the runners come in, and everyone catches their breath, they have to leave the track pretty quickly so the officials can get set up for the next event.

"But one guy didn't get up," Stephen explained. "He was just laying on his back, totally wiped. They needed to set up for the women's 5,000 meter race but they had to get this guy off the track first ... and he wasn't moving."

Apparently, one of the officials came up to him and told him he needed to get going, but he still didn't move. Finally, medical personnel came to check on him. Eventually, this exhausted runner gathered the strength to crawl off the track onto the infield ... where he continued to lay as the next race started.

"He had just given it *everything*," Stephen said.

You see, runners have two fears. First, they fear that they won't have enough energy to make it to the finish line. Second, they fear that they'll make it to the finish line with energy left to spare—energy they could have used. This guy had definitely used all the strength he had. Don't you want to enter Heaven's gates that way?

When Olympic marathon runners prepare for a race, they pour their lives into it. They work out extensively, learn proper habits and techniques, eat the right food, acquire the right accessories, and have their eyes set on the goal—to win. If athletes do all of this just to win an earthly award, shouldn't we have the same kind of dedication to win an eternal reward?

HOW TO KEEP RUNNING!

In general, people are able to run a pretty fast sprint. It's easy to do … once. We put all our energy into it and try to beat the person running beside us. But when it comes to long distances, we get tired and we're tempted to quit. In the same way, anyone can go out witnessing … once. But God isn't calling us to a one-time thing! He is calling us to a *lifetime* of faithfulness. How can we have the strength we will need to persevere for the long haul? Let's talk about four principles of perseverance.

1. Refuel
2. Lay Off Weights
3. Believe the Unseen
4. Look to Jesus

1. REFUEL

God sent manna to the Israelites once a week, right? No. He provided for them *every* day (double the day before the Sabbath). If we read our Bible once a month, that will be enough, right? No. How about once a week? Not if we want to be spiritually *strong*. Jesus instructed us to pray, "Give us *today* our daily bread." How can we have energy if we don't eat? First Peter 2:2 tells us to crave the Word like newborn babies cry for milk. That's a pretty intense desire!

If we want to be an oil lamp burning brightly, we need to be continually refilled by spending time with the Lord—in His Word and in prayer. We should also spend time with believers who build us up spiritually. There's nothing we have in and of ourselves to give to people—it is only what the Lord puts in us. We are just little clay lamps. The flame is entirely a product of the work of God in our lives. It is only through the nourishment that comes from Him that we will be able to keep burning strongly. "But we have this treasure in earthen vessels, that the excellency of the power may be of God, and not of us" (2 Corinthians 4:7).

2. LAY OFF WEIGHTS

Driving in four lanes of heavy, fast-moving traffic, my dad was heading toward downtown Indianapolis. The year was 1968. He was in college. It was the opening day of the Indy 500 Time Trials and my dad was on his way there—along with a quarter million other people. There was a bus on his right and a car on his left. All of a sudden, the bus merged into Dad's lane, forcing my dad to merge left. The car to his left slowed down to let him in. My dad sped up and squeezed in. In the process, the sides of the two cars rubbed.

They both pulled to the side and got out to look at their cars. My dad's black car now had a nice new white stripe. The other guy's white car now had a nice new black stripe. They stood there for a minute looking at the paint damage ... but only for a minute, because both my dad and the other driver were in a big hurry to get to the Time Trials.

"Let's forget it and go," the other man said.

That was just fine with my dad! The other guy's car was nicer anyway. So they hurried off to the race. They were so anxious to get to the Time Trials, nothing else mattered.

How many things in life should we just "forget and go," because there is something else more important? That is the attitude conveyed in Hebrews 12. It says, "Let us lay aside every weight, and the sin which doth so easily beset us, and let us run with patience the race that is set before us, looking unto Jesus ... " (Hebrews 12:1-2). Notice that it says to lay aside weights *and* the sin that entangles us. In other words, not every weight is sin. Weights could be "okay" things—but if they are weighing us down, we should lay them aside. Each one of us has to continually ask ourselves which activities are consuming our time and affections, keeping us from what is most important. It could be certain friends, TV, music, social media, novels, boyfriend/girlfriend relationships, various forms of entertainment or hobbies. Even "nice" things—such as blogging or keeping in touch with people on Facebook—can sap our time and be an enemy of the best. It is way more important to keep in touch with Jesus than with all our friends. Speaking of that, Jesus did not actually tell us to make friends. He told us to make *disciples*. In summary, a good question to ask ourselves is not, *What's wrong with this activity?* but rather, *Will this advance the kingdom of God?*

3. BELIEVE THE UNSEEN

Jenny, a high-school student, was backpacking in Northern Canada with friends. One evening while she and her friends were cooking over a fire at their campsite, a college-age brother and sister from another site came over to meet them. These friendly young people began talking about Jesus and sharing Scripture. Jenny thought they were nice, but she didn't understand what they were saying—at all. Looking back, she says she remembers making some pretty dumb statements in response to them.

After that encounter, Jenny got involved in an ungodly group of humanistic people at college and from there her life continued to go downhill. However, she never forgot the joyful brother and sister who talked with her at the campsite. They had given her a copy of *More than a Carpenter* by Josh McDowell and a little John 3:16 card—which became the only Scripture verse she knew. Jenny didn't read the book, but she didn't get rid of it either. Once in awhile a thought would come back to her about that conversation. Something about Jesus lingered in the back of her mind. The seed they had planted was germinating in her heart.

Two years later, Jenny became a Christian. Now Jenny is a friend of mine—a godly wife and mother of fourteen children, seven of whom are adopted from Liberia. Her love for the Lord is very evident.

"I know I am going to see that brother and sister in Heaven one day," Jenny told me. "And I am going to be able to tell them how God used them to plant that seed in my heart. It's likely they went away from that encounter discouraged, thinking, *She didn't get it at all!*"

But one day that brother and sister will have the joy of hearing the rest of the story.

Each of us is only one link in the chain—just one of the many influences God will use to speak into someone's life. Sometimes it's only the *last* "link" who has the joy of seeing the person come to Christ. The rest of us don't get to see the fruit of our efforts. Yet!

We must trust that God *is* working in this world. His Word *will* accomplish what He sends it to do (Isaiah 55:11). If we don't believe this, if we don't have faith, we will not persevere. We'll conclude that it's not working and quit. To keep pressing on, we must believe the unseen by faith.

Throughout history, who are the ones the Lord has chosen to use? Those who have faith. Hebrews 11 presents a list of ordinary people through whom God did extraordinary things—because they believed in God's power and trusted in His promises. These are the men and women who conquered kingdoms, saw the dead raised, and saw lions' mouths shut. Some were mocked and tortured, yet they refused to accept earthly deliverance, because they had their eyes fixed on an eternal reward. They persevered and conquered—and they did it by *faith.* Hebrews 11 concludes by pointing out that these people didn't even know about Jesus yet; they were Old Testament saints who merely looked forward to the coming of the Messiah.

Fast-forward a couple thousand years and look at what God has given to *us!* The Messiah has come, and He has conquered! It was more beautiful, terrible and magnificent than any of the ancient prophets dared to dream. *They* had only prophecies of a coming Messiah ... but *we* have seen the astonishing way our Savior, Jesus Christ—fully God and fully Man—demonstrated His love by performing the greatest rescue of all time. (And the story is not over yet!) It is this message, the gospel, that is now in *our* hands to deliver to the world.

Although the men and women listed in Hebrews 11 did not have a full understanding of the cross, they exercised faith and obeyed God. And God points us to their example. Countless thousands *since* Christ have followed in their footsteps, demonstrating the same faith. Many of them have laid down their lives for the sake of Christ. They have held tightly to the Word of God, and carried the message of the gospel. Now the gospel has been placed in the hands of *our generation* ... and it is our turn. Will our generation speak? Yes. How? We will run the same way they did: by faith.

4. LOOKING UNTO JESUS

Whatever happens, we must not fail to think about the One we will meet at the finish line and how amazing that will be. "Let us run with patience the race that is set before us, looking unto Jesus the author and finisher of our faith" (Hebrews 12:1b-2a). Jesus authored our faith, and He will finish it. Jesus Himself is both the Rewarder and the Reward of those who seek Him. It is our love for Him that gives us the passion and motivation we need. The more we delight in Jesus, the harder and stronger we run.

Jesus "for the joy that was set before Him endured the cross" (Hebrews 12:2). "If ye then be risen with Christ, seek those things which are above, where Christ sitteth on the right hand of God. Set your affection on things above, not on things on the earth" (Colossians 3:1-2).

When our eyes are on Christ, everything else comes into perspective. In contrast, when we compare ourselves with the people around us, we often become complacent, discouraged, or proud. Let's take a closer look at how this happens.

- **Complacency:** It could be that you already witness more than anyone else you know. You may be tempted to think, *I can take it easy now.* Since no one is expecting any more from you, you begin to relax and slow down. The cure to this kind of attitude is to bring your focus back to Christ and what *He* desires from you (Acts 20:24). Jesus Christ has extremely high expectations for each of us (John 14:12)—not because we are so capable, but because HE is so capable. He will do it through us. "Faithful is He that calleth you, who also will do it" (1 Thessalonians 5:24). Remember, the goal is not merely to witness more, but also to *be* a better witness. We all still have a long way to go.

- **Discouragement:** If we compare ourselves with other people, there is also the danger of becoming discouraged, thinking, *I could never witness like they do!* Have you ever thought that? I have. But remember—any wisdom or ability "they" have comes from God working in them. And the same God is working in you!

- **Pride:** Yet another hazard of comparing ourselves with others is that it can lead to pride. The way to combat pride is not to degrade or criticize ourselves, but rather to take our eyes off ourselves entirely (whether we are failing or succeeding) and place them on Christ. When we look at Jesus' suffering on the cross we are confronted with our true identity: we are sinful humans deserving God's wrath. All we have to boast in is the cross (Galatians 6:14). We needed God's forgiveness just as much as others. A grateful, worshipping heart has no room for pride. May our prayer be the same as the hymn writer: *"May His beauty rest upon me as I seek the lost to win, And may they forget the channel, seeing only Him."*
  —Kate B. Wilkinson

Again, what's the answer to avoiding these traps? Keeping our eyes on Christ. Hebrews 12:3-4 says, "Consider Him that endured such contradiction of sinners against Himself, lest ye be wearied and faint in your minds. Ye have not yet resisted unto blood, striving against sin."

A hundred thousand years from now most things from this life will no longer matter. One thing, however, will still matter: who is in Heaven and who is in Hell. Remember—we as young people have a voice to which the world listens! One day there will be no more lost souls to win. That work will be done forever. If we want to be a part of it, we have to do it now!

DAN

"All right, are we done?" I asked Sarah as we neared the end of the street.

"I think we should do this one last house near the corner," she replied, pointing to a little mustard-colored house.

"Okay, you can do that one and we'll go on to the next," Stephen and I decided.

It was a warm September morning and the three of us were knocking on doors around our church. We were inviting neighbors to an outreach barbeque and trying to get into conversations about the gospel. Stephen and I knocked on a few more doors, but no one else was home. However, as we looked back, we noticed that Sarah was still talking to the man in the house near the corner. Stephen and I decided to join the conversation. The man at the door looked about fifty, had long hair and sloppy clothes, and did not appear to be very friendly. As I began listening, I sensed that the discussion wasn't going very well. But since I figured it would be our only chance to talk with this man, I thought I'd throw out a question and see if it went anywhere.

"Would you say you are 100% sure you are going to Heaven?" I asked.

"Oh, no one could ever know that," he replied dismally.

"Well, we do!" we answered. "But it's not because we deserve it. It's because Jesus took the penalty we deserved."

Surprisingly, he began to soften a little and ask questions. He even asked if we would like to sit down on his lawn chairs to keep talking!

Good thing he has lawn chairs, I thought, *because I'm not going in that man's house!*

He brought up many questions and arguments, but he was open to hearing our views. We talked for about an hour and did our best to answer his questions, many of which were about evolution and how we could trust the Bible.

"It was great talking to you," he told us as we left. "Thank you for stopping by. Come back anytime!"

"We enjoyed talking with you too!" we replied.

"I'm Dan," he said, and shook our hands warmly.

Wow, he's a lot nicer than he seemed at first, I thought.

We drove home encouraged. We told our parents about the good conversation, and a few days later we dropped off some pamphlets and a family newsletter at his house.

To our great surprise, a few weeks later we found a letter in our mailbox … from Dan! Excitement ran through our house as we read the six-page letter, carefully written in very neat handwriting. He explained that he really appreciated our talk and the pamphlets we gave him, even though he didn't agree with all of it. He said he was having surgery and there was a 20% chance he wouldn't live through it, due to some possible complications.

"You should take the little harp and visit him in the hospital!" Dad suggested.

We agreed. As we softly entered his room with our little harp, we hoped Dan wouldn't be disturbed by our visit. He was absolutely delighted and also seemed touched by the Bible verse card we left him.

Dan made it through the surgery successfully, and we decided to invite him over for dinner.

Will he come? we wondered. Our "strategy" was to introduce him to our dad first, figuring he would then feel more comfortable to accept the invitation. So Dad and I were nominated to go to his door and invite him.

I hope this isn't awkward, I thought as I knocked on his door, my dad standing behind me. I made introductions, and Dan and my dad hit it off immediately. Dan complimented Dad's hat, made a joke, and they both laughed.

"We were wondering if you would like to come to our house for dinner," I explained.

He agreed and plans were arranged. Dan was a little nervous the night he came over, and he was very conscientious about being courteous. During dinner, his spoon slipped and a few kernels of corn flew off his plate and hit the wall. Mortified, he muttered, "I was afraid I'd do something like that." *[smile]* But he seemed to really enjoy his time at our house, complimenting everything—down to the herbs in the salad.

We enjoyed the evening too. Though Dan claimed to be a "hermit" he was actually a great conversationalist, and we were surprised by how knowledgeable he was on so many different topics. As he left, we thought, *Wow! That went great! We are going to have to invite him over again soon!*

We began dropping off audio messages of sermons from our church for Dan, which he really liked. Then he accompanied my dad on an errand to a town three hours away.

"You know, you have a lot of good questions," my dad told him. "Would you be interested in meeting for breakfast and studying the book of John in the Bible with me?"

Dan agreed, and every Tuesday morning the two of them studied John over eggs, toast and coffee. Each week my dad would come home and give us a report of how it went. This continued for the next eight or nine months.

Dan was not able to have a job because his health was declining. This gave him lots of time to read the Bible on his own too.

One time Dan spoke to my dad of his loneliness, having no family. He lived alone with his dog.

"Others are so blessed," he remarked.

"You just hit on a great topic—relationship," my dad said, and explained about the *ultimate* relationship. He emphasized to Dan that Heaven isn't a "where" but a "Who"—not a place, but a Person. It's all about a relationship—with God.

"God could never forgive someone like me, could He?" Dan asked one time.

Another time he stated, "You know, I think I'm half saved."

My dad laughed and explained how that was impossible. But as you can see, Dan was moving in the right direction! We were just waiting for the day Dan would realize that he was *not* saved. Finally, that day came. One afternoon after hearing another man share his salvation testimony at a men's Bible study, Dan told my dad, "You know, I don't think I'm saved."

He wanted to do something about it right away. He wanted to pray. In fact, he wanted to get on his knees and pray. So, right there in the park, Dan and my dad knelt down on the grass by a picnic table while Dan asked God for forgiveness and salvation.

When they stood up, Dan was shaking.

"Is it cold out here?" he asked.

"No," my dad answered.

"Maybe I'm just excited," he concluded.

He wasn't the only excited one. We were thrilled when we heard the news. Our good friend Dan was now our brother in Christ!

Our relationship continued to grow to a much closer level. Dan was baptized and became an avid student of God's Word. He always brought his Bible along when he came to our house, because he loved having Bible studies. We spent dozens of fun family evenings with Dan—eating dinner, having Bible studies, sitting around campfires, and celebrating birthdays and holidays.

"You know, it's amazing, I'm not afraid to die anymore," Dan told my mom and me while we were sipping milkshakes at Dairy Queen after a bike ride.

Dan quickly became very popular at our church. He was gentle, considerate and a great listener. He liked to draw pictures for the kids. Everyone loved him!

"I want to do more for the Lord. I feel like I'm not doing anything!" Dan would frequently tell us.

Yet the Lord was actually using Dan a lot. He began witnessing to his friends and started studying the book of John with one of them—just as he had been discipled by my dad.

Dan also helped our family by illustrating Sarah's book on purity, *Before You Meet Prince Charming*. He spent hours and hours drawing knights, princesses and castles for us.

Because of Dan's declining health, my mom regularly brought him homemade bread. In the spring of 2008 he was diagnosed with liver cancer and it progressed rapidly. One week at church, everyone went downstairs for a fellowship dinner after the service was over, but Dan and I stayed upstairs talking in the quiet of the auditorium.

"You're only nineteen and you have so much ahead for you, Grace," he told me. "But I've wasted my life. I wish I had done more for the Lord."

"But you *have*, Dan," I assured him. "You've been a huge blessing to everyone here at church—to my family especially—and you've been witnessing to your friends and encouraging everyone you meet. You've been such a great testimony for the Lord! And whenever we tell the story of how you were saved, everyone is so encouraged."

"Sometimes I just feel *so* discouraged," he admitted, "but sometimes," he added, full of emotion, "sometimes I just feel this … this … extreme joy." The tears rolling down his cheeks made me start crying along with him.

"I remember praying so hard that you would come to know the Lord," I recalled. "And then my dad came home from that Bible study and told us about your prayer to be saved. We were all so excited!"

I opened my Bible to Isaiah 51 and began to share a comforting passage that I had been thinking about. Dan interrupted after a few sentences, "You know, I've wondered what that verse meant."

I was surprised that he recognized that verse from Isaiah.

"You know, Dan, for only being a believer for four years, you sure know the Word well!" I told him.

He smiled and we discussed the verse, like we'd done with so many passages in the past. That was my last conversation with Dan. He died shortly afterward. But I'm confident that the "extreme joy" Dan mentioned only multiplied when he entered Heaven's gates.

In awe, I reflect with wonder at the amazing gift God has given us—to be able to lead someone to His Son and then see them go on to Heaven ahead of us.

We held a memorial dinner in our church basement for Dan. The basement was packed with Dan's friends and relatives, many of whom we had never met, and many of whom were unsaved. Several of Dan's old friends stood up and shared the huge change they had observed in Dan's life. One couple shared that they had started attending church now because of Dan's example. They all expressed gratefulness to our little church for whatever "we" did that changed Dan so dramatically. My dad shared how much Dan had meant to us and explained the whole story of how Dan came to place his faith in Jesus Christ for salvation.

Because of Dan's faith in Jesus, many more have heard the message of the gospel. After the memorial dinner, a few of Dan's relatives from out of town stayed around to talk … and guess what? We learned that they were believers and that they had been praying for "Danny" to come to the Lord for years!

Praise God for directing us to knock on the door of that little mustard-colored house near the corner.

NOTES

Chapter 1

1. Carl Kerby and Ken Ham, "Introduction: The 'Evolutionizing' of a Culture" *Answers in Genesis: www.answersingenesis.org/articles/nab2/the-evolutionizing-of-a-culture* (April 4, 2012).
2. Tertullian, *The Apology* (197 A.D.) Chapter 50, 13 *www.tertullian.org*.
3. 2011 Scripture Access Statistics *Wycliffe Global Alliance: www.wycliffe.net/resources/scriptureaccessstatistics/tabid/99/Default.aspx* (April 4, 2012).

Chapter 3

1. Bright Lights is a young ladies discipleship ministry which my older sister, Sarah, began in 1996. As of spring 2012, there are 500 Bright Lights groups worldwide. For more information, see *www.brightlightsministry.com*.
2. Jon Speed, *Evangelism in the New Testament* (Justin, TX: The Lost Cause Ministries, 2008), 8.
3. Ibid., 36.

Chapter 4

1. The Ten Commandments Coin is produced by Living Waters Publications. See *www.livingwaters.com*.
2. The IQ Quiz is produced by Living Waters Publications. See *www.livingwaters.com*.
3. *Joe Average* is an evangelistic DVD, produced by Living Waters Publications. See *www.livingwaters.com*.
4. See more information in *The New Answers Book 1* by Ken Ham, (Green Forest, AR: Master Books, 2006), 162.

Chapter 5

1. A phrase from the hymn "Who is on the Lord's Side?" by Frances Havergal.
2. *Christianity.com: www.christianity.com/churchhistory/11630083/print/* (April 5, 2012).
3. John Bunyan, *The Pilgrim's Progress Part II* (Green Forest, AR: Master Books, 2005), 371.

Chapter 6

1. Even though I was using that question to make a point, God doesn't actually draw a line based on our performance. The line is drawn between those who "have the Son" and those who don't. "He that hath the Son hath life; and he that hath not the Son of God hath not life" (1 John 5:12).
2. I borrowed the parachute illustration from Ray Comfort's message, *Hell's Best Kept Secret, www.livingwaters.com/learn/hellsbestkeptsecret.htm*.
3. You can listen online to Penn Jillette talk about this encounter: *http://fishwithtrish.blogspot.com/2008/12/youve-got-to-see-this-clip-from-well.html*.
4. Randy Alcorn, *The Grace and Truth Paradox: Responding with Christlike Balance* (Colorado Springs, CO: Multnomah Books, 2003), 16.

Chapter 8
1. William MacDonald, *Believer's Bible Commentary* (Nashville TN: Thomas Nelson, 1995), 1952.

Chapter 11
1. One aspect of the Bright Lights ministry is the Strong in the Lord conferences and the Radiant Purity conferences which we teach for mothers and daughters.

Chapter 12
1. For information about the bridge diagram, see *www.willourgenerationspeak.com*.
2. Go to *www.willourgenerationspeak.com* for information about some good websites to direct unbelievers to after witnessing to them.
3. Phil Telfer has a great ministry helping young people be wise in their use of media. The film *Captivated* is especially powerful—illustrating the way media has "enslaved" many in this generation. *MediaTalk101: www.mediatalk101.org*.
4. Amy Vest explains this well in her videocast entitled "Mastering Media for the Glory of God" *Loving the Lord Ministries: www.lovinglordministries.org*.

Chapter 13
1. See *www.willourgenerationspeak.com* for more details.

Chapter 14
1. The elements of random chance mutation and what is called "natural selection" depend on time. In the words of evolutionist George Wald: "Time is in fact the hero of the plot ... What we regard as impossible on the basis of human experience is meaningless here. Given so much time, the 'impossible' becomes possible, the possible probable, and the probable virtually certain. One has only to wait: time itself performs miracles" ("The Origin of Life," *Scientific American*, Vol. 190, August 1954, 48).

   Not only is the time not available, but these processes wouldn't actually work even with time. For more information see *Radioisotopes and the Age of the Earth* (by Larry Vardiman, published by the Institute for Creation Research), *Earth's Catastrophic Past* (by Andrew Snelling, published by the Institute for Creation Research), *The New Answers Book Volumes 1 and 2* (by Ken Ham, published by Master Books), *The Young Earth* (by John Morris, published by Master Books) and *Darwin's Black Box* (by Michael Behe, published by Free Press).
2. George Wald, "The Origin of Life," *Scientific American*, Vol. 190, August 1954, 48.

Chapter 15
1. The Barna Group, "Barna Survey Examines Changes in Worldview Among Christians over the Past 13 Years," March 6th, 2009 *www.barna.org*.
2. This list of questions came from Brian Thomas, a friend from the Institute for Creation Research.
3. *Jesus Rant* (Aliso Viego, CA: The Veracity Project) *www.veracityproject.com*.
4. Josh McDowell, *The New Evidence that Demands a Verdict* (Nashville, TN: Thomas Nelson Publishers, 1999) 77-82.
5. David Reid, *Ready to Give an Answer* (Dubuque, IA: ECS Min. 2003), 15-16.
6. Josh McDowell, *Evidence that Demands a Verdict Volume 1* (San Bernardino, CA:

Here's Life Publishers, Inc.) p. 65, quoting Nelson Glueck, *Rivers in the Desert; History of Negev,* (Philadelphia: Jewish Publications Society of America, 1969).

7. For further study about fulfilled prophecies, see *The New Evidence that Demands a Verdict* (by Josh McDowell, published by Thomas Nelson), 164-202.

8. Voddie T. Baucham Jr., *Why I Choose to Believe the Bible* recorded at 2007 Worldview Weekend *www.worldviewweekend.com.*

9. John Woodmorappe, *Noah's Ark: A Feasibility Study* (Dallas, TX: Institute for Creation Research, 1996), 16.

Chapter 16

1. Great Commission Statistics, *Joshua Project: www.joshuaproject.net/great-commission-statistics.php* (March 31, 2012).

2. Gospel For Asia: *www.gfa.org/about* (March 30th, 2012).

3. Jason Mandryk, *Operation World: The Definitive Prayer Guide to Every Nation,* 7th ed. (Colorado Springs, CO: Biblica Publishing, 2010), 830-831. See also *Operation World: www.operationworld.org/turk* (March 30th, 2012).

4. Ibid., 888-890. See also *www.operationworld.org/yeme* (March 30th, 2012).

5. Ibid, 58.

6. Joshua Project: *www.joshuaproject.net/continents.php* (April 3, 2012). See also "Tears of the Saints," a six-minute video, *Asia Link: www.asialink.org* (April 3, 2012).

7. Dr. and Mrs. Howard Taylor, *The Growth of a Soul* (Littleton, CO: OMF International, 1911, 2000), 71-72.

8. *Wisdom Booklet 39* (Oak Brook, IL: Advanced Training Institute 2006), 21.

9. The annual survey report published by the Institute of International Education (IIE) with funding from the U.S. Department of State's Bureau of Educational and Cultural Affairs.

10. I learned about Vanya Moseivyev from *Vanya: A True Story* (by Myrna Grant, published by Charisma house). I'd recommend the book, though I cannot necessarily say I endorse everything about it.

11. Jason Mandryk, "The State of the Gospel" *Harvest Media Ministry www.harvestmediaministry.com/State_Gospel_Full.htm* (March 30th, 2012).

12. Jason Mandryk, *Operation World: The Definitive Prayer Guide to Every Nation,* 7th ed. (Colorado Springs, CO: Biblica Publishing, 2010), 465.

13. Ibid., 216.

14. Ibid., 951.

15. Ibid., 951. See also "The State of the Gospel" *Harvest Media Ministry www harvestmediaministry.com/State_Gospel_Full.htm* (March 30th, 2012).

16. Ibid., 643. See also "The State of the Gospel."

17. I learned about Bert Elliot from my good friend, Danielle Sobie, who lived with Elisabeth Elliot and her husband for one year and spent a couple weeks with Bert and his wife in Peru in February of 2011 *(www.theinvisiblereality.blogspot.com).* See also *WORLD* Magazine (March 10, 2012 issue), 16.

Chapter 17

1. Illustration from my good friend, Lalo Gunther, who works for the Institute for Creation Research. See *www.youroriginsmatter.com.*

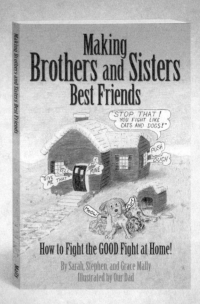

MAKING BROTHERS AND SISTERS BEST FRIENDS

By Sarah, Stephen and Grace Mally

In 2002, my older siblings and I wrote this book together in an effort to encourage families to be strong in the Lord. The three of us share many personal stories about struggles we faced and ways the Lord worked in our lives. Every chapter contains a section by Sarah, Stephen, and myself—giving the book three perspectives and three personalities. This book digs deeper into the principles discussed in chapter 16 of *Will Our Generation Speak?* (Start At Home but Aim for the World).

Making Brothers and Sisters Best Friends includes biblical insights, personal stories, practical ideas, and cartoons. It challenges families to work through pride, offenses, and irritations in their relationships and learn to become best friends—for the glory of God. "By this shall all men know that ye are My disciples, if ye have love one to another" (John 13:35).

"This painfully honest, hilarious book offers a creative look at how to build relationships between siblings. We read a few pages every day, and I am always delightfully surprised by how well the children apply what we have read."
—Beall Phillips, Vision Forum

272 pages, for whole families
Illustrated by our dad
Accompanying resources include *Making Brothers and Sisters Best Friends Coloring Book* and a 1-hour CD or DVD presentation on this topic.

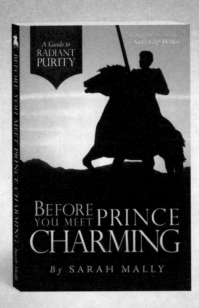

BEFORE YOU MEET PRINCE CHARMING
By Sarah Mally

One area of struggle for nearly every Christian young person is knowing how to properly handle relationships with the opposite gender. This area can either be a source of great distraction and difficulty, or one in which God is greatly glorified in our lives. In chapter eight of *Will Our Generation Speak?*, I talk about the need for personal purity if we desire to be fruitful witnesses for the Lord. Sarah writes about many important aspects of that in this book.

Through a captivating fairy tale, biblical insights, practical instruction, and humor, Sarah challenges young ladies to guard their hearts and minds, to identify and avoid the world's thinking, to use their single years wisely, to wait for God's best in marriage, and to focus their energies and affections on loving Jesus—our heavenly Prince—with all their hearts. She shares practical insights about how to handle friendships with young men in a wise and godly way.

> *"Sarah Mally is a 'bright light' in our day—a winsome, counter-cultural young woman with a passion for Christ and for truth."*
> —Nancy Leigh DeMoss, Author, Host of *Revive Our Hearts* Radio

> *"Creatively accomplished and very helpful."*
> —Gregg Harris, father of Joshua, Alex, and Brett Harris

272 pages, for young ladies of all ages
Accompanying resources include *Before You Meet Prince Charming Study Guide* and a 1-hour CD presentation on this topic.

BRIGHT LIGHTS LEADERSHIP KIT

We have been called not only to share the gospel, but also to *disciple* others—teaching them all things the Lord has commanded us (Matthew 28:20). The Bright Lights curriculum was developed by Sarah Mally to be a tool to assist older girls or mothers who desire to start a discipleship study with younger girls. The kit includes 12 training CDs taught by Sarah, covering many practical topics: principles of ministry, insights on discipleship, the responsibilities of a leader, rewards and demands of ministry, leading an effective meeting, and ways to reach the hearts of young ladies. It also includes a Leader's Manual and a copy of the Bright Lights curriculum.

OTHER SUGGESTED RESOURCES

The Light Shop Curriculum—A tool for young men or fathers to use to encourage boys to be leaders in godliness, holiness and testimony. Written by Harold Mally.

Knights, Maidens and Dragons DVD—1 hour session on purity, by Harold and Grace Mally, with skits and biblical teaching (for youth and parents).

Learning from Dad—A notebook and CD for fathers to use in training their families in godliness. Written by Harold Mally.

Let My Life Be A Light—Vocal and instrumental CD, a combined effort of the Bright Lights ministry and Wissmann family. Songbook also available.

WWW.TOMORROWSFOREFATHERS.COM/STORE

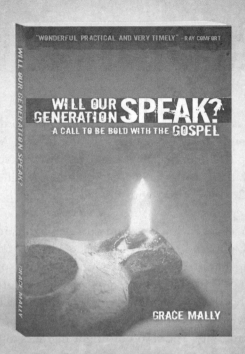

BUNDLES AND CASES

IF YOU WOULD LIKE TO DISTRIBUTE *WILL OUR GENERATION SPEAK?* TO YOUR FRIENDS, CHURCH, OR YOUTH GROUP, SEE OUR ONLINE STORE FOR DISCOUNTED PRICES.

> BUNDLE (15 BOOKS)
> CASE (52 BOOKS)

OTHER RECOMMENDED BOOKS, EVANGELISM TOOLS, TRACTS, LINKS, AND WITNESSING RESOURCES ARE LISTED ON OUR WEBSITE AND AVAILABLE ON OUR ONLINE STORE.

WWW.WILLOURGENERATIONSPEAK.COM

ABOUT THE AUTHOR

Grace Mally, 23, is grateful for the opportunities the Lord has given her to be involved in youth discipleship ministry. She lives in Marion, Iowa and attends Cedar Rapids Bible Chapel. She and her family have a ministry called Tomorrow's Forefathers, with the goal of equipping families to be strong in the Lord. In 2002, Grace, along with her older siblings, Sarah and Stephen, coauthored *Making Brothers and Sisters Best Friends*.

Grace likes to arrange witnessing and outreach events in her community, speaks at Bright Lights and family conferences, and helps to lead the Bright Lights discipleship ministry, which was founded by her older sister, Sarah. As of 2012, about 500 Bright Lights groups have started around the country and internationally. These groups of young ladies are usually led by an older girl (or mother) who has the desire to invest in the lives of younger girls in her church or community. The vision of Bright Lights is to encourage girls to be radiant in godliness, holiness, and testimony—to be strong in the Lord in their youth.

In 2008, the Lord provided a commercial building that has now become the Bright Lights office and a bookstore named Noah's Archive Christian Books. The Lord has continued to provide staff to work alongside the Mallys as they write new discipleship materials, lead Bright Lights "Strong in the Lord Conferences" and "Radiant Purity Conferences," and organize various discipleship and evangelism events for their church and community.

SEE GRACE'S BLOG:

Grace maintains a blog where she records updates on what God is doing in her life and the life of her family at *www.gracemally.com*.

CONTACT GRACE:

Grace Mally
PO Box 11451
Cedar Rapids, IA
52410-1451

grace@willourgenerationspeak.com